OpenCV 4 for Secret Agents
Second Edition

Use OpenCV 4 in secret projects to classify cats, reveal the unseen, and react to rogue drivers

Joseph Howse

BIRMINGHAM - MUMBAI

OpenCV 4 for Secret Agents
Second Edition

Copyright © 2019 Packt Publishing

All rights reserved. No part of this book may be reproduced, stored in a retrieval system, or transmitted in any form or by any means, without the prior written permission of the publisher, except in the case of brief quotations embedded in critical articles or reviews.

Every effort has been made in the preparation of this book to ensure the accuracy of the information presented. However, the information contained in this book is sold without warranty, either express or implied. Neither the author, nor Packt Publishing or its dealers and distributors, will be held liable for any damages caused or alleged to have been caused directly or indirectly by this book.

Packt Publishing has endeavored to provide trademark information about all of the companies and products mentioned in this book by the appropriate use of capitals. However, Packt Publishing cannot guarantee the accuracy of this information.

Commissioning Editor: Richa Tripathi
Acquisition Editor: Chaitanya Nair
Content Development Editors: Digvijay Bagul
Technical Editor: Riddesh Dawne
Copy Editor: Safis Editing
Project Coordinator: Prajakta Naik
Proofreader: Safis Editing
Indexer: Pratik Shirodkar
Graphics: Tom Scaria
Production Coordinator: Nilesh Mohite

First published: January 2015
Second edition: April 2019

Production reference: 1300419

Published by Packt Publishing Ltd.
Livery Place
35 Livery Street
Birmingham
B3 2PB, UK.

ISBN 978-1-78934-536-0

www.packtpub.com

I dedicate my work to Sam, Jan, Bob, Bunny, and the cats, who have been my lifelong guides and companions.

Let us remember Plasma Tigerlily Zoya (2004-2017), a pioneer of feline computer vision, and a cat of great virtue.

– Joseph Howse

mapt.io

Mapt is an online digital library that gives you full access to over 5,000 books and videos, as well as industry leading tools to help you plan your personal development and advance your career. For more information, please visit our website.

Why subscribe?

- Spend less time learning and more time coding with practical eBooks and Videos from over 4,000 industry professionals

- Improve your learning with Skill Plans built especially for you

- Get a free eBook or video every month

- Mapt is fully searchable

- Copy and paste, print, and bookmark content

PacktPub.com

Did you know that Packt offers eBook versions of every book published, with PDF and ePub files available? You can upgrade to the eBook version at www.PacktPub.com and as a print book customer, you are entitled to a discount on the eBook copy. Get in touch with us at service@packtpub.com for more details.

At www.PacktPub.com, you can also read a collection of free technical articles, sign up for a range of free newsletters, and receive exclusive discounts and offers on Packt books and eBooks.

Contributors

About the author

Joseph Howse lives in a Canadian fishing village with four cats; the cats like fish, but they prefer chicken.

Joseph provides computer vision expertise through his company, Nummist Media. His books include *OpenCV 4 for Secret Agents*, *OpenCV 3 Blueprints*, *Android Application Programming with OpenCV 3*, *iOS Application Development with OpenCV 3*, *Learning OpenCV 3 Computer Vision with Python*, and *Python Game Programming by Example*, published by Packt.

> *I want to thank the readers – such as Dan and Cindy Davis of Farmington, Utah – who shared their enthusiasm for this book's first edition and told me of their own adventures in computer vision. I am grateful to the editors, technical reviewers, and marketers of both editions, as well as my colleagues at Market Beat (El Salvador) and at General Motors who gave feedback on drafts. Above all, my family makes my work possible and I dedicate it to them.*

About the reviewers

Christian Stehno studied computer science, receiving his diploma from Oldenburg University, Germany, in 2000. Since then, he's worked in different fields of computer science, first as a researcher on theoretical computer science at an academic institution, before switching later on to embedded system design at a research institute. In 2010, he started his own company, CoSynth, which develops embedded systems and intelligent cameras for industrial automation. In addition, he is a long-time member of the Irrlicht 3D engine developer team.

Arun Ponnusamy works as a computer vision research engineer at an AI start-up in India. He is a lifelong learner, passionate about image processing, computer vision, and machine learning. He is an engineering graduate from PSG College of Technology, Coimbatore. He started his career at MulticoreWare Inc., where he spent most of his time on image processing, OpenCV, software optimization, and GPU computing.

Arun loves to build his understanding of computer vision concepts clearly, allowing him to explain it in an intuitive way on his blog and in meetups. He has created an open source Python library for computer vision, named *cvlib*, which is aimed at simplicity and user friendliness. He is currently working on object detection, action recognition, and generative networks.

Packt is searching for authors like you

If you're interested in becoming an author for Packt, please visit `authors.packtpub.com` and apply today. We have worked with thousands of developers and tech professionals, just like you, to help them share their insight with the global tech community. You can make a general application, apply for a specific hot topic that we are recruiting an author for, or submit your own idea.

Table of Contents

Preface   1

Section 1: The Briefing

Chapter 1: Preparing for the Mission   9
  Technical requirements   10
  Setting up a development machine   11
    Setting up Python and OpenCV on Windows   13
      Building OpenCV on Windows with CMake and Visual Studio   14
    Setting up Python and OpenCV on Mac   17
      Mac with MacPorts   18
      Mac with Homebrew   20
    Setting up Python and OpenCV on Debian Jessie and its derivatives, including Raspbian, Ubuntu, and Linux Mint   22
      Building OpenCV on Debian Jessie and its derivatives with CMake and GCC   23
    Setting up Python and OpenCV on Fedora and its derivatives, including RHEL and CentOS   26
    Setting up Python and OpenCV on openSUSE and its derivatives   27
  Setting up Android Studio and OpenCV   28
  Setting up Unity and OpenCV   29
  Setting up a Raspberry Pi   30
    Setting up the Raspberry Pi camera module   34
  Finding OpenCV documentation, help, and updates   36
  Alternatives to Raspberry Pi   37
  Summary   38

Chapter 2: Searching for Luxury Accommodations Worldwide   39
  Technical requirements   40
  Planning the Luxocator app   40
  Creating, comparing, and storing histograms   42
  Training the classifier with reference images   48
  Acquiring images from the web   50
  Acquiring images from Bing Image Search   52
  Preparing images and resources for the app   59
  Integrating everything into the GUI   61
  Running Luxocator and troubleshooting SSL problems   70
  Building Luxocator for distribution   71
  Summary   74

Section 2: The Chase

Chapter 3: Training a Smart Alarm to Recognize the Villain and His Cat — 77
- Technical requirements — 78
- Understanding machine learning in general — 79
- Planning the Interactive Recognizer app — 80
- Understanding Haar cascades and LBPH — 82
- Implementing the Interactive Recognizer app — 86
- Planning the cat-detection model — 101
- Implementing the training script for the cat-detection model — 103
- Planning the Angora Blue app — 117
- Implementing the Angora Blue app — 118
- Building Angora Blue for distribution — 125
- Further fun with finding felines — 125
- Summary — 126

Chapter 4: Controlling a Phone App with Your Suave Gestures — 127
- Technical requirements — 128
- Planning the Goldgesture app — 128
- Understanding optical flow — 130
- Setting up the project in Android Studio — 132
- Getting a cascade file and audio files — 138
- Specifying the app's requirements — 139
- Laying out a camera preview as the main view — 140
- Tracking back-and-forth gestures — 141
- Playing audio clips as questions and answers — 144
- Capturing images and tracking faces in an activity — 149
- Summary — 166

Chapter 5: Equipping Your Car with a Rearview Camera and Hazard Detection — 167
- Technical requirements — 168
- Planning The Living Headlights app — 169
- Detecting lights as blobs — 171
- Estimating distances (a cheap approach) — 174
- Implementing The Living Headlights app — 177
- Testing The Living Headlights app at home — 192
- Testing The Living Headlights app in a car — 195
- Summary — 200

Chapter 6: Creating a Physics Simulation Based on a Pen and Paper Sketch — 201
- Technical requirements — 202
- Planning the Rollingball app — 203

Detecting circles and lines	206
Setting up OpenCV for Unity	209
Configuring and building the Unity project	212
Creating the Rollingball scene in Unity	216
Creating Unity assets and adding them to the scene	219
Writing shaders and creating materials	219
Creating physics materials	222
Creating prefabs	224
Writing our first Unity script	228
Writing the main Rollingball script	230
Creating the launcher scene in Unity	248
Tidying up and testing	251
Summary	252

Section 3: The Big Reveal

Chapter 7: Seeing a Heartbeat with a Motion-Amplifying Camera	255
Technical requirements	257
Planning the Lazy Eyes app	257
Understanding what Eulerian video magnification can do	259
Extracting repeating signals from video using the fast Fourier transform	260
Choosing and setting up an FFT library	261
Compositing two images using image pyramids	264
Implementing the Lazy Eyes app	265
Configuring and testing the app for various motions	275
Summary	283
Seeing things in different light	283
Chapter 8: Stopping Time and Seeing like a Bee	285
Technical requirements	286
Planning the Sunbaker app	287
Understanding the spectrum	289
Finding specialized cameras	291
XNiteUSB2S-MUV	293
Sony PlayStation Eye	295
Point Grey Grasshopper 3 GS3-U3-23S6M-C	295
Installing Spinnaker SDK and PySpin	297
Capturing images from industrial cameras using PySpin	299
Adapting the Lazy Eyes app to make Sunbaker	304
Summary	308
Appendix A: Making WxUtils.py Compatible with Raspberry Pi	309
Appendix B: Learning More about Feature Detection in OpenCV	311

Table of Contents

Appendix C: Running with Snakes (or, First Steps with Python) — 313
Other Books You May Enjoy — 315
Index — 319

Preface

Computer vision systems are deployed in the Arctic Ocean to spot icebergs at night. They are flown over the Amazon rainforest to create aerial maps of fires, blights, and illegal logging. They are set up in ports and airports worldwide to scan for suspects and contraband. They are sent to the depths of the Marianas Trench to guide autonomous submarines. They are used in operating rooms to help surgeons visualize the planned procedure and the patient's current condition. They are launched from battlefields as the steering systems of heat-seeking, anti-aircraft rockets.

We might seldom—or never—visit these places. However, stories often encourage us to imagine extreme environments and a person's dependence on tools in these unforgiving conditions. Perhaps fittingly, one of contemporary fiction's most popular characters is an almost ordinary man (handsome, but not *too* handsome; clever, but not *too* clever) who wears a suit, works for the British Government, always chooses the same drink, the same kind of woman, the same tone for delivering a pun, and is sent to do dangerous jobs with a peculiar collection of gadgets.

> *Bond. James Bond.*

This book discusses seriously useful technologies and techniques, with a healthy dose of inspiration from spy fiction. The Bond franchise is rich in ideas about detection, disguise, smart devices, image capture, and sometimes, even computer vision specifically. With imagination, plus dedication to learning new skills, we can become the next generation of gadget makers to rival Bond's engineer, Q!

Who this book is for

This book is for tinkerers (and spies) who want to make computer vision a practical and fun part of their lifestyle. You should already be comfortable with 2D graphical concepts, object-oriented languages, GUIs, networking, and the command line. This book does not assume experience with any specific libraries or platforms. Detailed instructions cover everything from setting up the development environment to deploying finished apps.

A desire to learn multiple technologies and techniques, and then integrate them, is highly beneficial! This book will help you branch out to understand several types of systems and application domains where computer vision is relevant, and will help you to apply several approaches to detect, recognize, track, and augment faces, objects, and motions.

What this book covers

Chapter 1, *Preparing for the Mission*, helps us to install OpenCV, a Python development environment, and an Android development environment on Windows, macOS, or Linux systems. In this chapter, we also install a Unity development environment on Windows or macOS.

Chapter 2, *Searching for Luxury Accommodations Worldwide*, helps us to classify images of real estate based on color schemes. Are we outside a luxury dwelling or inside a Stalinist apartment? In this chapter, we use the classifier in a search engine that labels its image results.

Chapter 3, *Training a Smart Alarm to Recognize the Villain and His Cat*, helps us to detect and recognize human faces and cat faces as a means of controlling an alarm. Has Ernst Stavro Blofeld returned, with his blue-eyed Angora cat?

Chapter 4, *Controlling a Phone App with Your Suave Gestures*, helps us to detect motion and recognize gestures as a means of controlling a guessing game on a smartphone. The phone knows why Bond is nodding, even if no one else does.

Chapter 5, *Equipping Your Car with a Rearview Camera and Hazard Detection*, helps us to detect car headlights, classify their color, estimate distances to them, and provide feedback to the driver. Is that car tailing us?

Chapter 6, *Creating a Physics Simulation Based on a Pen and Paper Sketch*, helps us to draw a ball-in-a-maze puzzle on paper, and see it come to life as a physics simulation on a smartphone. Physics and timing are everything!

Chapter 7, *Seeing a Heartbeat with a Motion-Amplifying Camera*, helps us to amplify motion in live video, in real time, so that a person's heartbeat and breathing become clearly visible. See the passion!

Chapter 8, *Stopping Time and Seeing like a Bee*, helps us improve the previous chapter's project by adopting specialized cameras for high-speed, infrared, or ultraviolet imaging. Surpass the limits of human vision!

Appendix A, *Making WxUtils.py Compatible with Raspberry Pi*, helps us solve a compatibility issue that affects the wxPython GUI library in some Raspberry Pi environments.

Appendix B, *Learning More about Feature Detection in OpenCV*, helps us discover more of OpenCV's feature-detection capabilities, beyond the ones we use in this book's projects.

Appendix C, *Running with Snakes (or, First Steps with Python)*, helps us learn to run Python code and test an OpenCV installation in a Python environment.

To get the most out of this book

This book supports several operating systems as development environments, including Windows 7 SP 1 or later, macOS X 10.7 (Lion) or later, Debian Jessie, Raspbian, Ubuntu 14.04 or later, Linux Mint 17 or later, Fedora 28 or later, **Red Hat Enterprise Linux** (**RHEL**) 8 or a later version, CentOS 8 or later, openSUSE Leap 42.3, openSUSE Leap 15.0 or later, and openSUSE Tumbleweed.

The book contains six projects with the following requirements:

- Four of these six projects run on Windows, macOS, or Linux, and require a webcam. Optionally, these projects can use Raspberry Pi or another single-board computer that runs Linux.
- One project runs on Android 5.0 (Lollipop) or a later version, and requires a front-facing camera (which most Android devices have).
- One project runs on Android 4.1 (Jelly Bean) or a later version, and requires a rear-facing camera and gravity sensor (which most Android devices have). For development, it requires a Windows or macOS machine and approximately $95 worth of game development software.

Setup instructions for all required libraries and tools are covered in the book. Optional setup instructions for Raspberry Pi are also included.

Download the example code files

You can download the example code files for this book from your account at www.packtpub.com. If you purchased this book elsewhere, you can visit www.packtpub.com/support and register to have the files emailed directly to you.

You can download the code files by following these steps:

1. Log in or register at www.packtpub.com.
2. Select the **SUPPORT** tab.
3. Click on **Code Downloads & Errata**.
4. Enter the name of the book in the **Search** box and follow the onscreen instructions.

Once the file is downloaded, please make sure that you unzip or extract the folder using the latest version of:

- WinRAR/7-Zip for Windows
- Zipeg/iZip/UnRarX for Mac
- 7-Zip/PeaZip for Linux

The code bundle for the book is also hosted on GitHub at https://github.com/PacktPublishing/OpenCV-4-for-Secret-Agents-Second-Edition. In case there's an update to the code, it will be updated on the existing GitHub repository.

We also have other code bundles from our rich catalog of books and videos available at https://github.com/PacktPublishing/. Check them out!

Download the color images

We also provide a PDF file that has color images of the screenshots/diagrams used in this book. You can download it here: http://www.packtpub.com/sites/default/files/downloads/9781789345360_ColorImages.pdf.

Conventions used

There are a number of text conventions used throughout this book.

`CodeInText`: Indicates code words in text, database table names, folder names, filenames, file extensions, pathnames, dummy URLs, user input, and Twitter handles. Here is an example: "You can edit `/etc/modules` to check whether `bcm2835-v4l2` is already listed there."

A block of code is set as follows:

```
set PYINSTALLER=pyinstaller

REM Remove any previous build of the app.
rmdir build /s /q
rmdir dist /s /q

REM Train the classifier.
python HistogramClassifier.py
```

When we wish to draw your attention to a particular part of a code block, the relevant lines or items are set in bold:

```
<activity
    android:name=".CameraActivity"
    android:screenOrientation="landscape"
    android:theme="@android:style/Theme.NoTitleBar.Fullscreen">
    <intent-filter>
        <action android:name="android.intent.action.MAIN" />

        <category android:name="android.intent.category.LAUNCHER" />
    </intent-filter>
</activity>
```

Any command-line input or output is written as follows:

```
$ echo "bcm2835-v4l2" | sudo tee -a /etc/modules
```

Bold: Indicates a new term, an important word, or words that you see onscreen. For example, words in menus or dialog boxes appear in the text like this. Here is an example: "Click the **Android** platform and then the **Switch Platform** button."

Warnings or important notes appear like this.

Tips and tricks appear like this.

Get in touch

Feedback from our readers is always welcome.

General feedback: Email feedback@packtpub.com and mention the book title in the subject of your message. If you have questions about any aspect of this book, please email us at questions@packtpub.com.

Errata: Although we have taken every care to ensure the accuracy of our content, mistakes do happen. If you have found a mistake in this book, we would be grateful if you would report this to us. Please visit www.packtpub.com/submit-errata, selecting your book, clicking on the Errata Submission Form link, and entering the details.

Contacting the author: You can email Joseph Howse directly at josephhowse@nummist.com. He maintains this book's GitHub repository at https://github.com/PacktPublishing/OpenCV-4-for-Secret-Agents-Second-Edition, as well as his own support webpage for his books at http://nummist.com/opencv, so you may want to look for updates from him on these sites.

Piracy: If you come across any illegal copies of our works in any form on the Internet, we would be grateful if you would provide us with the location address or website name. Please contact us at copyright@packtpub.com with a link to the material.

If you are interested in becoming an author: If there is a topic that you have expertise in and you are interested in either writing or contributing to a book, please visit authors.packtpub.com.

Reviews

Please leave a review. Once you have read and used this book, why not leave a review on the site that you purchased it from? Potential readers can then see and use your unbiased opinion to make purchase decisions, we at Packt can understand what you think about our products, and our authors can see your feedback on their book. Thank you!

For more information about Packt, please visit packtpub.com.

Section 1: The Briefing

Set up a multi-platform development environment. Integrate OpenCV with other libraries to make an application that classifies images from the web.

The following chapters will be covered in this section:

- `Chapter 1`, *Preparing for the Mission*
- `Chapter 2`, *Searching for Luxury Accommodations Worldwide*

1
Preparing for the Mission

"Q: I've been saying for years, sir, that our special equipment is obsolete. And now, computer analysis reveals an entirely new approach: miniaturization."
— *On Her Majesty's Secret Service* (1969)

James Bond is not a pedestrian. He cruises in a submarine car; he straps on a rocket belt; and, oh, how he skis, how he skis! He always has the latest stuff, and he is never afraid to put a dent in it, much to the dismay of Q, the engineer.

As software developers in the 2010s, we have witnessed an explosion of the adoption of new platforms. Under one family's roof, we might find a mix of Windows, Mac, iOS, and Android devices. Mom and Dad's workplaces provide different platforms. The kids have three game consoles, or five, if you count the mobile versions. The toddler has a LeapFrog learning tablet. Smart glasses are becoming more affordable.

We must not be afraid to try new platforms and consider new ways to combine them. After all, our users do.

This book embraces multiplatform development. It presents weird and wonderful applications that we can deploy in unexpected places. It uses several of the computer's senses, but especially computer vision, to breathe new life into the humdrum, heterogeneous clutter of devices that surrounds us.

Before Agent 007 runs amok with the gadgets, he is obligated to listen to Q's briefing. This chapter will performs Q's role. It is the setup chapter.

Preparing for the Mission

By the end of this chapter, you will have obtained all the tools to develop OpenCV applications in Python for Windows, Mac, or Linux, and in Java for Android. You will also be the proud new user of a Raspberry Pi single-board computer. (This additional hardware is optional.) You will even know a bit about Unity, a game engine into which we can integrate OpenCV. Specifically, this chapter will cover the following approaches to setting up a development environment:

- Setting up Python and OpenCV on Windows. Optionally, this will include configuring and building OpenCV from a source with CMake and Visual Studio.
- Setting up Python and OpenCV on Mac. This will include using either MacPorts or Homebrew as a package manager.
- Setting up Python and OpenCV on Debian Jessie or one of its derivatives, such as Raspbian, Ubuntu, or Linux Mint. This will include using the **Advanced Package Tool** (**APT**) package manager. Optionally, it will also include configuring and building OpenCV from a source with CMake and GCC.
- Setting up Python and OpenCV on Fedora or one of its derivatives, such as **Red Hat Enterprise Linux** (**RHEL**) or CentOS. This will include using the yum package manager.
- Setting up Python and OpenCV on openSUSE. This will include using the yum package manager.
- Setting up Android Studio and OpenCV's Android libraries on Windows, Mac, or Linux.
- Setting up Unity and OpenCV on Windows or Mac.
- Setting up a Raspberry Pi.

If you find yourself a bit daunted by the extent of this setup chapter, be reassured that not all of the tools are required, and no single project uses all of them in combination. Although Q and I live for the big event of setting up multiple technologies at once, you can just skim this chapter and refer back to it later when the tools become useful, one by one, in our projects.

Technical requirements

This is the setup chapter. There are no particular software prerequisites at the outset; we will set up everything as we go along.

Basic instructions for running Python code are covered in Appendix C, *Running with Snakes (or, First Steps with Python)*. After we set up a Python environment with OpenCV, you may want to refer to this appendix so that you know how to minimally test the environment.

Setting up a development machine

We can develop our OpenCV applications on a desktop, a notebook, or even the humble Raspberry Pi (covered later, in the *Setting up a Raspberry Pi* section). Most of our apps have a memory footprint of less than 128 MB, so they can still run (albeit slowly) on old or low-powered machines. To save time, develop on your fastest machine first and test on slower machines later.

This book assumes that you have one of the following operating systems on your development machine:

- Windows 7 SP 1, or a later version.
- Mac OS 10.7 (Lion), or a later version.
- Debian Jessie, a later version, or a derivative such as the following:
    - Raspbian 2015-09-25, or a later version
    - Ubuntu 14.04, or a later version
    - Linux Mint 17, or a later version
- Fedora 28, a later version, or a derivative such as the following:
    - RHEL 8, or a later version
    - CentOS 8, or a later version
- openSUSE Leap 42.3, openSUSE Leap 15.0, or a later version; openSUSE Tumbleweed, or a derivative.

Other Unix-like systems might also work, but they will not be covered in this book.

You should have a USB webcam and any necessary drivers. Most webcams come with instructions for installing drivers on Windows and Mac. Linux distributions typically include the **USB Video Class** (**UVC**) Linux driver, which supports many webcams, listed at http://www.ideasonboard.org/uvc/#devices.

We are going to set up the following components:

- On Mac, a third-party package manager to help us install libraries and their dependencies; we will use either MacPorts or Homebrew.
- A Python development environment—at the time of writing this book, OpenCV supports Python 2.7, 3.4, 3.5, 3.6, and 3.7. The Python code in this book supports all of these versions. As part of the Python development environment, we will use Python's package manager, pip.
- Popular Python libraries, such as NumPy (for numeric functions), SciPy (for numeric and scientific functions), Requests (for web requests), and wxPython (for cross-platform GUIs).

Preparing for the Mission

- PyInstaller, a cross-platform tool for bundling Python scripts, libraries, and data as redistributable apps, such that user machines do not require installations of Python, OpenCV, and other libraries. For this book's purposes, building redistributables of Python projects is an optional topic. We will cover the basics in Chapter 2, *Searching for Luxury Accommodations Worldwide*, but you might need to do your own testing and debugging, as PyInstaller (like other Python bundling tools) does not show entirely consistent behavior across operating systems, Python versions, and library versions. It is not well supported on Raspberry Pi or other ARM devices.
- Optionally, we can use a C++ development environment to enable us to build OpenCV from a source. On Windows, we use Visual Studio 2015 or later. On Mac, we use Xcode. On Linux, we use GCC, which comes as standard.
- A build of OpenCV and opencv_contrib (a set of extra OpenCV modules) with Python support, plus optimizations for certain desktop hardware. At the time of writing this book, OpenCV 4.0.x is the latest stable branch, and our instructions are tailored for this branch. However, generally, the code in this book also works with the previous stable branch, OpenCV 3.4.x, which is more widely available from package managers for users who prefer a prepackaged build.
- Another build of OpenCV with Java support, plus optimizations for certain Android hardware. At the time of writing, OpenCV 4.0.1 is the most recent release.
- An Android development environment, including Android Studio and Android SDK.
- On 64-bit Windows or Mac, a three-dimensional game engine called **Unity**.

> Android Studio has a big memory footprint. Even if you want to use Raspberry Pi for developing desktop and Pi apps, use something with more RAM for developing Android apps.

Let's break this setup down into three sets of platform dependent steps for a Python and OpenCV environment, plus a set of platform independent steps for an Android Studio and OpenCV environment, and another set of platform independent steps for a Unity and OpenCV environment.

Setting up Python and OpenCV on Windows

On Windows, we have the option of setting up a 32-bit development environment (to make apps that are compatible with both 32-bit and 64-bit Windows) or a 64-bit development environment (to make optimized apps that are only compatible with 64-bit Windows). OpenCV is available in 32-bit and 64-bit versions.

We also have a choice of either using binary installers or compiling OpenCV from source. For our Windows apps in this book, the binary installers provide everything we need. However, we also discuss the option of compiling from source because it enables us to configure additional features, which may be relevant to your future work or to our projects in other books.

Regardless of our approach to obtaining OpenCV, we need a general-purpose Python development environment. We will set up this environment using a binary installer. The installers for Python are available from http://www.python.org/getit/. Download and run the latest revision of Python 3.7, in either the 32-bit variant or the 64-bit variant.

To make Python scripts run using our new Python 3.7 installation by default, let's edit the system's Path variable and append ;C:\Python3.7 (assuming Python 3.7 is installed in the default location). Remove any previous Python paths, such as ;C:\Python2.7. Log out and log back in (or reboot).

Python comes with a package manager called pip, which simplifies the task of installing Python modules and their dependencies. Open Command Prompt and run the following command to install numpy, scipy, requests, wxPython, and pyinstaller:

```
> pip install --user numpy scipy requests wxPython pyinstaller
```

Now, we have a choice. We can either install the binaries of OpenCV and opencv_contrib as a prebuilt Python module, or we can build this module from source. To install a prebuilt module, simply run the following command:

```
> pip install --user opencv-contrib-python
```

Alternatively, to build OpenCV and opencv_contrib from source, follow the instructions in the section *Building OpenCV on Windows with CMake and Visual Studio*, as follow.

After either installing a prebuilt `OpenCV` and `opencv_contrib` module or building it from source, we will have everything we need to develop OpenCV applications for Windows. To develop for Android, we need to set up Android Studio as described in the section *Setting up Android Studio, and OpenCV*, later in this chapter.

Building OpenCV on Windows with CMake and Visual Studio

To compile OpenCV from source, we need a general purpose C++ development environment. As our C++ development environment, we will use Visual Studio 2015 or later. Use any installation media you may have purchased, or go to the downloads page at `https://visualstudio.microsoft.com/downloads/`. Download and run the installer for one of the following:

- Visual Studio Community 2017, which is free
- Any of the paid Visual Studio 2017 versions, which have 30-day free trials

If the installer lists optional C++ components, we should opt to install them all. After the installer runs to completion, reboot.

OpenCV uses a set of build tools called **CMake**, which we must install. Optionally, we may install several third-party libraries in order to enable extra features in OpenCV. As an example, let's install Intel **Thread Building Blocks (TBB)**, which OpenCV can leverage in order to optimize some functions for multicore CPUs. After installing TBB, we will configure and build OpenCV. Lastly, we will ensure that our C++ and Python environments can find our build of OpenCV.

Here are the detailed steps:

1. Download and install the latest stable version of CMake from `https://cmake.org/download/`. CMake 3 or a newer version is required. Even if we are using 64-bit libraries and compilers, 32-bit CMake is compatible. When the installer asks about modifying PATH, select either **Add CMake to the system PATH for all users** or **Add CMake to the system PATH for current user**.
2. If your system uses a proxy server to access the internet, define two environment variables, `HTTP_PROXY` and `HTTPS_PROXY`, with values equal to the proxy server's URL, such as `http://myproxy.com:8080`. This ensures that CMake can use the proxy server to download some additional dependencies for OpenCV. (If in doubt, do not define these environment variables; you are probably not using a proxy server.)

3. Download the OpenCV Win pack from `http://opencv.org/releases.html`. (Choose the latest version.) The downloaded file may have an `.exe` extension, but actually, it is a self-extracting ZIP. Double-click on the file and, when prompted, enter any destination folder, which we will refer to as `<opencv_unzip_destination>`. A subfolder, `<opencv_unzip_destination>/opencv`, will be created.

4. Download `opencv_contrib` as a ZIP from `https://github.com/opencv/opencv_contrib/releases`. (Choose the latest version.) Unzip it to any destination folder, which we will refer to as `<opencv_contrib_unzip_destination>`.

5. Download the latest stable version of TBB from `https://www.threadingbuildingblocks.org/download`. It includes both 32-bit and 64-bit binaries. Unzip it to any destination, which we will refer to as `<tbb_unzip_destination>`.

6. Open Command Prompt. Create a folder to store our build:

   ```
   > mkdir <build_folder>
   ```

   Change directories to the newly created build folder:

   ```
   > cd <build_folder>
   ```

7. Having set up our dependencies, we can now configure OpenCV's build system. To understand all the configuration options, we can read the code in `<opencv_unzip_destination>/opencv/sources/CMakeLists.txt`. However, as an example, we will just use the options for a release build that includes Python bindings and multiprocessing through TBB:

   - To create a 32-bit project for Visual Studio 2017, run the following command (but replace the angle brackets and their contents with the actual paths):

   ```
   > CALL <tbb_unzip_destination>\bin\tbbvars.bat ia32 vs2017
   > cmake -DCMAKE_BUILD_TYPE=RELEASE DWITH_OPENGL=ON -DWITH_TBB=ON
   -DOPENCV_SKIP_PYTHON_LOADER=ON
   -DPYTHON3_LIBRARY=C:/Python37/libs/python37.lib
   -DPYTHON3_INCLUDE_DIR=C:/Python37/include -
   DOPENCV_EXTRA_MODULES_PATH="<opencv_contrib_unzip_destination>/modules" -G "Visual Studio 15 2017"
   "<opencv_unzip_destination>/opencv/sources"
   ```

- Alternatively, to create a 64-bit project for Visual Studio 2017, run the following command (but replace the angle brackets and their contents with the actual paths):

  ```
  > CALL <tbb_unzip_destination>\bin\tbbvars.bat intel64 vs2017
  > cmake -DCMAKE_BUILD_TYPE=RELEASE DWITH_OPENGL=ON -
  DWITH_TBB=ON
  -DOPENCV_SKIP_PYTHON_LOADER=ON
  -DPYTHON3_LIBRARY=C:/Python37/libs/python37.lib
  -DPYTHON3_INCLUDE_DIR=C:/Python37/include -
  DOPENCV_EXTRA_MODULES_PATH="<opencv_contrib_unzip_destination>/
  modules" -G "Visual Studio 15 2017 Win64"
  "<opencv_unzip_destination>/opencv/sources"
  ```

- CMake will produce a report on the dependencies that it did or did not find. OpenCV has many optional dependencies, so do not panic (yet) about missing dependencies. However, if the build does not finish successfully, try installing missing dependencies. (Many are available as prebuilt binaries.) Then, repeat this step.

8. Now that our build system is configured, we can compile OpenCV. Open `<build_folder>/OpenCV.sln` in Visual Studio. Select the **Release** configuration and build the solution. (You may get errors if you select another build configuration besides **Release**, because most Python installations do not include debug libraries.)

9. We should ensure that our Python installation does not already include some other version of OpenCV. Find and delete any OpenCV files in your Python `DLLs` folder and your Python `site-packages` folder. For example, the paths to these files might match the `C:\Python37\DLLs\opencv_*.dll`, `C:\Python37\Lib\site-packages\opencv`, and `C:\Python37\Lib\site-packages\cv2.pyd` patterns.

10. Finally, we need to install OpenCV to a location where Python and other processes can find it. To do this, right-click on the OpenCV solution's **INSTALL** project (in the **Solution Explorer** pane of Visual Studio) and build it. When this build finishes, quit Visual Studio. Edit the system's `Path` variable and append `;<build_folder>\install\x86\vc15\bin` (for a 32-bit build) or `;<build_folder>\install\x64\vc15\bin` (for a 64-bit build), which is the location where the OpenCV DLL files are located. Also, append `;<tbb_unzip_destination>\lib\ia32\vc14` (32-bit) or `;<tbb_unzip_ destination>\lib\intel64\vc14`(64-bit), which is the location where the TBB DLL files are located. Log out and log back in (or reboot). The OpenCV Python module is located at a path such as `C:\Python37\Lib\site-packages\cv2.pyd`. Python will find it there, so you do not need to take any further steps.

If you are using Visual Studio 2015, replace `vs2017` with `vs2015`, replace `Visual Studio 15 2017` with `Visual Studio 14 2015`, and replace `vc15` with `vc14`. However, for TBB, note that the folder named `vc14` contains the DLL files that work for both Visual Studio 2015 and Visual Studio 2017.

You might want to look at the code samples in `<opencv_unzip_destination>/opencv/sources/samples/python`.

At this point, we have everything we need to develop OpenCV applications for Windows. To also develop for Android, we need to set up Android Studio, as described in the *Setting up Android Studio and OpenCV* section, later in this chapter.

Setting up Python and OpenCV on Mac

Mac comes with Python preinstalled. However, the preinstalled Python has been customized by Apple for the system's internal needs. Normally, we should not install any libraries on top of Apple's Python. If we do, our libraries might break during system updates, or worse, they might conflict with preinstalled libraries that the system requires. Instead, we should install standard Python 3.7 and then install our libraries on top of it.

For Mac, there are several possible approaches to obtaining standard Python 3.7 and Python-compatible libraries, such as OpenCV. All approaches ultimately require some components to be compiled from source, using Xcode developer tools. However, depending on the approach we choose, the task of building these components is automated for us by third-party tools in various ways.

Preparing for the Mission

Let's begin by setting up Xcode and the Xcode command-line tools, which give us a complete C++ development environment:

1. Download and install Xcode from the Mac App Store or `https://developer.apple.com/xcode/`. If the installer provides an option to install command-line tools, select it.
2. Open Xcode. If a license agreement is presented, accept it.
3. If command-line tools were not already installed, we must install them now. Go to **Xcode** | **Preferences** | **Downloads** and click on the **Install** button next to command-line tools. Wait for the installation to finish. Then, quit Xcode. Alternatively, if you do not find an option to install command-line tools from inside Xcode, open the Terminal and run the following command:

```
$ xcode-select install
```

Now, we will look at ways to automate our builds using MacPorts or Homebrew. These two tools are package managers, which help us resolve dependencies and separate our development libraries from the system libraries.

Generally, I recommend MacPorts. Compared to Homebrew, MacPorts offers more patches and configuration options for OpenCV. On the other hand, Homebrew offers more timely updates for OpenCV. At the time of writing, Homebrew offers a package for OpenCV 4.0.1, but MacPorts is still lagging at OpenCV 3.4.3. Homebrew and MacPorts can coexist with the Python package manager, pip, and we can use pip to get OpenCV 4.0.1, even though MacPorts does not package this version yet. Normally, MacPorts and Homebrew should not be installed on the same machine.

Our installation methods for Mac do not give us the OpenCV sample projects. To get these, download the latest source code archive from `https://opencv.org/releases.html` and unzip it to any location. Find the samples in `<opencv_unzip_destination>/samples/python`.

Now, depending on your preference, let's proceed to either the *Mac with MacPorts* section or the *Mac with Homebrew* section.

Mac with MacPorts

MacPorts provides Terminal commands that automate the process of downloading, compiling, and installing various pieces of **open source software** (**OSS**). MacPorts also installs dependencies, as needed. For each piece of software, the dependencies and build recipe are defined in a configuration file called a **Portfile**. A MacPorts repository is a collection of Portfiles.

Starting from a system where Xcode and its command-line tools are already set up, the following steps will give us an OpenCV installation through MacPorts:

1. Download and install MacPorts from http://www.macports.org/install.php.
2. Open the Terminal and run the following command to update MacPorts:

   ```
   $ sudo port selfupdate
   ```

   When prompted, enter your password.

3. Run the following commands to install Python 3.7, pip, NumPy, SciPy, and Requests:

   ```
   $ sudo port install python37
   $ sudo port install py37-pip
   $ sudo port install py37-numpy
   $ sudo port install py37-scipy
   $ sudo port install py37-requests
   ```

4. The Python installation executable is named python3.7. To link the default python executable to python3.7, and to link the default pip executable to this Python pip installation, let's also run the following:

   ```
   $ sudo port install python_select
   $ sudo port select python python37
   $ sudo port install pip_select
   $ sudo port select pip pip37
   ```

5. At the time of writing, MacPorts only has packages for relatively old versions of wxPython and PyInstaller. Let's use the following `pip` command to install more recent versions:

   ```
   $ pip install --user wxPython pyinstaller
   ```

6. To check whether MacPorts has an OpenCV 4 package, run `$ port list opencv`. At the time of writing, this produces the following output:

   ```
   opencv                    @3.4.3          graphics/opencv
   ```

   - Here, `@3.4.3` means that OpenCV 3.4.3 is the latest available package from MacPorts. However, if your output shows `@4.0.0` or a more recent version, you can use MacPorts to configure, build, and install OpenCV 4, by running a command such as the following:

     ```
     $ sudo port install opencv +avx2 +contrib +opencl +python37
     ```

Preparing for the Mission

- By adding `+avx2 +contrib +opencl +python37` to the command, we are specifying that we want the `opencv` variant (build configuration) with AVX2 CPU optimizations, `opencv_contrib` extra modules, OpenCL GPU optimizations, and Python 3.7 bindings. To see the full list of available variants before installing, we can enter the following:

    ```
    $ port variants opencv
    ```

- Depending on our customization needs, we can add other variants to the `install` command.
- On the other hand, if the output from `$ port list opencv` showed that MacPorts does not have an OpenCV 4 package yet, we can instead install OpenCV 4 and the `opencv_contrib` extra modules with pip, by running the following command:

    ```
    $ pip install --user opencv-contrib-python
    ```

Now, we have everything we need to develop OpenCV applications for Mac. To also develop for Android, we need to set up Android Studio, as we will describe in the following *Android Studio* section.

Mac with Homebrew

Like MacPorts, Homebrew is a package manager that provides Terminal commands to automate the process of downloading, compiling, and installing various pieces of open source software.

Starting from a system where Xcode and its command-line tools are already set up, the following steps will give us an OpenCV installation through Homebrew:

1. Open Terminal and run the following command to install Homebrew:

    ```
    $ /usr/bin/ruby -e "$(curl -fsSL
    https://raw.githubusercontent.com/Homebrew/install/master/install)"
    ```

2. Unlike MacPorts, Homebrew does not automatically put its executables in `PATH`. To do so, create or edit the `~/.profile` file and add this line at the top:

    ```
    export PATH=/usr/local/bin:/usr/local/sbin:$PATH
    ```

- Save the file and run this command to refresh `PATH`:

  ```
  $ source ~/.profile
  ```

- Note that executables installed by Homebrew now take precedence over executables installed by the system.

3. For Homebrew's self-diagnostic report, run:

   ```
   $ brew doctor
   ```

   Follow any troubleshooting advice it gives.

4. Now, update Homebrew:

   ```
   $ brew update
   ```

5. Run the following command to install Python 3.7:

   ```
   $ brew install python
   ```

6. Now, we can use Homebrew to install OpenCV and its dependencies, including NumPy. Run the following command:

   ```
   $ brew install opencv --with-contrib
   ```

7. Similarly, run the following command to install SciPy:

   ```
   $ pip install --user scipy
   ```

8. At the time of writing, Homebrew does not have packages for `requests` and `pyinstaller`, and its `wxPython` package is a relatively old version, so instead, we will use `pip` to install these modules. Run the following command:

   ```
   $ pip install --user requests wxPython pyinstaller
   ```

Now, we have everything we need to develop OpenCV applications for Mac. To also develop for Android, we need to set up **Tegra Android Development Pack (TADP)**, as described in the following *Tegra Android Development Pack* section.

Setting up Python and OpenCV on Debian Jessie and its derivatives, including Raspbian, Ubuntu, and Linux Mint

 For information on setting up the Raspbian operating system, see the *Setting up a Raspberry Pi* section, later in this chapter.

On Debian Jessie, Raspbian, Ubuntu, Linux Mint, and their derivatives, the python executable is Python 2.7, which comes preinstalled. We can use the system package manager, apt, to install NumPy, SciPy, and Requests from the standard repository. To update the apt package index and install the packages, run the following commands in Terminal:

```
$ sudo apt-get update
$ sudo apt-get install python-numpy python-scipy python-requests
```

The standard repository's latest packaged version of wxPython varies, depending on the operating system. On Ubuntu 14.04 and its derivatives, including Linux Mint 17, the latest packaged version is wxPython 2.8. Install it by running the following command:

```
$ sudo apt-get install python-wxgtk2.8
```

On Ubuntu 18.04 and newer versions, as well as derivatives such as Linux Mint 19, the latest packaged version is wxPython 4.0. Install it by running the following command:

```
$ sudo apt-get install python-wxgtk4.0
```

On most other systems in the Debian Jessie family, wxPython 3.0 is the latest packaged version. Install it by running the following command:

```
$ sudo apt-get install python-wxgtk3.0
```

The standard repository does not offer a PyInstaller package. Instead, let's use Python's own package manager, `pip`, to obtain PyInstaller. First, to ensure that `pip` is installed, run the following command:

```
$ sudo apt-get install python-pip
```

Now, install PyInstaller by running the following command:

```
$ pip install --user pyinstaller
```

The standard repository contains a python-opencv package, but it is an old version (3.2.0 or older, depending on the operating system) and it is missing the opencv_contrib modules, so it lacks some of the functionality used in this book. Thus, we have a choice of either using pip to obtain OpenCV 4 with the opencv_contrib modules, or building the same from source. To install a prebuilt version of OpenCV 4 and opencv_contrib with pip, run the following command:

```
$ pip install --user opencv-contrib-python
```

 If you prefer to use the python3 executable, which is Python 3.4 or a newer version (depending on the operating system), modify all the apt-get commands in the preceding instructions to use package names like python3-numpy, instead of names like python-numpy. Similarly, replace the pip commands with the pip3 commands.

Alternatively, to build OpenCV and opencv_contrib from source, follow the instructions in the following *Building OpenCV on Debian Jessie and its derivates with CMake and GCC* section.

After either installing a prebuilt OpenCV and opencv_contrib module or building it from source, we will have everything we need to develop OpenCV applications for Debian Jessie or a derivative. To also develop for Android, we need to set up Android Studio, as described in the *Setting up Android Studio and OpenCV* section, later in this chapter.

Building OpenCV on Debian Jessie and its derivatives with CMake and GCC

To compile OpenCV from source, we need a general-purpose C++ development environment. On Linux, the standard C++ development environment includes the g++ compiler and the Make build system, which defines build instructions in a file format known as **Makefile**.

OpenCV uses a set of build tools called **CMake**, which automates the use of Make, g++, and other tools. CMake 3 or a newer version is required, and we must install it. Also, we will install several third-party libraries. Some of these are required for standard OpenCV features, while others are optional dependencies that enable extra features.

As an example, let's install the following optional dependencies:

- `libdc1394`: This is a library to programmatically control IEEE 1394 (FireWire) cameras, which are quite common in industrial use. OpenCV can leverage this library to capture photos or video from some of these cameras.

- `libgphoto2`: This is a library to programmatically control photo cameras through a wired or wireless connection. The `libgphoto2` library supports a large number of cameras from Canon, Fuji, Leica, Nikon, Olympus, Panasonic, Sony, and other manufacturers. OpenCV can leverage this library to capture photos or video from some of these cameras.

After installing dependencies, we will configure, build, and install `OpenCV`. Here are the detailed steps:

1. On Ubuntu 14.04 and its derivatives, including Linux Mint 17, the `cmake` package in the standard repository is CMake 2, which is too old for our purposes. We need to ensure that the `cmake` package is not installed, and then we need to install the `cmake3` package, as well as other essential development and packaging tools. To accomplish this, run the following commands:

    ```
    $ sudo apt-get remove cmake
    $ sudo apt-get install build-essential cmake3 pkg-config
    ```

    On more recent versions of Ubuntu and its derivatives, and on Debian Jessie, the `cmake3` package does not exist; rather, the `cmake` package is CMake 3. Install it, as well as other essential development and packaging tools, by running the following command:

    ```
    $ sudo apt-get install build-essential cmake pkg-config
    ```

2. If your system uses a proxy server to access the internet, define two environment variables, `HTTP_PROXY` and `HTTPS_PROXY`, with values equal to the proxy server URL, such as `http://myproxy.com:8080`. This ensures that CMake can use the proxy server to download some additional dependencies for OpenCV. (If in doubt, do *not* define these environment variables; you are probably *not* using a proxy server.)

3. Run the following command to install OpenCV's dependencies for Python bindings and for video capture from **Video4Linux** (**V4L**)-compatible cameras, including most webcams:

   `$ sudo apt-get install python-dev libv4l-dev`

    If you prefer to use Python 3, replace `python-dev` with `python3-dev` in the preceding command.

4. Run the following command to install optional OpenCV dependencies:

   `$ sudo apt-get install libdc1394-22-dev libgphoto2-dev`

5. Download the OpenCV source's ZIP from http://opencv.org/releases.html. (Choose the latest version.) Unzip it to any destination folder, which we will refer to as `<opencv_unzip_destination>`.

6. Download `opencv_contrib` as a ZIP from https://github.com/opencv/opencv_contrib/releases. (Choose the latest version.) Unzip it to any destination folder, which we will refer to as `<opencv_contrib_unzip_destination>`.

7. Open Command Prompt. Create a folder to store our build:

   `$ mkdir <build_folder>`

   Change the directory to the newly created build folder:

   `$ cd <build_folder>`

8. Having set up our dependencies, we can now configure OpenCV's build system. To understand all the configuration options, we can read the code in `<opencv_unzip_destination>/opencv/sources/CMakeLists.txt`. However, as an example, we will just use the options for a release build that includes Python bindings, support for OpenGL interoperability, and support for extra camera types and video types. To create Makefiles for OpenCV with Python 2.7 bindings, run the following command (but replace the angle brackets and their contents with the actual paths):

   ```
   $ cmake -D CMAKE_BUILD_TYPE=RELEASE -D BUILD_EXAMPLES=ON -D
   WITH_1394=ON
   -D WITH_GPHOTO2=ON -D BUILD_opencv_python2=ON
   -D PYTHON2_EXECUTABLE=/usr/bin/python2.7
   -D PYTHON_LIBRARY2=/usr/lib/python2.7/config-x86_64-linux-
   ```

```
gnu/libpython2.7.so -D PYTHON_INCLUDE_DIR2=/usr/include/python2.7 -
D BUILD_opencv_python3=OFF
-D
OPENCV_EXTRA_MODULES_PATH=<opencv_contrib_unzip_destination>/module
s <opencv_unzip_destination>
```

Alternatively, to create Makefiles for OpenCV with bindings for Python 3, run the following command (but replace the angle brackets and their contents with the actual paths, and replace 3.6 with your actual Python 3 version, if it is not 3.6):

```
$ cmake -D CMAKE_BUILD_TYPE=RELEASE -D BUILD_EXAMPLES=ON -D
WITH_1394=ON -D WITH_GPHOTO2=ON -D BUILD_opencv_python2=OFF
-D BUILD_opencv_python3=ON -D PYTHON3_EXECUTABLE=/usr/bin/python3.6
-D PYTHON3_INCLUDE_DIR=/usr/include/python3.6
-D PYTHON3_LIBRARY=/usr/lib/python3.6/config-3.6m-x86_64-linux-
gnu/libpython3.6.so -D
OPENCV_EXTRA_MODULES_PATH=<opencv_contrib_unzip_destination>
<opencv_unzip_destination>
```

9. Run the following commands to build and install OpenCV in the manner specified by the Makefiles:

```
$ make -j8
$ sudo make install
```

At this point, we have everything we need to develop OpenCV applications for Debian Jessie or a derivative. To also develop for Android, we need to set up Android Studio, as described in the *Setting up Android Studio and OpenCV* section, later in this chapter.

Setting up Python and OpenCV on Fedora and its derivatives, including RHEL and CentOS

On Fedora, RHEL, and CentOS, the `python` executable is Python 2.7, which comes preinstalled. We can use the system package manager, yum, to install NumPy, SciPy, Requests, and wxPython from the standard repository. To do this, open Terminal and run the following command:

```
$ sudo yum install numpy scipy python-requests wxPython
```

The standard repository does not offer a PyInstaller package. Instead, let's use Python's own package manager, `pip`, to obtain PyInstaller. First, to ensure that `pip` is installed, run the following command:

```
$ sudo yum install python-pip
```

Now, install PyInstaller by running the following command:

```
$ pip install --user pyinstaller
```

The standard repository contains an `opencv` package, which includes the `opencv_contrib` modules and Python bindings, but it is an old version (3.4.4 or older, depending on the operating system). Thus, we want to use `pip` to obtain OpenCV 4 with the `opencv_contrib` modules. Run the following command:

```
$ pip install --user opencv-contrib-python
```

If you prefer to use the `python3` executable, which is Python 3.6 or 3.7 (depending on the operating system), replace the preceding `pip` commands with the `pip3` commands. You do not need to modify the `yum` commands, as the relevant packages, such as `numpy`, include sub-packages for both Python 2 and Python 3.

Now, we have everything we need to develop OpenCV applications for Fedora or a derivative. To also develop for Android, we need to set up Android Studio, as described in the following *Setting up Android Studio and OpenCV* section.

Setting up Python and OpenCV on openSUSE and its derivatives

On openSUSE, the `python` executable is Python 2.7, which comes preinstalled. We can use the system package manager, yum, to install NumPy, SciPy, Requests, and wxPython from the standard repository. To do this, open Terminal and run the following command:

```
$ sudo yum install python-numpy python-scipy python-requests python-wxWidgets
```

Although openSUSE and Fedora both use the yum package manager, they use different standard repositories with different package names.

The standard repository does not offer a PyInstaller package. Instead, let's use Python's own package manager, `pip`, to obtain PyInstaller. First, to ensure that pip is installed, run the following command:

```
$ sudo yum install python-pip
```

[27]

Now, install PyInstaller by running the following command:

```
$ pip install --user pyinstaller
```

The standard repository contains a `python2-opencv` package (and a `python3-opencv` package for Python 3), but it is an old version of OpenCV (3.4.3 or older, depending on the operating system). Thus, we want to use pip to obtain OpenCV 4 with the `opencv_contrib` modules. Run the following command:

```
$ pip install --user opencv-contrib-python
```

If you prefer to use the `python3` executable, which is Python 3.4, 3.6, or 3.7 (depending on the operating system), replace the preceding `pip` commands with the `pip3` commands. You do not need to modify the `yum` commands, as the relevant packages, such as `python-numpy`, include sub-packages for both Python 2 and Python 3.

Now, we have everything we need to develop OpenCV applications for openSUSE or a derivative. Next, we need to follow the cross-platform steps for setting up an Android development environment.

Setting up Android Studio and OpenCV

Android Studio is Google's official **integrated development environment** (IDE) for Android app development. Since its first stable release in 2014, Android Studio has grown in popularity and has replaced Eclipse as the IDE of choice for Android developers. Although some of the OpenCV documentation still contains outdated tutorials on Android development in Eclipse, nowadays, the OpenCV Android library and Android sample projects are primarily intended for use with Android Studio, instead.

Google provides a good cross-platform tutorial on Android Studio installation at `https://developer.android.com/studio/install`. Follow the part of the tutorial that is relevant to your operating system.

Download the latest version of the OpenCV Android pack from `https://opencv.org/releases.html`. Unzip it to any destination, which we will refer to as `<opencv_android_pack_unzip_destination>`. This has two subfolders:

- `<opencv_android_pack_unzip_destination>/sdk` contains the `OpenCV4Android` SDK. This consists of Java and C++ libraries, as well as build instructions, which we can import into Android Studio projects.

- `<opencv_android_pack_unzip_destination>/samples` contains sample projects that can be built in Android Studio. Unfortunately, as of OpenCV 4.0.1, these samples are outdated. On Android 6.0 and newer versions, the samples fail to access the camera, because they do not request user permission at runtime in the required manner.

At this point, we have obtained the core components of our development environment for the OpenCV Android apps. Next, let's look at Unity, a game engine that can deploy to Android and other platforms.

Setting up Unity and OpenCV

Unity (`https://unity3d.com`) is a three-dimensional game engine that supports development on 64-bit Windows or Mac, and deployment to many platforms, including Windows, Mac, Linux, iOS, Android, WebGL, and several game consoles. For one of our projects, we will use Unity along with a plugin called **OpenCV for Unity**, which is developed by Enox Software (`http://enoxsoftware.com/`.) The main programming language for Unity projects is C#, and OpenCV for Unity provides a C# API that is modeled on the OpenCV Java API for Android.

Unity has three license plans, Personal, Plus, and Pro, which all support the plugin that we want to use. The different editions are for different sizes of companies, as described in the licensing information at `https://store.unity.com`. The Personal license is free. The Plus and Pro licenses have subscription costs. If you are not already a Unity subscriber, you may want to wait and purchase a subscription when you are ready to start working on our Unity project in `Chapter 6`, *Creating a Physics Simulation Based on a Pen and Paper Sketch*. Once you are ready, obtain your license from `https://store.unity.com` and download Unity Hub from `https://unity3d.com/get-unity/download`. Unity Hub is an application to manage your Unity licenses and installations. Use it to set up Unity on your system. You can purchase OpenCV for Unity from the Unity Asset Store at `https://assetstore.unity.com/packages/tools/integration/opencv-for-unity-21088`, but we will cover details about obtaining the plugin in `Chapter 6`, *Creating a Physics Simulation Based on a Pen and Paper Sketch*, when we set up a Unity project.

Preparing for the Mission

Even before installing Unity, we can get inspiration from the demos at `https://unity3d.com/unity/demos/`. These demos include videos, articles about the development process, and in some cases, playable games that you can download for various platforms. They also include source code and art assets that you can open in Unity. After installing Unity, we can learn from these and other demo projects. Take a look at the resources available for download at `https://unity3d.com/learn/resources/downloads`. Also, check out the tutorials, videos, and documentation at `https://unity3d.com/learn`.

As you can see, there are a lot of official resources for Unity beginners, so I will let you explore these on your own for now.

Setting up a Raspberry Pi

Raspberry Pi is a **single-board computer** (**SBC**) with a low cost and low power consumption. It can be used as a desktop, a server, or an embedded system that controls other electronics. The Pi comes in several models. Currently, the flagship is Model 3 B+, which costs about $35. Compared to other models, it offers a faster CPU, more memory, and a faster Ethernet port, so it is a good candidate for computer vision experiments that rely on either local computing resources or the cloud. However, other models are also usable for computer vision projects.

Several operating systems are available for Raspberry Pi. We will use Raspbian, which is a port of Debian Stretch (a major Linux distribution) to ARM.

Download the latest Raspbian disk image from `http://downloads.raspberrypi.org/raspbian_latest`. You do not need to unzip the downloaded file. At the time of writing, the ZIP is called `2018-11-13-raspbian-stretch.zip`. Since your filenames may differ, we will refer to the file as `<raspbian_zip>`.

The `<raspbian_zip>` file contains a disk image, which we need to burn to an SD card with a capacity of at least 4 GB. (Note that 8 GB or larger is preferable, to allow plenty of room for OpenCV and our projects.) Any existing data on the card will be lost in the process. To burn the card, let's use a cross-platform, open source application called **Etcher**. Download it from `https://www.balena.io/etcher/` and set it up. (An installer is available for Windows or Mac. Alternatively, a portable application is available for Windows, Mac, or Linux). Insert an SD card and open Etcher. You should see the following window:

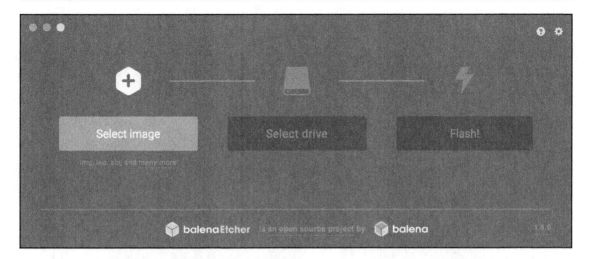

Etcher's user interface is so self-explanatory that even James Bond might struggle to find a double meaning in it. Click on the **Select image** button and select `<raspbian_zip>`. Click on the **Select drive** button and select your SD drive. Click on the **Flash!** button to burn the image to the SD card. Wait for the burning process to finish. Quit Etcher and eject the card.

Now, let's turn our attention to the Raspberry Pi hardware. Ensure that the Raspberry Pi micro-USB power cable is disconnected. Connect an HDMI monitor or TV, USB keyboard, USB mouse, and (optionally) Ethernet cable. Then, insert the SD card firmly into the slot on the bottom of the Pi. Connect the Pi power cable. The Pi should start booting from the SD card. During this first bootup, the filesystem expands to fill the entire SD card. When the Raspbian desktop appears for the first time, the system displays a series of setup dialogs. Follow the instructions in the dialogs in order to set your login password, and select an appropriate locale, time zone, and keyboard. Raspbian defaults to a UK keyboard layout, which will cause problems if you have a US or other keyboard. If you have an internet connection, you can also use the setup dialogs to perform a system update.

Preparing for the Mission

Once the setup is complete, take some time to admire the Raspbian desktop wallpaper and explore the system's infinite horizons, as I am doing in the following photograph:

In its heart (or in its seeds), Raspbian is just Debian Linux with an LXDE desktop and some special developer tools. If you are familiar with Debian or derivatives such as Ubuntu, you should feel right at home. Otherwise, you might want to explore the documentation and guides for beginners that are posted on the Raspberry Pi website, at https://www.raspberrypi.org/help/.

Now, as an exercise, let's share our Raspbian desktop through **Virtual Network Computing** (**VNC**) so that we can control it from a Windows, Mac, or Linux machine.

On the Pi, we need to first determine our local network address, which we will refer to as <pi_ip_address>. Open LXTerminal and run the following command:

```
$ ifconfig
```

The output should include a line beginning with something like `inet addr:192.168.1.93`, although the numbers will probably differ. In this example, `<pi_ip_address>` is `192.168.1.93`.

Now, we need to install a VNC server on the Pi by running the following command:

```
$ sudo apt-get install tightvncserver
```

To start the server, run this command:

```
$ tightvncserver
```

When prompted, enter a password, which other users must enter when connecting to this VNC server. Later, if you want to change the password, run this command:

```
$ vncpasswd
```

Unless the Pi (or the Ethernet socket to which it is connected) has a static IP address, the address may change whenever we reboot. Thus, upon reboot, we would need to run `ifconfig` again to determine the new address. Also, after rebooting, we need to run `tightvncserver` to relaunch the VNC server. For instructions on making the Pi's IP address static and automatically running `tightvncserver` upon boot, see Neil Black's online Raspberry Pi Beginner Guide, at `http://www.neil-black.co.uk/raspberrypi/raspberry-pi-beginners-guide/`.

Now, on another machine on the same local network, we can access the Pi's desktop through a VNC client. The steps are platform dependent, as follows:

1. On Windows, download VNC Viewer from `https://www.realvnc.com/download/`. Unzip it to any destination and run the executable file (such as `VNC-Server-6.4.0-Windows.exe`), which is inside the unzipped folder. Enter `vnc://<pi_ip_address>:5901` in the VNC server field and click on the **Connect** button. When prompted, enter the VNC password that you created earlier.
2. On Mac, open Safari and enter `vnc://<pi_ip_address>:5901` in the address bar. A window, **Connect to Shared Computer**, should appear. Click on the **Connect** button. When prompted, enter the VNC password that you created earlier.

3. Ubuntu normally comes with a VNC client called **Vinagre**. However, if we do not already have Vinagre, we can install it on Ubuntu or any Debian-based system by running the following command in Terminal:

   ```
   $ sudo apt-get install vinagre
   ```

   Open Vinagre (it might be listed as **Remote Desktop Viewer** in the system's applications menu or launcher). Click on the **Connect** button in the toolbar. Enter `vnc://<pi_ip_address>:5901` in the **Host:** field. Click on the **Connect** button in the lower-right corner.

Now you know how to prepare and serve Pi.

Setting up the Raspberry Pi camera module

Raspbian supports most USB webcams out of the box. Also, it supports the following **Camera Serial Interface** (**CSI**) cameras, which offer faster transfer speeds:

- **Raspberry Pi camera module**: A $25 RGB camera
- **Pi NoIR**: A $30 variant of the same camera, with the **infrared radiation** (**IR**) block filter removed so that it is sensitive to not only visible light, but also the nearest-to-visible part of the infrared spectrum, **near infrared** (**NIR**)

Compared to a USB webcam, the camera module or NoIR improves our chances of achieving high enough frame rates for interactive computer vision on the Pi. For this reason, I recommend these Pi-specific CSI cameras. However, in accordance with the low price, they have poor color rendition, mediocre auto-exposure, and fixed focus.

If in doubt, choose the camera module over the NoIR, because depending on the subject and lighting, NIR may interfere with vision, rather than aid it.

See the official tutorial at `http://www.raspberrypi.org/help/camera-module-setup/` for details about setting up either the camera module or the NoIR. Once the hardware is set up, you need to configure Raspbian to use the camera. From the Raspbian launch menu, select **Preferences** | **Raspbian Pi Configuration**, as shown in the following screenshot:

Chapter 1

The **Raspberry Pi Configuration** window should appear. Go to the **Interfaces** tab and select **Camera: Enable**, as shown in the following screenshot:

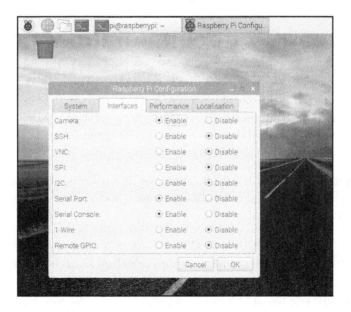

Click on **OK** and, when prompted, reboot the system.

Preparing for the Mission

At the time of writing, the camera module and NoIR do not work out of the box with OpenCV. We need to load a kernel module that adds support for the cameras through the **Video for Linux 2 (V4L2)** drivers. To do this for a single session, run the following command in Terminal:

```
$ sudo modprobe bcm2835-v4l2
```

Alternatively, to always load the kernel module upon bootup, run the following command, which appends the module to the `/etc/modules` file:

```
$ echo "bcm2835-v4l2" | sudo tee -a /etc/modules
```

Future versions of Raspbian (later than version 2018-11-13) might be preconfigured to use this kernel module. You can edit `/etc/modules` to check whether `bcm2835-v4l2` is already listed there.

Reboot the system again so that the kernel module is loaded. Now, we can use the `Camera` module or the NoIR with any camera software that supports V4L2 drivers, including OpenCV.

Finding OpenCV documentation, help, and updates

OpenCV's documentation is online, at `https://docs.opencv.org/master/`. The documentation includes a combined API reference for the latest OpenCV C++ API and its latest Python API (which is based on the C++ API). The latest Java API documentation is online, at `http://docs.opencv.org/master/javadoc/`.

If the documentation seems to leave your questions unanswered, try reaching out to the OpenCV community instead. The following sites are good venues for questions, answers, and shared experience:

- The official OpenCV forum, at `http://answers.opencv.org/questions/`
- The PyImageSearch site, where Adrian Rosebrock teaches computer vision and machine learning, at `https://www.pyimagesearch.com/`
- The support site for my OpenCV books, at `http://nummist.com/opencv/`

Finally, if you are an advanced user who wants to try new features, bug-fixes, and sample scripts from the latest (unstable) OpenCV source code, have a look at the project's repository at https://github.com/opencv/opencv/, as well as the repository for the opencv_contrib modules at https://github.com/opencv/opencv_contrib/.

Alternatives to Raspberry Pi

Besides Raspberry Pi, many other low-cost SBCs are suitable for running a desktop Linux distribution and OpenCV applications. The Raspberry Pi 3 models offer a quad-core ARMv8 processor and 1 GB RAM. However, some of the competing SBCs offer octa-core ARM processors and 2 GB RAM and can run more complex computer vision algorithms in real time. Moreover, unlike any current model of Pi, some of the competitors offer a USB 3 interface, which supports a wide range of high-resolution or high-speed cameras. These advantages tend to come with a higher price tag and higher power consumption. Here are some examples:

- Odroid XU4 (https://www.hardkernel.com/shop/odroid-xu4-special-price/): An octa-core SBC with 2 GB RAM and a USB 3 interface. It can run Ubuntu and other Linux distributions. At the time of writing, it is available from Odroid at a promotional price of $49.
- Banana Pi M3 (http://www.banana-pi.org/m3.html): An octa-core SBC with 2 GB RAM and a SATA interface for fast storage devices. It is compatible with many Raspberry Pi accessories and can run Ubuntu, Raspbian, and other Linux distributions. It typically costs around $75, if ordered factory-direct.
- Orange Pi 3 (http://www.orangepi.org/Orange%20Pi%203/): A quad-core SBC with 2 GB RAM and a USB 3 interface. It can run Ubuntu and other Linux distributions. It typically costs around $40, if ordered factory-direct.

If you would like to share your experience with using SBCs in computer vision projects, please write to me at josephhowse@nummist.com. I will post the community's wisdom to http://nummist.com/opencv/.

Summary

This was all a setup! I hear you gasp. Yes, but we did it for good reason. Now, we have a diverse set of development tools that will enable us to explore OpenCV in many contexts. Besides, it never hurts to learn some things about a lot of application frameworks and to have them all set up, in case someone asks us to do a project in a hurry.

Remember, James Bond has encyclopedic knowledge. In a highly symbolic conversation about rare and deadly fish, he goes toe-to-toe with Karl Stromberg, the diabolical oceanographer (*The Spy Who Loved Me*, 1977). Although we never see Bond studying the fish books, he must do it as bedtime reading after the camera cuts out.

The moral is, be prepared. Next, we will use OpenCV, along with several of the Python libraries and tools that we have installed, to build a GUI application that finds and classifies images on the web.

2
Searching for Luxury Accommodations Worldwide

Today the bridal suite, tomorrow a prison. A secret agent's sleeping arrangements are horribly unpredictable.

Each day, someone in MI6 gets the job of booking a stellar hotel room and, conversely, some evil henchman has to pick a warehouse or dilapidated apartment, plus a lamp, a chair, and implements of bondage. For mini missions or brief beatings, it is tolerable to leave the choice of venue to a fallible human being. However, for long-term rentals or acquisitions, would it not be wiser to develop a specialized search engine that takes the legwork and the guesswork out of the equation?

With this motivation, we are going to develop a desktop app called `Luxocator: The Luxury Locator`. It is a search engine that finds images on the web by keyword search and classifies each image as a luxury, interior scene; luxury, exterior scene; Stalinist, interior scene; or Stalinist, exterior scene, according to certain visual cues in the image.

Particularly, our classifier relies on comparing statistical distributions of color in different images or sets of images. This topic is called **color histogram analysis**. We will learn how to efficiently store and process our statistical model and how to redistribute it, along with our code, in an application bundle. Specifically, this chapter covers the following programming topics:

- Using OpenCV's Python bindings, along with the NumPy and SciPy libraries, to classify images based on color histogram analysis
- Using the Bing Image Search API to acquire images from a web search
- Building a GUI application with `wxPython`
- Using PyInstaller to bundle a Python application as an executable that can run on other systems

Technical requirements

This chapter's project has the following software dependencies:

- **A Python environment with the following modules**: OpenCV, NumPy, SciPy, Requests, wxPython, and optionally PyInstaller

Setup instructions are covered in `Chapter 1`, *Preparing for the Mission*. Refer to the setup instructions for any version requirements. Basic instructions for running Python code are covered in `Appendix C`, *Running with Snakes (or, First Steps with Python)*.

The completed project for this chapter can be found in this book's GitHub repository, `https://github.com/PacktPublishing/OpenCV-4-for-Secret-Agents-Second-Edition`, in the `Chapter002` folder.

Planning the Luxocator app

This chapter uses Python. Being a high-level, interpreted language with great third-party libraries for numeric and scientific computing, Python lets us focus on the functionality of the system rather than implementing subsystem details. For our first project, such a high-level perspective is precisely what we need.

Let's look at an overview of Luxocator's functionality and our choice of Python libraries that support this functionality. Like many computer vision applications, Luxocator has six basic steps:

1. **Acquire a static set of reference images**: For Luxocator, we (the developers) choose certain images that we deem to be luxury indoor scenes, other images that we consider Stalinist indoor scenes, and so on. We load these images into memory.
2. **Train a model based on the reference images**: For Luxocator, our model describes each image in terms of its normalized color histogram—that is, the distribution of colors across the image's pixels. We use OpenCV and NumPy to perform the calculations.
3. **Store the results of the training**: For Luxocator, we use SciPy to compress the reference histograms and write/read them to/from disk.
4. **Acquire a dynamic set of query images**: For Luxocator, we acquire query images using the Bing Search API through a Python wrapper. We also use the Requests library to download the full-resolution images.

5. **Compare the query images to the reference images**: For Luxocator, we compare each query image and each reference image based on the intersection of their histograms. We then make a classification based on the average results of these comparisons. We use NumPy to perform the calculations.
6. **Present the results of the comparison**: For Luxocator, we provide a GUI for initiating a search and navigating the results. This cross-platform GUI is developed in wxPython. A classification label, such as **Stalinist, exterior**, is shown below each image. See the following screenshot:

Optionally, we use PyInstaller to build Luxocator so that it can be deployed to users who do not have Python or the aforementioned libraries. However, remember that you might need to do extra troubleshooting of your own to make PyInstaller work in some environments, including Raspberry Pi or other ARM devices.

Creating, comparing, and storing histograms

"A grey-green color that often finds itself on the walls of public institutions-e.g., hospitals, schools, government buildings—and, where appropriated, on sundry supplies and equipment."
– *"institutional green", Segen's Medical Dictionary (2012)*

I hesitate to make sweeping statements about the ideal color of paint on a wall. It depends. I have found solace in many walls of many colors. My mother is a painter and I like paint in general.

But not all color is paint. Some color is dirt. Some color is concrete or marble, plywood or mahogany. Some color is the sky through big windows, the ocean, the golf course, the swimming pool, or Jacuzzi. Some color is discarded plastics and beer bottles, baked food on the stove, or perished vermin. Some color is unknown. Maybe the paint camouflages the dirt.

A typical camera can capture at least 16.7 million (*256 * 256 * 256*) distinct colors. For any given image, we can count the number of pixels of each color. This set of counts is called the **color histogram** of the image. Typically, most entries in the histogram will be zero because most scenes are not polychromatic (many-colored).

We can normalize the histogram by dividing the color counts by the total number of pixels. Since the number of pixels is factored out, normalized histograms are comparable even if the original images have different resolutions.

Given a pair of normalized histograms, we can measure the histograms' similarity on a scale of zero to one. One measure of similarity is called the **intersection** of the histograms. It is computed as follows:

$$d(H_1, H_2) = \sum_I min(H_1(I), H_2(I))$$

Here is the equivalent Python code (which we will optimize later):

```
def intersection(hist0, hist1):
    assert len(hist0) == len(hist1), \
        'Histogram lengths are mismatched'
    result = 0
    for i in range(len(hist0)):
        result += min(hist0[i], hist1[i])
    return result
```

For example, suppose that in one image, `50%` of the pixels are black and `50%` are white. In another image, `100%` of the pixels are black. The similarity is as follows:

```
min(50%, 100%) + min(50%, 0%) = 50% = 0.5
```

Here, a similarity of one does not mean that the images are identical; it means that their normalized histograms are identical. Relative to the first image, the second image could be a different size, could be flipped, or could even contain the same pixel values in a randomly different order.

Conversely, a similarity of zero does not mean that the images look completely different to a layperson; it just means that they have no color values in common. For example, an image that is all black and another image that is all charcoal-gray have histograms with a similarity of zero by our definition.

For the purpose of classifying images, we want to find the average similarity between a query histogram and a set of multiple reference histograms. A single reference histogram (and a single reference image) would be far too specific for a broad classification such as **Luxury, indoor**.

> Although we focus on one approach to comparing histograms, there are many alternatives. For a discussion of several algorithms and their implementations in Python, see this blog post by Adrian Rosebrock at `http://www.pyimagesearch.com/2014/07/14/3-ways-compare-histograms-using-opencv-python/`.

Let's write a class called `HistogramClassifier`, which creates and stores sets of references histograms and finds the average similarity between a query histogram and each set of reference histograms. To support this functionality, we will use OpenCV, NumPy, and SciPy. Create a file called `HistogramClassifier.py` and add the following shebang line (path to the Python interpreter) and `import` statements at the top:

```python
#!/usr/bin/env python


import numpy # Hint to PyInstaller
import cv2
import scipy.io
import scipy.sparse
```

Some versions of PyInstaller work better if we explicitly import the `numpy` module before the `cv2` module. Remember that OpenCV's Python bindings depend on NumPy. Also, note that the OpenCV Python module is called `cv2`, even though we are using OpenCV 4. The name `cv2` comes from a historical distinction between the parts of OpenCV that had an underlying C++ implementation (called `cv2`) and the parts that an older, underlying C implementation (called `cv`). As of OpenCV 4, everything is `cv2`.

An instance of `HistogramClassifier` stores several variables. A public Boolean called `verbose` controls the level of logging. A public float called `minimumSimilarityForPositiveLabel` defines a similarity threshold—if all the average similarities fall below this value, then the query image is given an `'Unknown'` classification. Several variables store values related to the color model. We assume that our images have three color channels with 8 bits (256 possible values) per channel. Finally, and most importantly, a dictionary called `_references` maps string keys such as `'Luxury, interior'` to lists of reference histograms. Let's declare the variables in the `HistogramClassifier` class's `__init__` method, as follows:

```
class HistogramClassifier(object):

    def __init__(self):

        self.verbose = False
        self.minimumSimilarityForPositiveLabel = 0.075

        self._channels = range(3)
        self._histSize = [256] * 3
        self._ranges = [0, 255] * 3
        self._references = {}
```

By convention, in a Python class, a variable or method name is prefixed with an underscore if the variable or method is meant to be protected (accessed only within the class and its subclasseses). However, this level of protection is not actually enforced. Most of our member variables and methods in this book are marked as protected, but a few are public. Python supports private variables and methods (denoted by a double-underscore prefix) that are meant to be inaccessible, even to subclasses. However, we avoid private variables and methods in this book because Python classes should typically be highly extensible.

`HistogramClassifier` has a method, `_createNormalizedHist`, which takes two arguments—an image and a Boolean indicating whether to store the resulting histogram in a **sparse** (compressed) format. The histogram is computed using an OpenCV function, `cv2.calcHist`. As arguments, it takes the image, the number of channels, the histogram size (that is, the dimensions of the color model), and the range of each color channel. We flatten the resulting histogram into a one-dimensional format that uses memory more efficiently. Then, optionally, we convert the histogram into a sparse format using a SciPy function called `scipy.sparse.csc_matrix`.

A sparse matrix uses a form of compression that relies on a default value, normally 0. That is to say, we do not bother storing all the zeroes individually; instead, we note the ranges that are full of zeroes. For histograms, this is an important optimization because in a typical image, most of the possible colors are absent. So, most of the histogram values are 0.

Compared to an uncompressed format, a sparse format offers better memory efficiency but worse computational efficiency. The same trade-off applies to compressed formats in general.

Here is the implementation of `_createNormalizedHist`:

```python
def _createNormalizedHist(self, image, sparse):
    # Create the histogram.
    hist = cv2.calcHist([image], self._channels, None,
                        self._histSize, self._ranges)
    # Normalize the histogram.
    hist[:] = hist * (1.0 / numpy.sum(hist))
    # Convert the histogram to one column for efficient storage.
    hist = hist.reshape(16777216, 1)   # 16777216 == pow(2, 24)
    if sparse:
        # Convert the histogram to a sparse matrix.
        hist = scipy.sparse.csc_matrix(hist)
    return hist
```

A public method, `addReference`, accepts two arguments—an image and a label (the label is a string describing the classification). We pass the image to `_createNormalizedHist` in order to create a normalized histogram in a sparse format. For a reference histogram, the sparse format is more appropriate because we want to keep many reference histograms in memory for the entire duration of a classification session. After creating the histogram, we add it to a list in `_references`, using the label as the key. Here is the implementation of `addReference`:

```
def addReference(self, image, label):
    hist = self._createNormalizedHist(image, True)
    if label not in self._references:
        self._references[label] = [hist]
    else:
        self._references[label] += [hist]
```

For the purposes of Luxocator, reference images come from files on disk. Let's give `HistogramClassifier` a public method, `addReferenceFromFile`, which accepts a file path instead of directly accepting an image. It also accepts a label. We load the image from file using an OpenCV method called `cv2.imread`, which accepts a path and a color format. Based on our earlier assumption about having three color channels, we always want to load images in color, not grayscale. This option is represented by the `cv2.IMREAD_COLOR` value. Having loaded the image, we pass it and the label to `addReference`. The implementation of `addReferenceFromFile` is as follows:

```
def addReferenceFromFile(self, path, label):
    image = cv2.imread(path, cv2.IMREAD_COLOR)
    self.addReference(image, label)
```

Now, we arrive at the crux of the matter—the `classify` public method, which accepts a query image, as well as an optional string to identify the image in log output. For each set of reference histograms, we compute the average similarity to the query histogram. If all similarity values fall below `minimumSimilarityForPositiveLabel`, we return the `'Unknown'` label. Otherwise, we return the label of the most similar set of reference histograms. If `verbose` is `True`, we also log all the labels and their respective average similarities. Here is the method's implementation:

```
def classify(self, queryImage, queryImageName=None):
    queryHist = self._createNormalizedHist(queryImage, False)
    bestLabel = 'Unknown'
    bestSimilarity = self.minimumSimilarityForPositiveLabel
    if self.verbose:
        print('===================================================')
        if queryImageName is not None:
            print('Query image:')
```

```
            print(' %s' % queryImageName)
        print('Mean similarity to reference images by label:')
    for label, referenceHists in self._references.items():
        similarity = 0.0
        for referenceHist in referenceHists:
            similarity += cv2.compareHist(
                    referenceHist.todense(), queryHist,
                    cv2.HISTCMP_INTERSECT)
        similarity /= len(referenceHists)
        if self.verbose:
            print(' %8f %s' % (similarity, label))
        if similarity > bestSimilarity:
            bestLabel = label
            bestSimilarity = similarity
    if self.verbose:
        print('=================================================')
    return bestLabel
```

Note the use of the `todense` method to decompress a sparse matrix.

We also provide a public method, `classifyFromFile`, which accepts a file path instead of directly accepting an image. Here is the implementation:

```
def classifyFromFile(self, path, queryImageName=None):
    if queryImageName is None:
        queryImageName = path
    queryImage = cv2.imread(path, cv2.IMREAD_COLOR)
    return self.classify(queryImage, queryImageName)
```

Computing all our reference histograms will take a bit of time. We do not want to recompute them every time we run Luxocator. So, we need to serialize and deserialize (save and load) the histograms to/from disk. For this purpose, SciPy provides two functions, `scipy.io.savemat` and `scipy.io.loadmat`. They accept a file and various optional arguments.

We can implement a `serialize` method with optional compression, as follows:

```
def serialize(self, path, compressed=False):
    file = open(path, 'wb')
    scipy.io.savemat(
        file, self._references, do_compression=compressed)
```

When deserializing, we get a dictionary from `scipy.io.loadmat`. However, this dictionary contains more than our original _references dictionary. It also contains some serialization metadata and some serialization metadata, and some additional arrays that wrap the lists that were originally in _references. We strip out these unwanted, added contents and store the result back in _references. The implementation is as follows:

```python
def deserialize(self, path):
    file = open(path, 'rb')
    self._references = scipy.io.loadmat(file)
    for key in list(self._references.keys()):
        value = self._references[key]
        if not isinstance(value, numpy.ndarray):
            # This entry is serialization metadata so delete it.
            del self._references[key]
            continue
        # The serializer wraps the data in an extra array.
        # Unwrap the data.
        self._references[key] = value[0]
```

That is our classifier. Next, we will test our classifier by feeding it some reference images and a query image.

Training the classifier with reference images

> *"Can you identify this coastline? Given time, yes."*
> *– Photo caption, Dante Stella*
> (http://www.dantestella.com/technical/hex352.html)

A small selection of reference images is included in this book's GitHub repository in a folder called `Chapter002/images`. Feel free to experiment with the classifier by adding more reference images, since a larger set may yield more reliable results. Bear in mind that our classifier relies on average similarity, so the more times you include a given color scheme in the reference images, the more heavily you are weighting the classifier in favor of that color scheme.

At the end of `HistogramClassifier.py`, let's add a `main` method to train and serialize a classifier using our reference images. We will also run the classifier on a couple of the images as a test. Here is a partial implementation:

```
def main():
    classifier = HistogramClassifier()
    classifier.verbose = True
    # 'Stalinist, interior' reference images
    classifier.addReferenceFromFile(
            'images/communal_apartments_01.jpg',
            'Stalinist, interior')
    # ...
    # Other reference images are omitted for brevity.
    # See the GitHub repository for the full implementation.
    # ...
    classifier.serialize('classifier.mat')
    classifier.deserialize('classifier.mat')
    classifier.classifyFromFile('images/dubai_damac_heights.jpg')
    classifier.classifyFromFile('images/communal_apartments_01.jpg')

if __name__ == '__main__':
    main()
```

Depending on the number of reference images, this method may take several minutes (or even longer) to run. Fortunately, since we are serializing the trained classifier, we will not have to run such a method every time we open our main application. Instead, we will simply deserialize the trained classifier from file, as we will see later in this chapter in the *Integrating everything into the GUI* section.

For a large number of training images, you might wish to modify the `main` function of `HistogramClassifier.py` to use all images in a specified folder. (For examples of iteration over all images in a folder, refer to the `describe.py` file in the code for Chapter 3, *Training a Smart Alarm to Recognize the Villain and His Cat*.) However, for a small number of training images, I find it more convenient to specify a list of images in code so that we can comment and uncomment individual images to see the effect on training.

Next, let's consider how our main application will acquire query images.

Acquiring images from the web

Our query images will come from a web search. Before we start implementing the search functionality, let's write some helper functions that let us fetch images through the `Requests` library and convert them into an OpenCV-compatible format. Because this functionality is highly reusable, we will put it in a module of static utility functions. Let's create a file called `RequestsUtils.py` and import OpenCV, NumPy, and Requests, as follows:

```
#!/usr/bin/env python


import numpy # Hint to PyInstaller
import cv2
import requests
import sys
```

As a global variable, let's store `HEADERS`, a dictionary of headers that we will use when making web requests. Some servers reject requests that appear to come from a bot. To improve the chance of our requests being accepted, let's set the `'User-Agent'` header to a value that mimics a web browser, as follows:

```
# Spoof a browser's User-Agent string.
# Otherwise, some sites will reject us as a bot.
HEADERS = {
    'User-Agent': 'Mozilla/5.0 ' \
                  '(Macintosh; Intel Mac OS X 10.9; rv:25.0) ' \
                  'Gecko/20100101 Firefox/25.0'
}
```

Whenever we receive a response to a web request, we want to check whether the status code is `200` OK. This is only a cursory test of whether the response is valid, but it is a good enough test for our purposes. We implement this test in the following method, `validateResponse`, which returns `True` if the response is deemed valid; otherwise, it logs an error message and returns `False`:

```
def validateResponse(response):
    statusCode = response.status_code
    if statusCode == 200:
        return True
    url = response.request.url
    sys.stderr.write(
            'Received unexpected status code (%d) when requesting %s\n' % \
            (statusCode, url))
    return False
```

With the help of HEADERS and validateResponse, we can try to get an image from a URL and return that image in an OpenCV-compatible format (failing that, we return None). As an intermediate step, we read raw data from a web response into a NumPy array using a function called numpy.fromstring. We then interpret this data as an image using a function called cv2.imdecode. Here is our implementation, a function called cvImageFromUrl that accepts a URL as an argument:

```python
def cvImageFromUrl(url):
    response = requests.get(url, headers=HEADERS)
    if not validateResponse(response):
        return None
    imageData = numpy.fromstring(response.content, numpy.uint8)
    image = cv2.imdecode(imageData, cv2.IMREAD_COLOR)
    if image is None:
        sys.stderr.write(
                'Failed to decode image from content of %s\n' % url)
    return image
```

To test these two functions, let's give RequestsUtils.py a main function that downloads an image from the web, converts it into an OpenCV-compatible format, and writes it to disk using an OpenCV function called imwrite. Here is our implementation:

```python
def main():
    image = cvImageFromUrl('http://nummist.com/images/ceiling.gaze.jpg')
    if image is not None:
        cv2.imwrite('image.png', image)

if __name__ == '__main__':
    main()
```

To confirm that everything worked, open image.png (which should be in the same directory as RequestsUtils.py) and compare it to the online image, which you can view in a web browser at http://nummist.com/images/ceiling.gaze.jpg.

Although we are putting a simple test of our RequestUtils module in a main function, a more sophisticated and maintainable approach to writing tests in Python is to use the classes in the unittest module of the standard library. For more information, refer to the official tutorial at https://docs.python.org/3/library/unittest.html.

Acquiring images from Bing Image Search

Microsoft's search engine, Bing, has an API that enables us to send queries and receive results in our own application. For a limited number of queries per month, the Bing Search API is free to use (currently, the limit is three thousand queries per month and three queries per second). However, we must register for it by performing the following steps:

1. Go to `https://azure.microsoft.com/` and log in. You will need to create a Microsoft account if you do not already have one.
2. Go to `https://azure.microsoft.com/en-us/services/cognitive-services/bing-image-search-api/`. Click the **Try Bing Image Search** button.
3. Next to the **Guest** option, click the **Get started** button to start a free seven-day trial. After you have started your trial, go to `https://azure.microsoft.com/en-us/try/cognitive-services/`. Select the **Search APIs** tab. Under the **Bing Image Search APIs v7** section, find the 32-character API key (you might find two keys labeled **Key 1** and **Key 2**. Either of these is fine). Copy the key and save it in a safe place. We will need to use it later to associate our Bing session with our Microsoft Account.
4. As an alternative to step three, or after your seven-day trial expires, you can create a free account. Next to the **Free Azure account** option, click the **Sign up** button to register for a free account with limited uses per month (of course, if you decide to use Luxocator obsessively, to the exclusion of normal activities, you can always upgrade to a paid account later). Even though the account is free, the registration process requires you to provide a phone number and a credit card in order to verify your identity. Once you have completed the registration process, click the **Portal** tab to go the Microsoft Azure control panel. Click **Cognitive Services**, then **Add**, then **Bing Search v7**, and then **Create**. Fill out the **Create** dialog by following the example in the following screenshot. Click the dialog's **Create** button. Click the **Go to resource** button. Click **Keys**. Find the 32-character API key (you might see two keys labeled **Key 1** and **Key 2**. Either of these is fine). Copy the key and save it in a safe place:

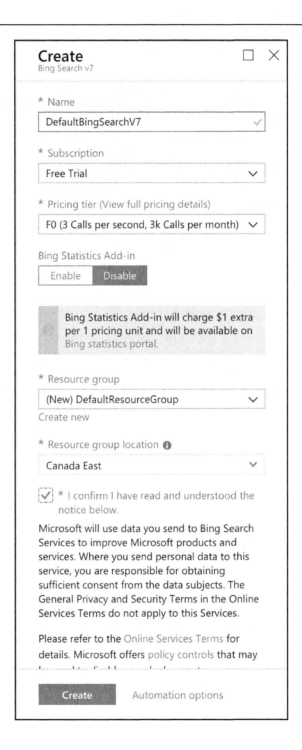

5. Create an environment variable named `BING_SEARCH_KEY`. Set its value equal to the API key that we created in step three or four (later, in our code, we will access the value of this environment variable in order to associate our Bing search session with our API key). Depending on your operating system, there are many different ways to create an environment variable. On Windows, you may want to use the Control Panel to add a user environment variable. On Unix-like systems, you may want to add a definition of the environment variable by editing the user's login script, which is called `~/.profile` on Mac, Ubuntu, and many other systems. After you have created the environment variable, reboot (or log out and log back in).

The Bing Search API and several other Microsoft APIs have a third-party Python wrapper called `py-ms-cognitive`. We can install it using Python's package manager, `pip`. Open a Terminal (on Unix-like systems) or Command Prompt (on Windows) and run the following command:

```
$ pip install --user py-ms-cognitive
```

Building atop `py-ms-cognitive`, we want a high-level interface for submitting a query string and navigating through a resulting list of images, which should be in an OpenCV-compatible format. We will make a class, `ImageSearchSession`, which offers such an interface. First, let's create a file, `ImageSearchSession.py`, and add the following `import` statements at the top:

```python
#!/usr/bin/env python

from py_ms_cognitive import PyMsCognitiveImageSearch
PyMsCognitiveImageSearch.SEARCH_IMAGE_BASE = \
        'https://api.cognitive.microsoft.com/bing/v7.0/images/search'

import numpy # Hint to PyInstaller
import cv2
import os
import pprint
import sys

import RequestsUtils
```

Note that we are modifying one of the `py_ms_cognitive` Python wrapper's static variables, `PyMsCognitiveImageSearch.SEARCH_IMAGE_BASE`. We do this because, by default, `py_ms_cognitive` uses an outdated base URL for the Bing Search API endpoint.

For `py_ms_cognitive`, we are using OpenCV, pretty-print (for logging JSON results from the search), system libraries, and our networking utility functions.

Like `HistogramClassifier`, `ImageSearchSession` has a public Boolean called `verbose` to control the level of logging. Moreover, `ImageSearchSession` has member variables to store the current query, metadata about the current image results, and metadata to help us navigate to the previous and next results. We can initialize these variables like so:

```python
class ImageSearchSession(object):

    def __init__(self):
        self.verbose = False
        self._query = ''
        self._results = []
        self._offset = 0
        self._numResultsRequested = 0
        self._numResultsReceived = 0
        self._numResultsAvailable = 0
```

We provide getters for many of the member variables, as follows:

```python
    @property
    def query(self):
        return self._query

    @property
    def offset(self):
        return self._offset

    @property
    def numResultsRequested(self):
        return self._numResultsRequested

    @property
    def numResultsReceived(self):
        return self._numResultsReceived

    @property
    def numResultsAvailable(self):
        return self._numResultsAvailable
```

Given these variables, we can navigate through a large set of results by fetching only a few at a time; that is, by looking through a window into the results. We can move our window to earlier or later results, as needed, by simply adjusting the offset by the number of requested results and clamping the offset to the valid range. Here are some implementations of the `searchPrev` and `searchNext` methods, which rely on a more general search method that we will implement afterwards:

```python
def searchPrev(self):
    if self._offset == 0:
        return
    offset = max(0, self._offset - self._numResultsRequested)
    self.search(self._query, self._numResultsRequested, offset)

def searchNext(self):
    if self._offset + self._numResultsRequested >= \
            self._numResultsAvailable:
        return
    offset = self._offset + self._numResultsRequested
    self.search(self._query, self._numResultsRequested, offset)
```

The more general-purpose `search` method accepts a query string, a maximum number of results, and an offset relative to the first available result. We store these arguments in member variables for reuse in the `searchPrev` and `searchNext` methods. The search method also uses the `BING_SEARCH_KEY` environment variable that we defined earlier. Here is this first part of the method's implementation:

```python
def search(self, query, numResultsRequested=50, offset=0):
    if 'BING_SEARCH_KEY' in os.environ:
        bingKey = os.environ['BING_SEARCH_KEY']
    else:
        sys.stderr.write(
                'Environment variable BING_SEARCH_KEY is undefined. '
                'Please define it, equal to your Bing Search API '
                'key.\n')
        return

    self._query = query
    self._numResultsRequested = numResultsRequested
    self._offset = offset
```

Then, we set up our search parameters, specifying that the results should be in JSON format and should include color photos only:

```
params = {'color':'ColorOnly', 'imageType':'Photo'}
```

We set up a search and request the results in JSON format. We handle any exceptions by printing an error message, setting the number of search results to 0, and returning prematurely:

```
searchService = PyMsCognitiveImageSearch(
        bingKey, query, custom_params=params)
searchService.current_offset = offset

try:
    self._results = searchService.search(numResultsRequested,
                                          'json')
except Exception as e:
    sys.stderr.write(
            'Error when requesting Bing image search for '
            '"%s":\n' % query)
    sys.stderr.write('%s\n' % str(e))
    self._offset = 0
    self._numResultsReceived = 0
    return
```

If the request succeeded, we proceed to parse the JSON. We store metadata about the actual number of results received and number of results available:

```
json = searchService.most_recent_json
self._numResultsReceived = len(self._results)
if self._numResultsRequested < self._numResultsReceived:
    # py_ms_cognitive modified the request to get more results.
    self._numResultsRequested = self._numResultsReceived
self._numResultsAvailable = int(json[u'totalEstimatedMatches'])
```

If the `verbose` public variable is `True`, we print the JSON results. Here is the end of the method's implementation:

```
if self.verbose:
    print('Received results of Bing image search for '
            '"%s":' % query)
    pprint.pprint(json)
```

Although the `search` method fetches a textual description of results, including image URLs, it does not actually fetch any full-sized images. This is good, because the full-sized images may be large and we do not need them all at once. Instead, we provide another method, `getCvImageAndUrl`, to retrieve the image and image URL that have a specified index in the current results. The index is given as an argument. As an optional second argument, this method accepts a Boolean indicating whether a thumbnail should be used instead of the full-sized image. We use `cvImageFromUrl` to fetch and convert the thumbnail or full-sized image. Here is our implementation:

```python
def getCvImageAndUrl(self, index, useThumbnail = False):
    if index >= self._numResultsReceived:
        return None, None
    result = self._results[index]
    if useThumbnail:
        url = result.thumbnail_url
    else:
        url = result.content_url
    return RequestsUtils.cvImageFromUrl(url), url
```

The caller of `getCvImageAndUrl` is responsible for dealing gracefully with image downloads that are slow or that fail. Recall that our `cvImageFromUrl` function just logs an error and returns `None` if the download fails.

To test `ImageSearchSession`, let's write a main function that instantiates the class, sets `verbose` to `True`, searches for `'luxury condo sales'`, and writes the first resulting image to disk. Here is the implementation:

```python
def main():
    session = ImageSearchSession()
    session.verbose = True
    session.search('luxury condo sales')
    image, url = session.getCvImageAndUrl(0)
    cv2.imwrite('image.png', image)

if __name__ == '__main__':
    main()
```

Now that we have a classifier and a search session, we are almost ready to proceed to the frontend of Luxocator. We just need a few more utility functions to help us prepare data and images for bundling and display.

Preparing images and resources for the app

Alongside `RequestsUtils.py` and `ImageSearchSession.py`, let's create another file called `ResizeUtils.py` with the following `import` statements:

```
import numpy # Hint to PyInstaller
import cv2
```

For display in a GUI, images usually have to be resized. One popular mode of resizing is called **aspect fill**. Here, we want to preserve the image's aspect ratio while changing its larger dimension (width for a landscape image or height for a portrait image) to a certain value. OpenCV does not directly provide this resizing mode, but it does provide a function, `cv2.resize`, which accepts an image, target dimensions, and optional arguments, including an interpolation method. We can write our own function, `cvResizeAspectFill`, which accepts an image, maximum size, and preferred interpolation methods for upsizing and downsizing. It determines the appropriate arguments for `cv2.resize` and passes them along. Here is the implementation:

```
def cvResizeAspectFill(src, maxSize,
                       upInterpolation=cv2.INTER_LANCZOS4,
                       downInterpolation=cv2.INTER_AREA):
    h, w = src.shape[:2]
    if w > h:
        if w > maxSize:
            interpolation=downInterpolation
        else:
            interpolation=upInterpolation
        h = int(maxSize * h / float(w))
        w = maxSize
    else:
        if h > maxSize:
            interpolation=downInterpolation
        else:
            interpolation=upInterpolation
        w = int(maxSize * w / float(h))
        h = maxSize
    dst = cv2.resize(src, (w, h), interpolation=interpolation)
    return dst
```

For a description of the interpolation methods that OpenCV supports, see the official documentation at https://docs.opencv.org/master/da/d54/group__imgproc__transform.html#ga47a974309e9102f5f08231edc7e7529d. For upsizing, we default to cv2.INTER_LANCZOS4, which produces sharp results. For downsizing, we default to cv2.INTER_AREA, which produces moiré-free results (moiré is an artifact that makes parallel lines or concentric curves look like crosshatching when they are sharpened at certain magnifications).

Now, let's create another file called WxUtils.py with the following import statements:

```
import numpy # Hint to PyInstaller
import cv2
import wx
```

Due to API changes between wxPython 3 and wxPython 4, it is important for us to check which version has been imported. We use the following code to get a version string, such as '4.0.3', and to parse the major version number, such as 4:

```
WX_MAJOR_VERSION = int(wx.__version__.split('.')[0])
```

OpenCV and wxPython use different image formats, so we will implement a conversion function, wxBitmapFromCvImage. While OpenCV stores color channels in BGR order, wxPython expects RGB order. We can use an OpenCV function, cv2.cvtColor, to reformat the image data accordingly. Then, we can use a wxPython function, wx.BitmapFromBuffer, to read the reformatted data into a wxPython bitmap, which we return. Here is the implementation:

```
def wxBitmapFromCvImage(image):
    image = cv2.cvtColor(image, cv2.COLOR_BGR2RGB)
    h, w = image.shape[:2]
    # The following conversion fails on Raspberry Pi.
    if WX_MAJOR_VERSION < 4:
        bitmap = wx.BitmapFromBuffer(w, h, image)
    else:
        bitmap = wx.Bitmap.FromBuffer(w, h, image)
    return bitmap
```

On some versions of Raspberry Pi and Raspbian, wx.BitmapFromBuffer suffers from a platform-specific bug that causes it to fail. For a workaround, see Appendix A, *Making WxUtils.py Compatible with Raspberry Pi*, at the end of this book.

[60]

We have one more utility module to make. Let's create a file, `PyInstallerUtils.py`, with `import` statements for the `os` and `sys` modules from Python's standard library:

```
import os
import sys
```

When we bundle our application using PyInstaller, the paths to resources will change. So, we need a function that correctly resolves paths, regardless of whether our application has been bundled or not. Let's add a function, `pyInstallerResourcePath`, which resolves a given path relative to the app directory (the `'_MEIPASS'` attribute) or, failing that, the current working directory (`'.'`). It is implemented as follows:

```
def resourcePath(relativePath):
    basePath = getattr(sys, '_MEIPASS', os.path.abspath('.'))
    return os.path.join(basePath, relativePath)
```

Our utilities modules are done now and we can move on to implementing the frontend of Luxocator.

Integrating everything into the GUI

For Luxocator's front end, let's create a file called `Luxocator.py`. This module depends on OpenCV, wxPython, and some of Python's standard OS and threading functionality. It also depends on all the other modules that we have written in this chapter. Add the following shebang line and `import` statements at the top of the file:

```
#!/usr/bin/env python


import numpy # Hint to PyInstaller
import cv2
import os
import threading
import wx

from HistogramClassifier import HistogramClassifier
from ImageSearchSession import ImageSearchSession
import PyInstallerUtils
import ResizeUtils
import WxUtils
```

Now, let's implement the `Luxocator` class as a subclass of `wx.Frame`, which represents a GUI frame such as the contents of a window. Most of our GUI code is in the `Luxocator` class's `__init__` method, which is, therefore, a big method but not very complicated. Our GUI elements include a search control, previous and next buttons, a bitmap, and a label to show the classification result. All of these GUI elements are stored in member variables. The bitmap is confined to a certain maximum size (by default, 768 pixels in the larger dimension), and the other elements are laid out below it. Several methods are registered as callbacks to handle events such as the window closing, the *Esc* key being pressed, a search string being entered, or the next or previous button being clicked. Besides the GUI elements, other member variables include instances of our `HistogramClassifier` and `ImageSearchSession` classes. Here is the implementation of the initializer, interspersed with some remarks on the GUI elements that we are using:

```python
class Luxocator(wx.Frame):

    def __init__(self, classifierPath, maxImageSize=768,
                 verboseSearchSession=False,
                 verboseClassifier=False):

        style = wx.CLOSE_BOX | wx.MINIMIZE_BOX | wx.CAPTION | \
            wx.SYSTEM_MENU | wx.CLIP_CHILDREN
        wx.Frame.__init__(self, None, title='Luxocator', style=style)
        self.SetBackgroundColour(wx.Colour(232, 232, 232))

        self._maxImageSize = maxImageSize
        border = 12
        defaultQuery = 'luxury condo sales'

        self._index = 0
        self._session = ImageSearchSession()
        self._session.verbose = verboseSearchSession
        self._session.search(defaultQuery)

        self._classifier = HistogramClassifier()
        self._classifier.verbose = verboseClassifier
        self._classifier.deserialize(classifierPath)

        self.Bind(wx.EVT_CLOSE, self._onCloseWindow)

        quitCommandID = wx.NewId()
        self.Bind(wx.EVT_MENU, self._onQuitCommand,
                  id=quitCommandID)
        acceleratorTable = wx.AcceleratorTable([
            (wx.ACCEL_NORMAL, wx.WXK_ESCAPE, quitCommandID)
        ])
        self.SetAcceleratorTable(acceleratorTable)
```

For more information about using bitmaps, controls, and layouts in wxPython, refer to the official wiki at http://wiki.wxpython.org/.

The search control (coming up next) deserves special attention because it contains multiple controls within it, and its behavior differs slightly across operating systems. It may have up to three sub-controls—a text field, a search button, and a cancel button. There may be a callback for the *Enter* key being pressed while the text field is active. If the search and cancel buttons are present, they have callbacks for being clicked. We can set up the search control and its callbacks as follows:

```
self._searchCtrl = wx.SearchCtrl(
    self, size=(self._maxImageSize / 3, -1),
    style=wx.TE_PROCESS_ENTER)
self._searchCtrl.SetValue(defaultQuery)
self._searchCtrl.Bind(wx.EVT_TEXT_ENTER,
                     self._onSearchEntered)
self._searchCtrl.Bind(wx.EVT_SEARCHCTRL_SEARCH_BTN,
                     self._onSearchEntered)
self._searchCtrl.Bind(wx.EVT_SEARCHCTRL_CANCEL_BTN,
                     self._onSearchCanceled)
```

By contrast, the label, previous and next buttons, and bitmap do not have any sub-controls that concern us. We can set them up as follows:

```
self._labelStaticText = wx.StaticText(self)

self._prevButton = wx.Button(self, label='Prev')
self._prevButton.Bind(wx.EVT_BUTTON,
                     self._onPrevButtonClicked)

self._nextButton = wx.Button(self, label='Next')
self._nextButton.Bind(wx.EVT_BUTTON,
                     self._onNextButtonClicked)

self._staticBitmap = wx.StaticBitmap(self)
```

Our controls are lined up horizontally, with the search control on the left edge of the window, the previous and next buttons on the right edge, and the label halfway in-between the search control and previous button. We use an instance of `wx.BoxSizer` to define this horizontal layout:

```
controlsSizer = wx.BoxSizer(wx.HORIZONTAL)
controlsSizer.Add(self._searchCtrl, 0,
                 wx.ALIGN_CENTER_VERTICAL | wx.RIGHT,
```

```
                    border)
controlsSizer.Add((0, 0), 1) # Spacer
controlsSizer.Add(
        self._labelStaticText, 0, wx.ALIGN_CENTER_VERTICAL)
controlsSizer.Add((0, 0), 1) # Spacer
controlsSizer.Add(
        self._prevButton, 0,
        wx.ALIGN_CENTER_VERTICAL | wx.LEFT | wx.RIGHT,
        border)
controlsSizer.Add(
        self._nextButton, 0, wx.ALIGN_CENTER_VERTICAL)
```

The best thing about layouts (and Russian dolls) is that they can be nested, one inside another. Our horizontal layout of controls needs to appear below the bitmap. This relationship is a vertical layout, which we define using another `wx.BoxSizer` instance:

```
self._rootSizer = wx.BoxSizer(wx.VERTICAL)
self._rootSizer.Add(self._staticBitmap, 0,
                    wx.TOP | wx.LEFT | wx.RIGHT, border)
self._rootSizer.Add(controlsSizer, 0, wx.EXPAND | wx.ALL,
                    border)

self.SetSizerAndFit(self._rootSizer)

self._updateImageAndControls()
```

That is the end of the `__init__` method.

As we can see in the following code, we provide getters and setters for the `verbose` property of our `ImageSearchSession` instance and our `HistogramClassifier` instance:

```
@property
def verboseSearchSession(self):
    return self._session.verbose

@verboseSearchSession.setter
def verboseSearchSession(self, value):
    self._session.verbose = value

@property
def verboseClassifier(self):
    return self._classifier.verbose

@verboseClassifier.setter
def verboseClassifier(self, value):
    self._classifier.verbose = value
```

Our `_onCloseWindow` callback just cleans up the application by calling the `Destroy` method of the superclass. Here is its implementation:

```
def _onCloseWindow(self, event):
    self.Destroy()
```

Similarly, we have connected the *Esc* key to the `_onQuitCommand` callback, which closes the window. This, in turn, will result in `_onCloseWindow` being called. Here is the implementation of `_onQuitCommand`:

```
def _onQuitCommand(self, event):
    self.Close()
```

Our `_onSearchEntered` callback submits the query string through the search method of `ImageSearchSession`. Then, it calls a helper method, `_updateImageAndControls`, which asynchronously fetches images and updates the GUI, as we will see later. Here is the implementation of `_onSearchEntered`:

```
def _onSearchEntered(self, event):
    query = event.GetString()
    if len(query) < 1:
        return
    self._session.search(query)
    self._index = 0
    self._updateImageAndControls()
```

Our `_onSearchCanceled` callback simply clears the search control's text field, as seen in the following code:

```
def _onSearchCanceled(self, event):
    self._searchCtrl.Clear()
```

Our remaining GUI event callbacks, `_onNextButtonClicked` and `_onPrevButtonClicked`, check whether more results are available and, if so, uses the `searchNext` or `searchPrev` method of `ImageSearchSession`. Then, using the `_updateImageAndControls` helper method, images are fetched asynchronously and the GUI is updated. Here are the implementations of the callbacks:

```
def _onNextButtonClicked(self, event):
    self._index += 1
    if self._index >= self._session.offset + \
            self._session.numResultsReceived - 1:
        self._session.searchNext()
    self._updateImageAndControls()

def _onPrevButtonClicked(self, event):
```

```
        self._index -= 1
        if self._index < self._session.offset:
            self._session.searchPrev()
        self._updateImageAndControls()
```

The `_disableControls` method disables the search control and the previous and next buttons, as follows:

```
def _disableControls(self):
    self._searchCtrl.Disable()
    self._prevButton.Disable()
    self._nextButton.Disable()
```

Conversely, the `_enableControls` method enables the search control, the previous button (if we are not already at the first available search result), and the next button (if we are not already at the last available search result). Here is the implementation:

```
def _enableControls(self):
    self._searchCtrl.Enable()
    if self._index > 0:
        self._prevButton.Enable()
    if self._index < self._session.numResultsAvailable - 1:
        self._nextButton.Enable()
```

The `_updateImageAndControls` method first disables the controls because we do not want to handle any new queries until the current query is handled. Then, a busy cursor is shown and another helper method, `_updateImageAndControlsAsync`, is started on a background thread. Here is the implementation:

```
def _updateImageAndControls(self):
    # Disable the controls.
    self._disableControls()
    # Show the busy cursor.
    wx.BeginBusyCursor()
    # Get the image in a background thread.
    threading.Thread(
            target=self._updateImageAndControlsAsync).start()
```

The background method, `_updateImageAndControlsAsync`, starts by fetching an image and converting it into OpenCV format. If the image cannot be fetched and converted, an error message is used as the label. Otherwise, the image is classified and resized to an appropriate size for display. Then, the resized image and the classification label are passed to a third and final helper method, `_updateImageAndControlsResync`, which updates the GUI on the main thread. Here is the implementation of `_updateImageAndControlsAsync`:

```
def _updateImageAndControlsAsync(self):
    if self._session.numResultsRequested == 0:
        image = None
        label = 'Search had no results'
    else:
        # Get the current image.
        image, url = self._session.getCvImageAndUrl(
            self._index % self._session.numResultsRequested)
        if image is None:
            # Provide an error message.
            label = 'Failed to decode image'
        else:
            # Classify the image.
            label = self._classifier.classify(image, url)
            # Resize the image while maintaining its aspect ratio.
            image = ResizeUtils.cvResizeAspectFill(
                image, self._maxImageSize)
    # Update the GUI on the main thread.
    wx.CallAfter(self._updateImageAndControlsResync, image,
                 label)
```

The synchronous callback, `_updateImageAndControlsResync`, hides the busy cursor, creates a wxPython bitmap from the fetched image (or just a black bitmap if no image was successfully fetched and converted), shows the image and its classification label, resizes GUI elements, re-enables controls, and refreshes the window. Here is its implementation:

```
def _updateImageAndControlsResync(self, image, label):
    # Hide the busy cursor.
    wx.EndBusyCursor()
    if image is None:
        # Provide a black bitmap.
        bitmap = wx.Bitmap(self._maxImageSize,
                           self._maxImageSize / 2)
    else:
        # Convert the image to bitmap format.
        bitmap = WxUtils.wxBitmapFromCvImage(image)
    # Show the bitmap.
    self._staticBitmap.SetBitmap(bitmap)
```

```
# Show the label.
self._labelStaticText.SetLabel(label)
# Resize the sizer and frame.
self._rootSizer.Fit(self)
# Re-enable the controls.
self._enableControls()
# Refresh.
self.Refresh()
```

When the image cannot be successfully fetched and converted, the user sees something like the following screenshot, containing a black placeholder image:

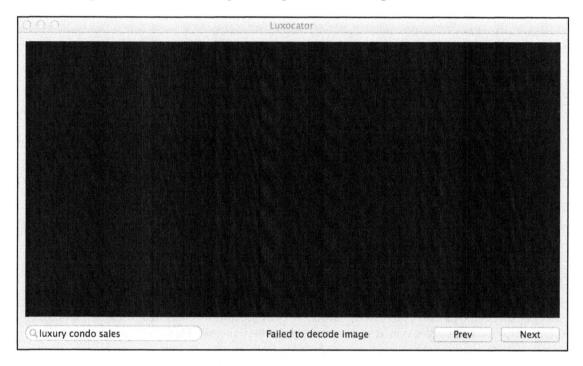

Conversely, when an image is successfully fetched and converted, the users sees the classification result, as shown in the following screenshot:

That completes the implementation of the `Luxocator` class. Now, let's write a `main` method to set resource paths and launch an instance of `Luxocator`:

```
def main():
    os.environ['REQUESTS_CA_BUNDLE'] = \
            PyInstallerUtils.resourcePath('cacert.pem')
    app = wx.App()
    luxocator = Luxocator(
            PyInstallerUtils.resourcePath('classifier.mat'),
            verboseSearchSession=False, verboseClassifier=False)
```

```
        luxocator.Show()
        app.MainLoop()

if __name__ == '__main__':
    main()
```

Note that one of the resources is a certificate bundle called `cacert.pem`. It is required by Requests in order to make an SSL connection, which is, in turn, required by Bing. You can find a copy of it inside this chapter's code bundle, which is downloadable from my website at http://nummist.com/opencv/7376_02.zip. Place `cacert.pem` in the same folder as `Luxocator.py`. Note that our code sets an environment variable, `REQUESTS_CA_BUNDLE`, which is used by Requests to locate the certificate bundle.

 Depending on how it is installed or how it is bundled with an app, Requests may or may not have an internal version of the certificate bundle. For predictability, it is better to provide this external version.

Running Luxocator and troubleshooting SSL problems

At this point, you can run `Luxocator.py`, enter search keywords, and navigate through the results. Watch for any errors that Luxocator might print to the Terminal. On some systems, notably Ubuntu 14.04 and its derivatives, such as Linux Mint 17, you might run into a bug in the Requests library when Luxocator attempts to access an HTTPS URL. The symptom of this bug is an error message similar to the following:

```
requests.exceptions.SSLError: [Errno 1] _ssl.c:510: error:14077410:SSL routines:SSL23_GET_SERVER_HELLO:sslv3 alert handshake failure
```

If you encounter this problem, you can try to resolve it by installing additional SSL-related packages and downgrading Requests to an earlier version. Some users of Ubuntu 14.04 and its derivatives report that they resolved the problem by running the following commands:

```
$ sudo apt-get install python-dev libssl-dev libffi-dev
$ pip install --user pyopenssl==0.13.1 pyasn1 ndg-httpsclient
```

Alternatively, some users of Ubuntu 14.04 and its derivatives report that they resolved the problem by upgrading to a newer version of the operating system. Note that the problem is not specific to Luxocator, but rather it affects any software that uses Requests, so it is potentially an issue of system-wide importance.

When you are satisfied with your results from testing Luxocator, let's proceed to build a Luxocator package that we can more easily distribute to other users' systems.

Building Luxocator for distribution

To tell PyInstaller how to build Luxocator, we must create a specification file, which we will call `Luxocator.spec`. Actually, the specification file is a Python script that uses a PyInstaller class called `Analysis` and the PyInstaller functions called `PYZ`, `EXE`, and `BUNDLE`. The `Analysis` class is responsible for analyzing one or more Python scripts (in our case, just `Luxocator.py`) and tracing all the dependencies that must be bundled with these scripts in order to make a redistributable application. Sometimes, `Analysis` makes mistakes or omissions, so we modify the list of dependencies after it is initialized. Then, we zip the scripts, make an executable, and (for Mac) make an app bundle using `PYZ`, `EXE`, and `BUNDLE`, respectively. Here is the implementation:

```
a = Analysis(['Luxocator.py'],
             pathex=['.'],
             hiddenimports=[],
             hookspath=None,
             runtime_hooks=None)

# Include SSL certificates for the sake of the 'requests' module.
a.datas.append(('cacert.pem', 'cacert.pem', 'DATA'))

# Include our app's classifier data.
a.datas.append(('classifier.mat', 'classifier.mat', 'DATA'))


pyz = PYZ(a.pure)

exe = EXE(pyz,
          a.scripts,
          a.binaries,
          a.zipfiles,
          a.datas,
          name='Luxocator',
          icon='win\icon-windowed.ico',
```

Searching for Luxury Accommodations Worldwide

```
            debug=False,
            strip=None,
            upx=True,
            console=False)
app = BUNDLE(exe,
             name='Luxocator.app',
             icon=None)
```

Note that this script specifies three resource files that must be bundled with the app: `cacert.pem`, `classifier.mat`, and `winicon-windowed.ico`. We have already discussed `cacert.pem` in the previous section, and `classifier.mat` is the output of our main function in `HistogramClassifier.py`. The Windows icon file, `winicon-windowed.ico`, is included in this book's GitHub repository in the `Chapter002/win` folder. Alternatively, you may provide your own icon file if you prefer.

> For more information about PyInstaller's `Analysis` class, specification files, and other functionality, see the official documentation at https://pyinstaller.readthedocs.io/.

Now, let's write a platform-specific shell script to clean any old builds, train our classifier, and then bundle the app using PyInstaller. On Windows, create a script called `build.bat`, containing the following commands:

```
set PYINSTALLER=pyinstaller

REM Remove any previous build of the app.
rmdir build /s /q
rmdir dist /s /q

REM Train the classifier.
python HistogramClassifier.py

REM Build the app.
"%PYINSTALLER%" --onefile --windowed Luxocator.spec

REM Make the app an executable.
rename dist\Luxocator Luxocator.exe
```

> If `pyinstaller.exe` is not in your system's `Path`, you will need to change the `build.bat` script's definition of the `PYINSTALLER` variable in order to provide a full path to `pyinstaller.exe`.

Similarly, on Mac or Linux, create a script called `build.sh`. Make it executable (for example, by running `$ chmod +x build.sh` in the Terminal). The file should contain the following commands:

```sh
#!/usr/bin/env sh


# Search for common names of PyInstaller in $PATH.
if [ -x "$(command -v "pyinstaller")" ]; then
    PYINSTALLER=pyinstaller
elif [ -x "$(command -v "pyinstaller-3.6")" ]; then
    PYINSTALLER=pyinstaller-3.6
elif [ -x "$(command -v "pyinstaller-3.5")" ]; then
    PYINSTALLER=pyinstaller-3.5
elif [ -x "$(command -v "pyinstaller-3.4")" ]; then
    PYINSTALLER=pyinstaller-3.4
elif [ -x "$(command -v "pyinstaller-2.7")" ]; then
    PYINSTALLER=pyinstaller-2.7
else
    echo "Failed to find PyInstaller in \$PATH"
    exit 1
fi
echo "Found PyInstaller in \$PATH with name \"$PYINSTALLER\""

# Remove any previous build of the app.
rm -rf build
rm -rf dist

# Train the classifier.
python HistogramClassifier.py

# Build the app.
"$PYINSTALLER" --onefile --windowed Luxocator.spec

# Determine the platform.
platform=`uname -s`

if [ "$platform" = 'Darwin' ]; then
    # We are on Mac.
    # Copy custom metadata and resources into the app bundle.
    cp -r mac/Contents dist/Luxocator.app
fi
```

> **TIP**
> If the `pyinstaller` executable (or a similar executable, such as `pyinstaller-3.6` for Python 3.6) is not in your system's `PATH`, you will need to change the `build.sh` script's definition of the `PYINSTALLER` variable in order to provide a full path to `pyinstaller`.

Note that on Mac (the Darwin platform), we are manually modifying the app bundle's contents as a post-build step. We do this in order to overwrite the default app icon and default properties file that PyInstaller puts in all Mac apps (notably, in some versions of PyInstaller, the default properties do not include support for Retina mode, so they make the app look pixelated on recent Mac hardware. Our customizations fix this issue). This book's GitHub repository includes the custom Mac app contents in a folder called `Chapter002/mac/Contents`. You may modify its files to provide any icon and properties you want.

After running the platform-specific build script, we should have a redistributable build of Luxocator at `dist/Luxocator.exe` (Windows), `dist/Luxocator.app` (Mac), or `dist/Luxocator` (Linux). If we are using 64-bit Python libraries on our development machine, this build will only work on 64-bit systems. Otherwise, it should work on both 32-bit and 64-bit systems. The best way to test the build is to run it on another machine that doesn't have any of the relevant libraries (such as OpenCV) installed.

Summary

So much can happen in a single mission! We trained an OpenCV/NumPy/SciPy histogram classifier, performed Bing Image Searches, built a `wxPython` app, and used PyInstaller to bundle it all for redistribution to Russia with love (or, indeed, to any destination with any sentiment). At this point, you are well-primed to create other Python applications that combine computer vision, web requests, and a GUI.

For our next mission, we will dig our claws deeper into OpenCV and computer vision by building a fully functional cat recognizer!

Section 2: The Chase

Detect, classify, recognize, and measure real-world objects in real-time. Integrate with a wider range of application frameworks and libraries.

The following chapters will be covered in this section:

- `Chapter 3`, *Training a Smart Alarm to Recognize the Villain and His Cat*
- `Chapter 4`, *Controlling a Phone App with Your Suave Gestures*
- `Chapter 5`, *Equipping Your Car with a Rearview Camera and Hazard Detection*
- `Chapter 6`, *Creating a Physics Simulation Based on a Pen and Paper Sketch*

3
Training a Smart Alarm to Recognize the Villain and His Cat

"The naming of cats is a difficult matter."
　　　　　　　　　　　 – T. S. Eliot, Old Possum's Book of Practical Cats (1939)

"Blofeld: I've taught you to love chickens, to love their flesh, their voice."
　　　　　　　　　　　 – On Her Majesty's Secret Service (1969)

Imagine that the date is January 1, 2015. The balance of world power is shifting again. Lithuania is joining the eurozone. Russia, Belarus, Armenia, Kazakhstan, and Kyrgyzstan are forming the Eurasian Economic Union. The first edition of *OpenCV for Secret Agents* is going to the printers. On this day, if you saw Ernst Stavro Blofeld, would you recognize him?

Let me remind you that Blofeld, as the number one man in the **Special Executive for Counterintelligence, Terrorism, Revenge, and Extortion** (**SPECTRE**), is a super-villain who eludes James Bond countless times before being written out of the movies due to an intellectual property dispute. Blofeld last appears as an anonymous character in the intro sequence of *For Your Eyes Only* (1981), where we see him fall from a helicopter and down a factory's smokestack as he shouts, *Mr. Booooooooooond!*

Despite this dramatic exit, the evidence of Blofeld's death is unclear. After all, Blofeld is a notoriously difficult man to recognize. His face is seldom caught on camera. As early as the 1960s, he was using plastic surgery to change his identity and to turn his henchmen into lookalikes of himself. Half a century later, we must ask, is Blofeld a dead man or is he just made-over, perhaps as a beautiful actress in a Colombian telenovela?

One thing is certain. If Blofeld is alive, he is accompanied by a blue-eyed, white Angora cat (preserved by a veterinary miracle or taxidermy). Patting this cat is Blofeld's telltale habit in every movie. His face may be different but his lap cat is the same. We last see the cat jumping out of Blofeld's lap just before the fateful helicopter ride.

Some commentators have noted a resemblance between Blofeld and Dr. Evil, the nemesis of Austin Powers. However, by comparing the respective lap cats, we can prove that these two villains are not the same.

The moral is that two approaches to recognition are better than one. Though we cannot see the man's face, we should not lose sight of his cat.

Of course, the suspense ended on October 26, 2015, when Blofeld made his comeback in *Spectre*. He and the cat looked remarkably unchanged after 34 years.

To automate the search for villains and their cats, we are going to develop a desktop or Raspberry Pi application called `Angora Blue` (an innocent-sounding code name that alludes to the blue eyes of Blofeld's cat). `Angora Blue` will send us an email alert when it recognizes a specified villain or a specified cat with a certain level of confidence. We will also develop a GUI app called `Interactive Recognizer`, which will train Angora Blue's recognition model based on camera images and names that we provide interactively. To distinguish faces from the background, `Interactive Recognizer` depends on a human face detection model that comes with OpenCV and a cat face detection model that we are going to train using an original script and third-party image databases.

Perhaps you have heard that OpenCV comes with a set of pretrained cat face detectors. This is true! I originally developed them for this book's first edition; I contributed them to OpenCV, and I have maintained them with improvements. This chapter covers the process that I used to train the latest version of these official OpenCV cat-face detectors.

This is a big chapter, but it is rewarding because you will learn a process that applies to detecting and recognizing any kind of animal face, and even any object!

Technical requirements

This chapter's project has the following software dependencies:

- **A Python environment with the following modules**: OpenCV (including opencv_contrib), NumPy, SciPy, Requests, wxPython, and optionally PyInstaller

Setup instructions are covered in `Chapter 1`, *Preparing for the Mission*. Refer to the setup instructions for any version requirements. Basic instructions for running Python code are covered in `Appendix C`, *Running with Snakes (or, First Steps with Python)*.

The completed project for this chapter can be found in this book's GitHub repository, `https://github.com/PacktPublishing/OpenCV-4-for-Secret-Agents-Second-Edition`, in the `Chapter003` folder.

Understanding machine learning in general

Our work throughout this chapter builds on the techniques of machine learning, meaning that the software makes predictions or decisions based on statistical models. Particularly, our approach is one of supervised learning, meaning that we (programmers and users) provide the software with examples of data and correct responses. The software creates the statistical model to extrapolate from these examples. The human provided examples are referred to as reference data or training data (or reference images or training images in the context of computer vision). Conversely, the software's extrapolations pertain to test data (or test images or scenes in the context of computer vision).

Supervised learning is much like the flashcard pedagogy used in early childhood education. The teacher shows the child a series of pictures (training images) and says,

> *"This is a cow. Moo! This is a horse. Neigh!"*

Then, on a field trip to a farm (a scene), the child can hopefully distinguish between a horse and a cow. However, I must confess that I once mistook a horse for a cow, and I was teased about this misclassification for many years thereafter.

Apart from supervised learning, which is widely used in problems of vision and semantics, there are two other broad approaches to machine learning—unsupervised learning and reinforcement learning. **Unsupervised learning** requires the software to find some structure, such as clusters, in data where no meaning or correct examples are assigned by a human. Analyzing biological structures, such as genomes, is a common problem for unsupervised learning. On the other hand, **reinforcement learning** requires the software to experimentally optimize a solution to some sequence of problems, where a human assigns the final goal but the software must set intermediate goals. Piloting a vehicle and playing a game are common problems for reinforcement learning.

Besides being a computer vision library, OpenCV offers a general purpose machine learning module that can process any kind of data, not necessarily images. For more information on this module and the underlying machine learning concepts, see the *Machine Learning* section of the official OpenCV-Python tutorials at `https://docs.opencv.org/4.0.0-beta/d6/de2/tutorial_py_table_of_contents_ml.html`. Meanwhile, our chapter proceeds with more specialized machine learning functionality and concepts that OpenCV users often apply to face detection and recognition.

Planning the Interactive Recognizer app

Let's begin this project with the middle layer, the `Interactive Recognizer` app, in order to see how all layers connect. Like Luxocator from the `Chapter 2`, *Searching for Luxury Accommodations Worldwide*, project, `Interactive Recognizer` is a GUI app built with wxPython. Refer to the following screenshot, featuring one of my colleagues, Chief Science Officer Sanibel San Delphinium Andromeda, high priestess of the Numm:

The app uses a face detection model, which is loaded from disk, and it maintains a face recognition model, which is saved to disk and later loaded back from disk. The user may specify the identity of any detected face, and this input is added to the face recognition model. A detection result is shown by outlining the face in the video feed, while a recognition result is shown by displaying the name of the face in the text below. To elaborate, we may say that the app has the following flow of execution:

1. Load a face detection model from file. The role of the detection model is to distinguish faces from the background.

2. Load a face recognition model from file if any such model was saved during a previous run of `Interactive Recognizer`. Otherwise, if there is no such model to load, create a new one. The role of the recognition model is to distinguish faces of different individuals from each other.

3. Capture and display a live video from a camera.

4. For each frame of video, detect the largest face, if any. If a face is detected:

    1. Draw a rectangle around the face.
    2. Permit the user to enter the face's identity as a short string (up to four characters), such as `Joe` or `Puss`. When the user hits the **Add to Model** button, train the model to recognize the face as whomever the user specified (`Joe`, `Puss`, or another identity).
    3. If the recognition model is trained for at least one face, display the recognizer's prediction for the current face—that is, display the most probable identity of the current face, according to the recognizer. Also, display a measure of distance (non-confidence) for this prediction.

5. If the recognition model is trained for at least one face, permit the user to hit the **Clear Model** button to delete the model (including any version saved to file) and create a new one.

6. On exit, if the recognition model is trained for at least one face, save the model to file so that it can be loaded in subsequent runs of `Interactive Recognizer` and `Angora Blue`.

We could generalize by using the term object instead of face. Depending on the models that it loads, `Interactive Recognizer` could detect and recognize any kind of object, not necessarily faces.

We use a type of detection model called a **Haar cascade** and a type of recognition model called **Local Binary Patterns** (**LBP**) or **Local Binary Pattern Histograms** (**LBPH**). Alternatively, we may use LBPH for both detection and recognition. As detection models, LBP cascades are faster but generally less reliable, compared to Haar cascades. OpenCV comes with some Haar cascade and LBP cascade files, including several face detection models. Command-line tools for generating such files are also included with OpenCV. The APIs offer high-level classes for loading and using Haar or LBP cascades and for loading, saving, training, and using LBPH recognition models. Let's look at the basic concepts of these models.

Understanding Haar cascades and LBPH

> *"Cookie Monster: Hey, you know what? A round cookie with one bite out of it looks like a C. A round donut with one bite out of it also looks like a C! But it is not as good as a cookie. Oh, and the moon sometimes looks like a C! But you can't eat that."*
>
> *– "C is for Cookie," Sesame Street*

Think about cloud-watching. If you lie on the ground and look up at the clouds, maybe you imagine that one cloud is shaped like a mound of mashed potatoes on a plate. If you board an airplane and fly to this cloud, you will still see some resemblance between the cloud's surface and the fluffy, lumpy texture of hearty mashed potatoes. However, if you could slice off a piece of cloud and examine it under a microscope, you might see ice crystals that do not resemble the microscopic structure of mashed potatoes at all.

Similarly, in an image made up of pixels, a person or a computer vision algorithm can see many distinctive shapes or patterns, partly depending on the level of magnification. During the creation of a Haar cascade, various parts of the image are cropped and/or scaled so that we consider only a few pixels at a time (though these pixels may represent any level of magnification). This sample of the image is called a **window**. We subtract some of the grayscale pixel values from others in order to measure the window's similarity to certain common shapes where a dark region meets a light region. Examples include an edge, a corner, or a thin line, as shown in the following diagram. If a window has a high similarity to one of these archetypes, it may be selected as a **feature**. We expect to find similar features at similar positions and magnifications relative to each other, across all images of the same subject:

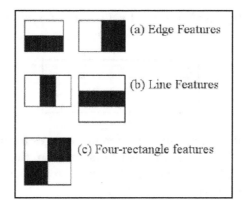

Not all features are equally significant. Across a set of images, we can see whether a feature is truly typical of images that include our subject (the **positive training set**) and atypical of images that exclude our subject (the **negative training set**). We give features a different rank or **stage** depending on how well they distinguish subjects from non-subjects. Together, a set of stages form a **cascade** or a series of comparison criteria. Every stage must be passed in order to reach a positive detection result. Conversely, a negative detection result can be reached in fewer stages, perhaps only a single stage (an important optimization). Like the training images, scenes are examined through various windows, and we may end up detecting multiple subjects in one scene.

 For more information about Haar cascades in OpenCV, see the official documentation at `https://docs.opencv.org/4.0.0-beta/d7/d8b/tutorial_py_face_detection.html`.

An LBPH model, as the name suggests, is based on a kind of histogram. For each pixel in a window, we note whether each neighboring pixel in a certain radius is brighter or darker. Our histogram counts the darker pixels in each neighboring position. For example, suppose a window contains the following two neighborhoods of a one-pixel radius:

Black	White	Black
White	White	White
Black	White	Black

Black	Black	Black
White	White	White
White	White	White

Counting these two neighborhoods (and not yet counting other neighborhoods in the window), our histogram can be visualized like this:

2	1	2
0	0	0
1	0	1

If we compute the LBPH of multiple sets of reference images for multiple subjects, we can determine which set of LBPH references is least distant from the LBPH of a piece of a scene, such as a detected face. Based on the least distant set of references, we can predict the identity of the face (or other object) in the scene.

An LBPH model is good at capturing fine texture detail in any subject, not just faces. Moreover, it is good for applications where the model needs to be updated, such as Interactive Recognizer. The histograms for any two images are computed independently, so a new reference image can be added without recomputing the rest of the model.

OpenCV also implements other models that are popular for face recognition, namely, Eigenfaces and Fisherfaces. We use LBPH because it supports updates in real time, whereas Eigenfaces and Fisherfaces do not. For more information on these three recognition models, see the official documentation at https://docs.opencv.org/4.0.0-beta/da/d60/tutorial_face_main.html.

Alternatively, for detection rather than recognition, we can organize LBPH models into a cascade of multiple tests, much like a Haar cascade. Unlike an LBPH recognition model, an LBP cascade cannot be updated in real time.

Haar cascades, LBP cascades, and LBPH recognition models are not robust with respect to rotation or flipping. For example, if we look at a face upside down, it will not be detected by a Haar cascade that was trained only with upright faces. Similarly, if we had an LBPH recognition model trained for a cat whose face is black on the cat's left-hand side and orange on the cat's right-hand side, the model might not recognize the same cat in a mirror. The exception is that we could include mirror images in the training set, but then we might get a false positive recognition for a different cat whose face is orange on the cat's left-hand side and black on the cat's right-hand side.

Chapter 3

 Unless otherwise noted, we may assume that a Haar cascade or LBPH model is trained for an *upright* subject. That is, the subject is not tilted or upside down in the image's coordinate space. If a man is standing on his head, we can take an upright photo of his face by turning the camera upside down or, equivalently, by applying a 180-degree rotation in software.

Some other directional terms are worth noting. A *frontal*, *rear*, or *profile* subject has its front, rear, or profile visible in the image. Most computer vision people, including the authors of OpenCV, express *left* and *right* in the image's coordinate space. For example, if we say *left eye*, for an upright, frontal, non-mirrored face, we mean the subject's right-hand eye, since left and right in image space are opposite from an upright, frontal, non-mirrored subject's left-hand and right-hand directions.

The following screenshot shows how we would label the *left eye* and *right eye* in a non-mirrored image (left) and mirrored image (right):

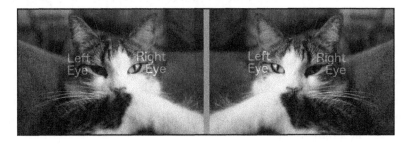

Our human and feline detectors deal with upright, frontal faces.

Of course, in a real-world photo, we cannot expect a face to be perfectly upright. The person's head or the camera might have been slightly tilted. Moreover, we cannot expect boundary regions, where a face meets a background, to be similar across images. We must take great care to preprocess the training images so that the face is rotated to a nearly perfect upright pose and boundary regions are cropped off. When cropping, we should place the major features of the face, such as eyes, in a consistent position. These considerations are addressed further in the *Planning the cat-detection model* section, later in this chapter.

If we must detect faces in various rotations, one option is to rotate the scene before sending it to the detector. For example, we can try to detect faces in the original scene, then in a version of the scene that has been rotated 15 degrees, then a version rotated—15 degrees (345 degrees), then a version rotated 30 degrees, and so on. Similarly, we can send mirrored versions of the scene to the detector. Depending on how many variations of the scene are tested, such an approach may be too slow for real-time use, and thus we do not use it in this chapter.

Implementing the Interactive Recognizer app

Let's create a new folder, where we will store this chapter's project, including the following subfolders and files that are relevant to `Interactive Recognizer`:

- `cascades/haarcascade_frontalface_alt.xml`: A detection model for a frontal human face. It should be included with OpenCV at a path such as `<opencv_unzip_destination>/data/haarcascades/haarcascade_frontalface_alt.xml` or for a MacPorts installation at `/opt/local/share/OpenCV/haarcascades/haarcascade_frontalface_alt.xml`. Copy or link to that version. (Alternatively, get it from this book's GitHub repository).
- `cascades/lbpcascade_frontalface.xml`: An alternative (faster but less reliable) detection model for a frontal human face. It should be included with OpenCV at a path such as `<opencv_unzip_destination>/data/lbpcascades/lbpcascade_frontalface.xml` or for a MacPorts installation at `/opt/local/share/OpenCV/lbpcascades/lbpcascade_frontalface.xml`. Copy or link to that version. Alternatively, get it from this book's GitHub repository.
- `cascades/haarcascade_frontalcatface.xml`: A detection model for a frontal, feline face. We will build it later in this chapter. Alternatively, you may get a prebuilt version from this book's GitHub repository.

- `cascades/haarcascade_frontalcatface_extended.xml`: An alternative detection model for a frontal feline face. This version is sensitive to diagonal patterns, potentially including whiskers and ears. We will build it later in this chapter. (Alternatively, you may get a prebuilt version from this book's GitHub repository.)
- `cascades/lbpcascade_frontalcatface.xml`: Another alternative (faster but less reliable) detection model for a frontal feline face. We will build it later in this chapter. (Alternatively, you may get a prebuilt version from this book's GitHub repository.)
- `recognizers/lbph_human_faces.xml`: A recognition model for the faces of certain human individuals. It is generated by `InteractiveHumanFaceRecognizer.py`, as follows later.
- `recognizers/lbph_cat_faces.xml`: A recognition model for the faces of certain feline individuals. It is generated by `InteractiveCatFaceRecognizer.py`, as follows later.
- `ResizeUtils.py`: Utility functions for resizing images. It copies or links to the previous chapter's version of `ResizeUtils.py`. We will add a function to resize the camera capture dimensions.
- `WxUtils.py`: Utility functions for wxPython GUI applications. It copies or links to the `Chapter 2`, *Searching for Luxury Accommodations Worldwide*, version of `WxUtils.py`.
- `BinasciiUtils.py`: Utility functions for converting human-readable identifiers into numbers and back.
- `InteractiveRecognizer.py`: A class that encapsulates the `Interactive Recognizer` app and exposes certain variables for configuration. We will implement it in this section.
- `InteractiveHumanFaceRecognizer.py`: A script to launch a version of Interactive Recognizer that is configured for frontal human faces. We will implement it in this section.
- `InteractiveCatFaceRecognizer.py`: A script to launch a version of `Interactive Recognizer` that is configured for frontal feline faces. We will implement it in this section.

Let's start with an addition to our existing `ResizeUtils` module. We want to be able to specify the resolution at which a camera captures images. Camera input is represented by an OpenCV class called `VideoCapture`, with the `get` and `set` methods that pertain to various camera parameters, including resolution. (Incidentally, `VideoCapture` can also represent a video file.) There is no guarantee that a given capture resolution is supported by a given camera. We need to check the success or failure of any attempt to set the capture resolution. Accordingly, let's add the following utility function to `ResizeUtils.py` to attempt to set a capture resolution and to return the actual capture resolution:

```python
def cvResizeCapture(capture, preferredSize):

    # Try to set the requested dimensions.
    w, h = preferredSize
    capture.set(cv2.CAP_PROP_FRAME_WIDTH, w)
    capture.set(cv2.CAP_PROP_FRAME_HEIGHT, h)

    # Sometimes the dimensions fluctuate at the start of capture.
    # Discard two frames to allow for this.
    capture.read()
    capture.read()

    # Try to return the actual dimensions of the third frame.
    success, image = capture.read()
    if success and image is not None:
        h, w = image.shape[:2]
    return (w, h)
```

Now, let's consider the requirements for our new `BinasciiUtils` module. OpenCV's recognizers use 32-bit integers as identifiers. For a GUI, asking the user to give a face a number, instead of a name, is not very friendly. We could keep a dictionary that maps numbers to names, and we could save this dictionary to disk, alongside the recognition model, but here is my lazier solution. Four or fewer ASCII characters can be cast to a 32-bit integer (and vice versa). For example, consider the name *Puss*, in which the letter ASCII codes are *80, 117, 115,* and *115*, respectively. Remembering that each letter is one byte or 8 bits, we can apply bitshift operations to the ASCII codes to get the following value:

$(80 << 24) + (117 << 16) + (115 << 8) + 115 = 1,349,874,547$

We will let the user enter names of up to four characters, and, behind the scenes, we will convert to and from the 32-bit integers that the model stores. Let's create `BinasciiUtils.py`, and put the following imports and conversion functions in it:

```
import binascii

def fourCharsToInt(s):
    return int(binascii.hexlify(bytearray(s, 'ascii')), 16)

def intToFourChars(i):
    return binascii.unhexlify(format(i, 'x')).decode('ascii')
```

Now, let's proceed to write `InteractiveRecognizer.py`. It should start with the following `import` statements:

```
import numpy
import cv2
import os
import sys
import threading
import wx

import BinasciiUtils
import ResizeUtils
import WxUtils
```

Our `InteractiveRecognizer` application class accepts several arguments that allow us to create different variants of the app with different titles, highlight colors, recognition models, detection models, and tweaks to the detection behavior. Let's look at the initializer's declaration:

```
class InteractiveRecognizer(wx.Frame):

    def __init__(self, recognizerPath, cascadePath,
                 scaleFactor=1.3, minNeighbors=4,
                 minSizeProportional=(0.25, 0.25),
                 rectColor=(0, 255, 0),
                 cameraDeviceID=0, imageSize=(1280, 720),
                 title='Interactive Recognizer'):
```

The initializer's arguments are defined as follows:

- `recognizerPath`: This is the file containing the recognition model. This file does not need to exist when the app starts. Rather, the recognition model (if any) is saved here when the app exits.

- `cascadePath`: This is the file containing the detection model. This file does need to exist when the app starts.
- `scaleFactor`: The detector searches for faces at several different scales. This argument specifies the ratio of each scale to the next smaller scale. A bigger ratio implies a faster search but fewer detections.
- `minNeighbors`: If the detector encounters two overlapping regions that both might pass detection as faces, they are called neighbors. The `minNeighbors` argument specifies the minimum number of neighbors that a face must have in order to pass detection. Where `minNeighbors>0`, the rationale is that a true face could be cropped in several alternative places and still look like a face. A greater number of required neighbors implies fewer detections and a lower proportion of false positives.
- `minSizeProportional`: A face's minimum width and height are expressed as a proportion of the camera's vertical resolution or horizontal resolution, whichever is less. For example, if the camera resolution is *640 x 480* and `minSizeProportional=(0.25, 0.25)`, the face must measure at least *120 x 120* (in pixels) in order to pass detection. A bigger minimum size implies a faster search but fewer detections. The `(0.25, 0.25)` default value is appropriate for a face that is close to a webcam.
- `rectColor`: This is for the color of the rectangle outlining a detected face. Like most color tuples in OpenCV, it is specified in **blue, green, and red** (BGR) order (not RGB).
- `cameraDeviceID`: The is the device ID of the camera that should be used for input. Typically, webcams are numbered starting from `0`, with any connected external webcams coming before any internal webcams. Some camera drivers reserve fixed device IDs. For example, OpenNI reserves `900` for Kinect and `910` for Asus Xtion.
- `imageSize`: The preferred resolution for captured images. If the camera does not support this resolution, another resolution is used.
- `title`: The app title, as seen in the window title bar.

We also provide a public Boolean variable to configure whether or not the camera feed is mirrored. By default, it is mirrored because users find a mirrored image of themselves to be more intuitive:

```
self.mirrored = True
```

Another Boolean tracks whether the app should still be running or whether it is closing. This information is relevant to cleaning up a background thread:

```
self._running = True
```

Using an OpenCV class called `cv2.VideoCapture`, we open a camera feed and get its resolution, as follows:

```
self._capture = cv2.VideoCapture(cameraDeviceID)
size = ResizeUtils.cvResizeCapture(
        self._capture, imageSize)
self._imageWidth, self._imageHeight = size
```

We define variables to store the images that we will capture, process, and display. Initially, these are `None`. In order to capture and process images on one thread, and then draw them to the screen on another thread, we will use a pattern known as **double buffering**. While one frame (the **back buffer**) is being prepared on one thread, another frame (the **front buffer**) will be being drawn on a second thread. When both threads have done a round of work, we will swap the buffers so that the old back buffer becomes the new front buffer and vice versa (by simply changing references, without copying data). To accomplish this in a thread-safe manner, we need to declare a **mutual exclusion lock** (also called a **mutex**), which represents a permission or resource (in this case, access to the front buffer) that only one thread can acquire at a time. We will see the lock in use later in this section, in the `_onVideoPanelPaint` and `_runCaptureLoop` methods. For now, here are the initial declarations of the images and lock:

```
self._image = None
self._grayImage = None
self._equalizedGrayImage = None

self._imageFrontBuffer = None
self._imageFrontBufferLock = threading.Lock()
```

Next, we set up variables related to detection and recognition. Many of these variables just store initialization arguments for later use. Also, we keep a reference to the currently detected face, which is initially `None`. We initialize an LBPH recognizer and load any recognition model that we may have saved on a previous run on the app. Likewise, we initialize a detector by loading a Haar cascade or LBP cascade from file. Here is the relevant code:

```
self._currDetectedObject = None

self._recognizerPath = recognizerPath
self._recognizer = cv2.face.LBPHFaceRecognizer_create()
if os.path.isfile(recognizerPath):
    self._recognizer.read(recognizerPath)
    self._recognizerTrained = True
else:
    self._recognizerTrained = False
```

```
self._detector = cv2.CascadeClassifier(cascadePath)
self._scaleFactor = scaleFactor
self._minNeighbors = minNeighbors
minImageSize = min(self._imageWidth, self._imageHeight)
self._minSize = (int(minImageSize * minSizeProportional[0]),
                 int(minImageSize * minSizeProportional[1]))
self._rectColor = rectColor
```

Having set up the variables that are relevant to computer vision, we proceed to the GUI implementation, which is mostly boilerplate code. First, in the following snippet, we set up the window with a certain style, size, title, and background color, and we bind a handler for its close event:

```
style = wx.CLOSE_BOX | wx.MINIMIZE_BOX | wx.CAPTION | \
    wx.SYSTEM_MENU | wx.CLIP_CHILDREN
wx.Frame.__init__(self, None, title=title,
                  style=style, size=size)
self.SetBackgroundColour(wx.Colour(232, 232, 232))

self.Bind(wx.EVT_CLOSE, self._onCloseWindow)
```

Next, we set a callback for the *Escape* key. Since a key is not a GUI widget, there is no `Bind` method directly associated with a key, and we need to set up the callback a bit differently than we have previously seen with wxWidgets. We bind a new menu event and callback to the `InteractiveRecognizer` instance, and we map a keyboard shortcut to the menu event using a class called `wx.AcceleratorTable`. (Note, however, that our app actually has no menu, nor is an actual menu item required for the keyboard shortcut to work.) Here is the code:

```
quitCommandID = wx.NewId()
self.Bind(wx.EVT_MENU, self._onQuitCommand,
          id=quitCommandID)
acceleratorTable = wx.AcceleratorTable([
    (wx.ACCEL_NORMAL, wx.WXK_ESCAPE, quitCommandID)
])
self.SetAcceleratorTable(acceleratorTable)
```

The following code initializes the GUI widgets (including a video panel, text field, buttons, and label) and sets their event callbacks:

```
self._videoPanel = wx.Panel(self, size=size)
self._videoPanel.Bind(
    wx.EVT_ERASE_BACKGROUND,
    self._onVideoPanelEraseBackground)
self._videoPanel.Bind(
    wx.EVT_PAINT, self._onVideoPanelPaint)
```

```
self._videoBitmap = None

self._referenceTextCtrl = wx.TextCtrl(
        self, style=wx.TE_PROCESS_ENTER)
self._referenceTextCtrl.SetMaxLength(4)
self._referenceTextCtrl.Bind(
        wx.EVT_KEY_UP, self._onReferenceTextCtrlKeyUp)

self._predictionStaticText = wx.StaticText(self)
# Insert an endline for consistent spacing.
self._predictionStaticText.SetLabel('\n')

self._updateModelButton = wx.Button(
        self, label='Add to Model')
self._updateModelButton.Bind(
        wx.EVT_BUTTON, self._updateModel)
self._updateModelButton.Disable()

self._clearModelButton = wx.Button(
        self, label='Clear Model')
self._clearModelButton.Bind(
        wx.EVT_BUTTON, self._clearModel)
if not self._recognizerTrained:
    self._clearModelButton.Disable()
```

Similar to Luxocator (the Chapter 2, *Searching for Luxury Accommodations Worldwide*, project), Interactive Recognizer lays out the image on top and a row of controls on the bottom. Here is the layout code:

```
border = 12

controlsSizer = wx.BoxSizer(wx.HORIZONTAL)
controlsSizer.Add(self._referenceTextCtrl, 0,
                  wx.ALIGN_CENTER_VERTICAL | wx.RIGHT,
                  border)
controlsSizer.Add(
        self._updateModelButton, 0,
        wx.ALIGN_CENTER_VERTICAL | wx.RIGHT, border)
controlsSizer.Add(self._predictionStaticText, 0,
                  wx.ALIGN_CENTER_VERTICAL)
controlsSizer.Add((0, 0), 1) # Spacer
controlsSizer.Add(self._clearModelButton, 0,
                  wx.ALIGN_CENTER_VERTICAL)

rootSizer = wx.BoxSizer(wx.VERTICAL)
rootSizer.Add(self._videoPanel)
rootSizer.Add(controlsSizer, 0, wx.EXPAND | wx.ALL, border)
self.SetSizerAndFit(rootSizer)
```

Finally, the initializer starts a background thread that performs image capture and image processing, including detection and recognition. It is important to perform the intensive computer vision work on a background thread so that it doesn't stall the handling of GUI events. Here is the code that starts the thread:

```
self._captureThread = threading.Thread(
        target=self._runCaptureLoop)
self._captureThread.start()
```

With a variety of input events and background work, InteractiveRecognizer has many methods that run in an indeterminate order. We will look at input event handlers first, before proceeding to the image pipeline (capture, processing, and display), which partly runs on the background thread.

When the window is closed, we ensure that the background thread stops. Then, if the recognition model is trained, we save it to file. Here is the implementation of the relevant callback:

```
def _onCloseWindow(self, event):
    self._running = False
    self._captureThread.join()
    if self._recognizerTrained:
        modelDir = os.path.dirname(self._recognizerPath)
        if not os.path.isdir(modelDir):
            os.makedirs(modelDir)
        self._recognizer.write(self._recognizerPath)
    self.Destroy()
```

Besides closing the window when its standard *X* button is clicked, we also close it in the _onQuitCommand callback, which we linked to the *Esc* button. The callback's implementation is shown in the following code:

```
def _onQuitCommand(self, event):
    self.Close()
```

We handle the video panel's erase event by doing nothing because we simply want to draw over the old video frame instead of erasing it. We handle the video panel's draw event by acquiring the lock that gives us thread-safe access to the front image buffer, converting the image into a wxPython bitmap, and then drawing the bitmap to the panel. Here are the implementations of the two relevant callbacks in the following code:

```
def _onVideoPanelEraseBackground(self, event):
    pass

def _onVideoPanelPaint(self, event):
```

```
        self._imageFrontBufferLock.acquire()

        if self._imageFrontBuffer is None:
            self._imageFrontBufferLock.release()
            return

        # Convert the image to bitmap format.
        self._videoBitmap = \
                WxUtils.wxBitmapFromCvImage(self._imageFrontBuffer)

        self._imageFrontBufferLock.release()

        # Show the bitmap.
        dc = wx.BufferedPaintDC(self._videoPanel)
        dc.DrawBitmap(self._videoBitmap, 0, 0)
```

When the user adds or deletes text in the text field, our `_onReferenceTextCtrlKeyUp` callback (as follows) calls a helper method to check whether the **Add to Model** button should be enabled or disabled:

```
        def _onReferenceTextCtrlKeyUp(self, event):
            self._enableOrDisableUpdateModelButton()
```

When the **Add to Model** button is clicked, its callback provides new training data to the recognition model. If the LBPH model has no prior training data, we must use the recognizer's `train` method; otherwise, we must use its `update` method. Both methods accept two arguments—a list of images (the faces) and a NumPy array of integers (the face identifiers). We train or update the model with just one image at a time so that the user can interactively test the effect of each incremental change to the model. The image is the most recently detected face, and the identifier is converted from the text in the text field using our `BinasciiUtils.fourCharsToInt` function. Here is the implementation of the **Add to Model** button's callback:

```
        def _updateModel(self, event):
            labelAsStr = self._referenceTextCtrl.GetValue()
            labelAsInt = BinasciiUtils.fourCharsToInt(labelAsStr)
            src = [self._currDetectedObject]
            labels = numpy.array([labelAsInt])
            if self._recognizerTrained:
                self._recognizer.update(src, labels)
            else:
                self._recognizer.train(src, labels)
                self._recognizerTrained = True
                self._clearModelButton.Enable()
```

When the **Clear Model** button is clicked, its callback deletes the recognition model (including any version that has been saved to disk) and creates a new one. Also, we record that the model is untrained and we disable the **Clear Model** button until the model is retrained. Here is the implementation in the following code:

```python
def _clearModel(self, event=None):
    self._recognizerTrained = False
    self._clearModelButton.Disable()
    if os.path.isfile(self._recognizerPath):
        os.remove(self._recognizerPath)
    self._recognizer = cv2.face.LBPHFaceRecognizer_create()
```

Our background thread runs a loop. On each iteration, we capture an image using the `VideoCapture` object's `read` method. Along with the image, the `read` method returns a `success` flag, which we do not need because instead we just check whether the image is `None`. If the image is not `None`, we call a helper method named `_detectAndRecognize`, and then we may mirror the image for display. We also acquire the lock to perform a thread-safe swap of the front and back image buffers. After the swap, we tell the video panel to refresh itself by drawing the bitmap from the new front buffer. Here is the implementation of the loop in the following code:

```python
def _runCaptureLoop(self):
    while self._running:
        success, self._image = self._capture.read(
                self._image)
        if self._image is not None:
            self._detectAndRecognize()
            if (self.mirrored):
                self._image[:] = numpy.fliplr(self._image)

            # Perform a thread-safe swap of the front and
            # back image buffers.
            self._imageFrontBufferLock.acquire()
            self._imageFrontBuffer, self._image = \
                    self._image, self._imageFrontBuffer
            self._imageFrontBufferLock.release()

            # Send a refresh event to the video panel so
            # that it will draw the image from the front
            # buffer.
            self._videoPanel.Refresh()
```

Chapter 3

By calling `self._capture.read(self._image)`, we are telling OpenCV to reuse the image buffer in `self._image` (if `self.image` is not `None` and is the right size) so that new memory doesn't have to be allocated every time we capture a new frame. Alternatively, it would be valid, but less efficient, to call `self._capture.read()` without arguments; in this case, new memory would be allocated every time we captured a new frame.

Recall that the loop ends after our `_onCloseWindow` callback sets `_running` to `False`.

The `_detectAndRecognize` helper method is also running on the background thread. It begins by creating an equalized grayscale version of the image. An **equalized** image has an approximately uniform histogram; that is to say, for some bin size, the number of pixels in each bin of gray values is approximately equal. It is a kind of contrast adjustment that makes a subject's appearance more predictable, despite different lighting conditions and exposure settings in different images; thus, it aids detection or recognition. We pass the equalized image to the classifier's `detectMultiScale` method, also using the `scaleFactor`, `minNeighbors`, and `minSize` arguments that were specified during initialization of `InteractiveRecognizer`. As the return value from `detectMultiScale`, we get a list of rectangle measurements, describing the bounds of the detected faces. For display, we draw green outlines around these faces. If at least one face is detected, we store an equalized grayscale version of the first face in the `_currDetectedObject` member variable. Here is the implementation of this first portion of the `_detectAndRecognize` method:

```
def _detectAndRecognize(self):
    self._grayImage = cv2.cvtColor(
            self._image, cv2.COLOR_BGR2GRAY,
            self._grayImage)
    self._equalizedGrayImage = cv2.equalizeHist(
            self._grayImage, self._equalizedGrayImage)
    rects = self._detector.detectMultiScale(
            self._equalizedGrayImage,
            scaleFactor=self._scaleFactor,
            minNeighbors=self._minNeighbors,
            minSize=self._minSize)
    for x, y, w, h in rects:
        cv2.rectangle(self._image, (x, y), (x+w, y+h),
                      self._rectColor, 1)
    if len(rects) > 0:
        x, y, w, h = rects[0]
        self._currDetectedObject = cv2.equalizeHist(
                self._grayImage[y:y+h, x:x+w])
```

Note that we perform equalization separately on the detected face region after we crop it. This enables us to get an equalization result that is better adapted to the local contrast of the face, instead of the global contrast of the whole image.

If a face is currently detected and the recognition model is trained for at least one individual, we can proceed to predict the identity of the face. We pass the equalized face to the `predict` method of the recognizer and get two return values—an integer identifier and a measure of distance (non-confidence). Using our `BinasciiUtils.intToFourChars` function, we convert the integer into a string (of at most four characters), which will be one of the face names that the user previously entered. We show the name and distance. If an error occurs (for example, if an invalid model was loaded from file), we delete and recreate the model. If the model is not yet trained, we show instructions about training the model. Here is the implementation of this middle portion of the `_detectAndRecognize` method:

```
if self._recognizerTrained:
    try:
        labelAsInt, distance = self._recognizer.predict(
                self._currDetectedObject)
        labelAsStr = BinasciiUtils.intToFourChars(labelAsInt)
        self._showMessage(
                'This looks most like %s.\n'
                'The distance is %.0f.' % \
                (labelAsStr, distance))
    except cv2.error:
        print >> sys.stderr, \
                'Recreating model due to error.'
        self._clearModel()
else:
    self._showInstructions()
```

If no face was detected, we set `_currDetectedObject` to `None` and show either the instructions (if the model hasn't been trained yet) or no descriptive text, otherwise. Under all conditions, we end the `_detectAndRecognize` method by ensuring that the **Add to Model** button is enabled or disabled, as appropriate. Here is this final portion of the method's implementation:

```
else:
    self._currDetectedObject = None
    if self._recognizerTrained:
        self._clearMessage()
    else:
        self._showInstructions()

self._enableOrDisableUpdateModelButton()
```

The **Add to Model** button should be enabled only when a face is detected and the text field is not empty. We can implement this logic in the following manner:

```
def _enableOrDisableUpdateModelButton(self):
    labelAsStr = self._referenceTextCtrl.GetValue()
    if len(labelAsStr) < 1 or \
            self._currDetectedObject is None:
        self._updateModelButton.Disable()
    else:
        self._updateModelButton.Enable()
```

Since we set the label's text under several different conditions, we use the following helper functions to reduce repetition of code, as shown in the following code:

```
def _showInstructions(self):
    self._showMessage(
            'When an object is highlighted, type its name\n'
            '(max 4 chars) and click "Add to Model".')

def _clearMessage(self):
    # Insert an endline for consistent spacing.
    self._showMessage('\n')

def _showMessage(self, message):
    wx.CallAfter(self._predictionStaticText.SetLabel, message)
```

Note the use of the `wx.CallAfter` function to ensure that the label is updated on the main thread.

That is all the functionality of `Interactive Recognizer`. Now, we just need to write the `main` functions for the two variants of the app, starting with the `Interactive Human Face Recognizer`. As arguments to the initializer of `InteractiveRecognizer`, we provide the app's title and PyInstaller-compatible paths to the relevant detection model and recognition model. We run the app. Here is the implementation, which we may put in `InteractiveHumanFaceRecognizer.py`:

```
#!/usr/bin/env python


import wx

from InteractiveRecognizer import InteractiveRecognizer
import PyInstallerUtils


def main():
    app = wx.App()
```

```
        recognizerPath = PyInstallerUtils.resourcePath(
                'recognizers/lbph_human_faces.xml')
        cascadePath = PyInstallerUtils.resourcePath(
                # Uncomment the next argument for LBP.
                #'cascades/lbpcascade_frontalface.xml')
                # Uncomment the next argument for Haar.
                'cascades/haarcascade_frontalface_alt.xml')
        interactiveRecognizer = InteractiveRecognizer(
                recognizerPath, cascadePath,
                title='Interactive Human Face Recognizer')
        interactiveRecognizer.Show()
        app.MainLoop()

if __name__ == '__main__':
    main()
```

Remember that `cascades/haarcascade_frontalface_alt.xml` or `cascades/lpbcascade_frontalface.xml` needs to be obtained from the OpenCV samples or from this book's GitHub repository. Feel free to test `Interactive Human Face Recognizer` now!

Our second variant of the app, `Interactive Cat Face Recognizer`, uses very similar code. We change the app's title and the paths of the detection and recognition models. Also, we lower the `scaleFactor` value to `1.2`, the `minNeighbors` value to `1`, and the `minSizeProportional` value to `(0.125, 0.125)` to make the detector a little more sensitive. (A cat face is smaller than a human face, and our cat face detection model turns out to be less prone to false positives than our human face detection model, so these adjustments are appropriate.) Here is the implementation, which we may put in `InteractiveCatFaceRecognizer.py`:

```
#!/usr/bin/env python

import wx

from InteractiveRecognizer import InteractiveRecognizer
import PyInstallerUtils


def main():
    app = wx.App()
    recognizerPath = PyInstallerUtils.resourcePath(
            'recognizers/lbph_cat_faces.xml')
    cascadePath = PyInstallerUtils.resourcePath(
            # Uncomment the next argument for LBP.
            #'cascades/lbpcascade_frontalcatface.xml')
```

```
            # Uncomment the next argument for Haar with basic
            # features.
            #'cascades/haarcascade_frontalcatface.xml')
            # Uncomment the next argument for Haar with extended
            # features.
            'cascades/haarcascade_frontalcatface_extended.xml')
    interactiveRecognizer = InteractiveRecognizer(
            recognizerPath, cascadePath,
            scaleFactor=1.2, minNeighbors=1,
            minSizeProportional=(0.125, 0.125),
            title='Interactive Cat Face Recognizer')
    interactiveRecognizer.Show()
    app.MainLoop()

if __name__ == '__main__':
    main()
```

At this stage, `Interactive Cat Face Recognizer` will not run properly because `cascades/haarcascade_frontalcatface.xml`, `cascades/haarcascade_frontalcatface_extended.xml`, or `cascades/lpbcascade_frontalcatface.xml` does not exist (unless you copied the prebuilt version from this book's GitHub repository). Soon, we will create it!

Planning the cat-detection model

When I said *soon*, I meant in a day or two. Training a Haar cascade takes a lot of processing time. Training an LBP cascade is relatively quick. However, in either case, we need to download some big collections of images before we even start. Settle down with a reliable internet connection, a power outlet, at least 4 GB of free disk space, and the fastest CPU and biggest RAM you can find. Do not attempt this segment of the project on a Raspberry Pi. Keep the computer away from external heat sources or things that might block its fans. My processing time for Haar cascade training was 24 hours (or more for the whisker-friendly version that is sensitive to diagonal patterns), with 100% usage on four cores, on a MacBook Pro with a 2.6 GHz Intel Core i7 CPU and 16 GB RAM.

We use the following sets of images, which are freely available for research purposes:

- The PASCAL **Visual Object Classes Challenge 2007 (VOC2007)** dataset. VOC2007 contains 10,000 images of diverse subjects against diverse backgrounds, under diverse lighting conditions, so it is suitable as the basis of our negative training set. The images come with annotation data, including a count of cats for each image (most often 0). Thus, in building our negative training set, we can easily omit images that contain cats.

- The frontal face dataset from the **California Institute of Technology (Caltech)** Faces 1999. This set contains 450 images of frontal human faces under diverse lighting conditions and against diverse backgrounds. These images make a useful addition to our negative training set because our frontal cat face detector may be deployed in places where frontal human faces are also likely to be present. None of the images contain cats.
- The Urtho negative training set, which was originally part of a face- and eye-detection project called **Urtho**. This set contains 3,000 images of diverse backgrounds. None of the images contain cats.
- The cat head dataset from Microsoft Research (*Microsoft Cat Dataset 2008*) has 10,000 images of cats against diverse backgrounds and under diverse lighting conditions. The rotation of the cat's head varies, but in all cases the nose, mouth, both eyes, and both ears are clearly visible. Thus, we may say that all the images include frontal faces and are suitable for use as our positive training set. Each image comes with annotation data, indicating coordinates of the center of the mouth, center of the eyes, and corners of the hollow of the ear (three corners per ear). Based on the annotation data, we can straighten and crop the cat's face in order to make the positive training images more similar to each other, as shown in the following screenshot:

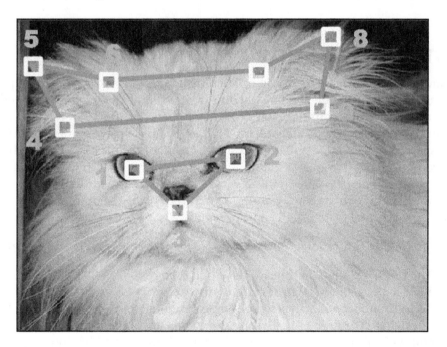

The author of the Urtho negative training set is unknown. The other annotated datasets are generously provided by the following authors, as part of the following publications:

- Everingham, M. and Van Gool, L. and Williams, C. K. I. and Winn, J., and Zisserman, A. *The PASCAL Visual Object Classes Challenge 2007 (VOC2007) Results.*
- Weber, Markus. *Frontal face dataset.* California Institute of Technology, 1999.
- Weiwei Zhang, Jian Sun, and Xiaoou Tang. *Cat Head Detection - How to Effectively Exploit Shape and Texture Features*, Proc. of European Conf. Computer Vision, vol. 4, pp. 802-816, 2008.

We will preprocess the images and generate files describing the positive and negative training sets. After preprocessing, all the training images are in equalized grayscale format, and the positive training images are upright and cropped. The description files conform to certain formats expected by the OpenCV training tools. With the training sets prepared, we will run the OpenCV training tools with the appropriate parameters. The output will be a Haar cascade file for detecting upright frontal cat faces.

Implementing the training script for the cat-detection model

> *"Praline: I've never seen so many aerials in me life. The man told me, their equipment could pinpoint a purr at 400 yards and Eric, being such a happy cat, was a piece of cake."*
> *– Fish License sketch, Monty Python's Flying Circus, Episode 23 (1970)*

This segment of the project uses tens of thousands of files, including images, annotation files, scripts, and intermediate and final outputs of the training process. Let's organize all of this new material by giving our project a subfolder, `cascade_training`, which will ultimately have the following contents:

- `cascade_training/CAT_DATASET_01`: This is the first half of the Microsoft Cat Dataset 2008.
- `cascade_training/CAT_DATASET_02`: This is the second half of the Microsoft Cat Dataset 2008.
- `cascade_training/faces`: This is the Caltech Faces 1999 dataset.

- `cascade_training/urtho_negatives`: This is the Urtho negatives dataset.
- `cascade_training/VOC2007`: This is the VOC2007 dataset.
- `cascade_training/describe.py`: A script to preprocess and describe the positive and negative training sets. As outputs, it creates new images in the previous dataset directories and in the following text description files.
- `cascade_training/negative_description.txt`: This is a generated text file describing the negative training set.
- `cascade_training/positive_description.txt`: This is a generated text file describing the positive training set.
- `cascade_training/train.bat` (Windows) or `cascade_training/train.sh` (Mac or Linux): This is a script to run the OpenCV cascade training tools with appropriate parameters. As input, it uses the previous text description files. As output, it generates a not-yet mentioned binary description file and cascade files.
- `cascade_training/binary_description`: This is a generated binary file describing the positive training set.
- `cascade_training/lbpcascade_frontalcatface/*.xml`: This gives the intermediate and final results of the LBP cascade training.
- `cascades/lbpcascade_frontalcatface.xml`: This is a copy of the final result of the LBP cascade training, in a location where our apps expect it.
- `cascade_training/haarcascade_frontalcatface/*.xml`: This shows the intermediate and final results of the Haar cascade training.
- `cascades/haarcascade_frontalcatface.xml`: This is a copy of the final result of the Haar cascade training, in a location where our apps expect it.

For up-to-date instructions on obtaining and extracting the Microsoft Cat Dataset 2008, the Caltech Faces 1999 dataset, the Urtho negatives dataset, and the VOC2007 dataset, refer to the README on this book's GitHub web page at https://github.com/PacktPublishing/OpenCV-4-for-Secret-Agents-Second-Edition/. Over time, some of the datasets' original websites and mirrors have gone down permanently, yet other mirrors continue to come online.

Once the datasets are downloaded and decompressed to the proper locations, let's write `describe.py`. It needs to start with the following shebang line and imports:

```
#!/usr/bin/env python

from __future__ import print_function
```

```
import cv2
import glob
import math
import sys
```

All our source images need some preprocessing to optimize them as training images. We need to save the preprocessed versions, so let's globally define an extension that we will use for these files:

```
outputImageExtension = '.out.jpg'
```

To give our training images a more predictable appearance despite differences in lighting conditions and exposure settings, we need to create equalized grayscale images at several points in this script. Let's write the following helper function for this purpose:

```
def equalizedGray(image):
    return cv2.equalizeHist(cv2.cvtColor(
        image, cv2.COLOR_BGR2GRAY))
```

Similarly, we need to append to the negative description file at more than one point in the script. Each line in the negative description is just an image path. Let's add the following helper method, which accepts an image path and a file object for the negative description, loads the image and saves an equalized version, and appends the equalized version's path to the description file:

```
def describeNegativeHelper(imagePath, output):
    outputImagePath = '%s%s' % (imagePath, outputImageExtension)
    image = cv2.imread(imagePath)
    # Save an equalized version of the image.
    cv2.imwrite(outputImagePath, equalizedGray(image))
    # Append the equalized image to the negative description.
    print(outputImagePath, file=output)
```

Now, let's write the `describeNegative` function that calls `describeNegativeHelper`. It begins by opening a file in write mode so that we can write the negative description. Then, we iterate over all the image paths in the Caltech Faces 1999 set, which contains no cats. We skip any paths to output images that were written on a previous call of this function. We pass the remaining image paths, along with the newly opened negative description file, to `describeNegativeHelper`, as follows:

```
def describeNegative():
    output = open('negative_description.txt', 'w')
    # Append all images from Caltech Faces 1999, since all are
    # non-cats.
    for imagePath in glob.glob('faces/*.jpg'):
        if imagePath.endswith(outputImageExtension):
```

```
            # This file is equalized, saved on a previous run.
            # Skip it.
            continue
        describeNegativeHelper(imagePath, output)
```

For every image in the Urtho negative training set, we pass the file path to `describeNegativeHelper`, as follows:

```
    # Append all images from the Urtho negative training set,
    # since all are non-cats.
    for imagePath in glob.glob('urtho_negatives/*.jpg'):
        if imagePath.endswith(outputImageExtension):
            # This file is equalized, saved on a previous run.
            # Skip it.
            continue
        describeNegativeHelper(imagePath, output)
```

The remainder of the `describeNegative` function is responsible for passing relevant file paths from the VOC2007 image set to `describeNegativeHelper`. Some images in VOC2007 do contain cats. An annotation file, `VOC2007/ImageSets/Main/cat_test.txt`, lists image IDs and a flag indicating whether any cats are present in the image. The flag may be—1 (no cats), 0 (one or more cats as background or secondary subjects of the image), or 1 (one or more cats as foreground or foreground subjects of the image). We parse this annotation data and, if an image contains no cats, we pass its path and the description file to `describeNegativeHelper`, as follows:

```
    # Append non-cat images from VOC2007.
    input = open('VOC2007/ImageSets/Main/cat_test.txt', 'r')
    while True:
        line = input.readline().rstrip()
        if not line:
            break
        imageNumber, flag = line.split()
        if int(flag) < 0:
            # There is no cat in this image.
            imagePath = 'VOC2007/JPEGImages/%s.jpg' % imageNumber
            describeNegativeHelper(imagePath, output)
```

Now, let's move on to helper functions for generating the positive description. When rotating a face to straighten it, we also need to rotate a list of coordinate pairs representing features of the face. The following helper function accepts such a list, along with a center of rotation and angle of rotation, and returns a new list of the rotated coordinate pairs:

```
    def rotateCoords(coords, center, angleRadians):
        # Positive y is down so reverse the angle, too.
        angleRadians = -angleRadians
```

```
    xs, ys = coords[::2], coords[1::2]
    newCoords = []
    n = min(len(xs), len(ys))
    i = 0
    centerX = center[0]
    centerY = center[1]
    cosAngle = math.cos(angleRadians)
    sinAngle = math.sin(angleRadians)
    while i < n:
        xOffset = xs[i] - centerX
        yOffset = ys[i] - centerY
        newX = xOffset * cosAngle - yOffset * sinAngle + centerX
        newY = xOffset * sinAngle + yOffset * cosAngle + centerY
        newCoords += [newX, newY]
        i += 1
    return newCoords
```

Next, let's write a long helper function to preprocess a single positive training image. This function accepts two arguments—a list of coordinate pairs (which is named `coords`) and an OpenCV image. Refer to the diagram of feature points on a cat face. The numbering of the points signifies their order in a line of annotation data and in `coords`. To begin the function, we get the coordinates for the eyes and mouth. If the face is upside down (not an uncommon pose in playful or sleepy cats), we swap our definitions of left and right eyes to be consistent with an upright pose. (In determining whether the face is upside down, we rely in part on the position of the mouth relative to the eyes.) Then, we find the angle between the eyes and we rotate the image so that the face becomes upright. An OpenCV function called `cv2.getRotationMatrix2D` is used to define the rotation, and another function called `cv2.warpAffine` is used to apply it. As a result of rotating border regions, some blank regions are introduced into the image. We may specify a fill color for these regions as an argument to `cv2.warpAffine`. We use 50% gray, since it has the least tendency to bias the equalization of the image. Here is the implementation of this first part of the `preprocessCatFace` function:

```
def preprocessCatFace(coords, image):
    leftEyeX, leftEyeY = coords[0], coords[1]
    rightEyeX, rightEyeY = coords[2], coords[3]
    mouthX = coords[4]
    if leftEyeX > rightEyeX and leftEyeY < rightEyeY and \
            mouthX > rightEyeX:
        # The "right eye" is in the second quadrant of the face,
        # while the "left eye" is in the fourth quadrant (from the
        # viewer's perspective.) Swap the eyes' labels in order to
        # simplify the rotation logic.
        leftEyeX, rightEyeX = rightEyeX, leftEyeX
        leftEyeY, rightEyeY = rightEyeY, leftEyeY
```

```
        eyesCenter = (0.5 * (leftEyeX + rightEyeX),
                0.5 * (leftEyeY + rightEyeY))
        eyesDeltaX = rightEyeX - leftEyeX
        eyesDeltaY = rightEyeY - leftEyeY
        eyesAngleRadians = math.atan2(eyesDeltaY, eyesDeltaX)
        eyesAngleDegrees = eyesAngleRadians * 180.0 / math.pi
        # Straighten the image and fill in gray for blank borders.
        rotation = cv2.getRotationMatrix2D(
                eyesCenter, eyesAngleDegrees, 1.0)
        imageSize = image.shape[1::-1]
        straight = cv2.warpAffine(image, rotation, imageSize,
                borderValue=(128, 128, 128))
```

As well as straightening the image, we call `rotateCoords` to make feature coordinates that match the straightened image. Here is the code for this function call:

```
        # Straighten the coordinates of the features.
        newCoords = rotateCoords(
                coords, eyesCenter, eyesAngleRadians)
```

At this stage, the image and feature coordinates are transformed so that the cat's eyes are level and upright. Next, let's crop the image to eliminate most of the background and to standardize the eyes' position relative to the bounds. Arbitrarily, we define the cropped face to be a square region, as wide as the distance between the outer base points of the cat's ears. This square is positioned so that half its area lies to the left of the midpoint between the cat's eyes, half lies to the right, 40% lies above, and 60% lies below. For an ideal frontal cat face, this crop excludes all background regions, but includes the eyes, chin, and several fleshy regions—the nose, mouth, and part of the inside of the ears. We equalize and return the cropped image. Accordingly, the implementation of `preprocessCatFace` proceeds as follows:

```
        # Make the face as wide as the space between the ear bases.
        # (The ear base positions are specified in the reference
        # coordinates.)
        w = abs(newCoords[16] - newCoords[6])
        # Make the face square.
        h = w
        # Put the center point between the eyes at (0.5, 0.4) in
        # proportion to the entire face.
        minX = eyesCenter[0] - w/2
        if minX < 0:
            w += minX
            minX = 0
        minY = eyesCenter[1] - h*2/5
        if minY < 0:
            h += minY
            minY = 0
```

```
# Crop the face.
crop = straight[int(minY):int(minY+h), int(minX):int(minX+w)]
# Convert the crop to equalized grayscale.
crop = equalizedGray(crop)
# Return the crop.
return crop
```

 During cropping, we usually eliminate the blank border region that was introduced during rotation. However, if the cat face was close to the border of the original image, some of the rotated gray border region may remain.

The following pair of screenshots is an example of input and output for the `processCatFace` function. First, there's the input:

The output is displayed in the following screenshot:

To generate the positive description file, we iterate over all the images in the Microsoft Cat Dataset 2008. For each image, we parse the cat feature coordinates from the corresponding .cat file and we generate the straightened, cropped, and equalized image by passing the coordinates and original image to our `processCatFace` function. We append each processed image path and measurements to the positive description file. Here is the implementation:

```python
def describePositive():
    output = open('positive_description.txt', 'w')
    dirs = ['CAT_DATASET_01/CAT_00',
            'CAT_DATASET_01/CAT_01',
            'CAT_DATASET_01/CAT_02',
            'CAT_DATASET_02/CAT_03',
            'CAT_DATASET_02/CAT_04',
            'CAT_DATASET_02/CAT_05',
            'CAT_DATASET_02/CAT_06']
    for dir in dirs:
        for imagePath in glob.glob('%s/*.jpg' % dir):
            if imagePath.endswith(outputImageExtension):
                # This file is a crop, saved on a previous run.
                # Skip it.
                continue
            # Open the '.cat' annotation file associated with this
            # image.
            input = open('%s.cat' % imagePath, 'r')
            # Read the coordinates of the cat features from the
            # file. Discard the first number, which is the number
            # of features.
            coords = [int(i) for i in input.readline().split()[1:]]
            # Read the image.
            image = cv2.imread(imagePath)
            # Straighten and crop the cat face.
            crop = preprocessCatFace(coords, image)
            if crop is None:
                sys.stderr.write(
                        'Failed to preprocess image at %s.\n' % \
                        imagePath)
                continue
            # Save the crop.
            cropPath = '%s%s' % (imagePath, outputImageExtension)
            cv2.imwrite(cropPath, crop)
            # Append the cropped face and its bounds to the
            # positive description.
            h, w = crop.shape[:2]
            print('%s 1 0 0 %d %d' % (cropPath, w, h), file=output)
```

Here, let's take note of the format of a positive description file. Each line contains a path to a training image, followed by a series of numbers indicating the count of positive objects in the image and the measurements (x, y, width, and height) of rectangles containing those objects. In our case, there is always one cat face filling the entire cropped image, so we get lines such as the following, which is for a *64 x 64* image:

```
CAT_DATASET_02/CAT_06/00001493_005.jpg.out.jpg 1 0 0 64 64
```

Hypothetically, if the image had two *8 x 8* pixel cat faces in opposite corners, its line in the description file would look like this:

```
CAT_DATASET_02/CAT_06/00001493_005.jpg.out.jpg 2 0 0 8 8 56 56 8 8
```

The main function of `describe.py` simply calls our `describeNegative` and `describePositive` functions, as follows:

```
def main():
    describeNegative()
    describePositive()

if __name__ == '__main__':
    main()
```

Run `describe.py` and then feel free to have a look at the generated files, including `negative_description.txt`, `positive_description.txt`, and the cropped cat faces whose filenames follow the `CAT_DATASET_*/CAT_*/*.out.jpg` pattern.

Next, we will use two of OpenCV's command-line tools. We will refer to them as `<opencv_createsamples>` and `<opencv_traincascade>`. They are responsible for converting the positive description to a binary format and generating the Haar cascade in an XML format, respectively. On Windows, these executables are named `opencv_createsamples.exe` and `opencv_traincascade.exe`. On Mac or Linux, the executables are named `opencv_createsamples` and `opencv_traincascade`.

> For up-to-date instructions on obtaining `<opencv_createsamples>` and `<opencv_traincascade>`, refer to the README on this book's GitHub web page at `https://github.com/PacktPublishing/OpenCV-4-for-Secret-Agents-Second-Edition/`. At the time of writing, there is not yet an OpenCV 4.x version of these two command-line tools, but the OpenCV 3.4 version of them is forward-compatible, and work on a 4.x version has been proposed for summer 2019.

Many flags can be used to provide arguments to <opencv_createsamples> and <opencv_traincascade>, as described in the official documentation at https://docs.opencv.org/master/dc/d88/tutorial_traincascade.html. We use the following flags and values:

- vec: This is the path to a binary description of the positive training images. This file is generated by <opencv_createsamples>.
- info: This is the path to a text description of the positive training images. We generated this file using describe.py.
- bg: The path to a text description of the negative training images. We generated this file using describe.py.
- num: The number of positive training images in info.
- numStages: The number of stages in the cascade. As we discussed earlier in *Conceptualizing Haar cascades and LBPH*, each stage is a test that is applied to an image region. If the region passes all tests, it is classified as a frontal cat face (or whatever class of object the positive training set represents). We use 20.
- numPos: The number of positive training images used in each stage. It should be significantly smaller than num. (Otherwise, the trainer will fail, complaining that it has run out of new images to use in new stages.) We use 90% of num.
- numNeg: The number of negative training images used in each stage. We use 90% of the number of negative training images in bg.
- minHitRate: The **hit rate** is also called the **sensitivity**, **recall**, or **true positive rate**. In our case, it is the proportion of cat faces that are correctly classified as such. The minHitRate parameter specifies the minimum hit rate that *each* stage must achieve. A higher proportion implies a longer training time but a better fit between the model and the training data. (A better fit is normally a good thing, though it is possible to **overfit** so that the model does not make correct extrapolations beyond the training data.) We use 0.995. With 20 stages, this implies an overall hit rate of *0.995 ^ 20* or approximately 99%.
- maxFalseAlarmRate: The **false alarm rate** is also called the **miss rate** or **false positive rate**. In our case, it is the proportion of backgrounds or non-cat faces that are misclassified as cat faces. The maxFalseAlarmRate parameter specifies the maximum false alarm rate for *each* stage. We use 0.5. With 20 stages, this implies an overall false alarm rate of *0.5 ^ 20* or approximately one in a million.
- featureType: The type of features used, either HAAR (the default) or LBP. As we discussed previously, Haar cascades tend to be more reliable but are much slower to train and somewhat slower at runtime.

- `mode`: This is the subset of Haar features used. (For LBP, this flag has no effect.) The valid options are BASIC (the default), CORE, and ALL. The CORE option makes the model slower to train and run, but the benefit is to make the model sensitive to little dots and thick lines. The ALL option goes further, making the model even slower to train and run but adding sensitivity to diagonal patterns (whereas BASIC and CORE are only sensitive to horizontal and vertical patterns). The ALL option has nothing to do with detecting non-upright subjects. Rather, it relates to detecting subjects that contain diagonal patterns. For example, a cat's whiskers and ears might qualify as diagonal patterns.

Let's write a shell script to run <opencv_createsamples> and <opencv_traincascade> with the appropriate flags and to copy the resulting Haar cascade to the path where Interactive Cat Face Recognizer expects it. On Windows, let's call our script train.bat and implement it as follows:

```
REM On Windows, opencv_createsamples and opencv_traincascades expect
REM absolute paths.
REM Set baseDir to be the absolute path to this script's directory.
set baseDir=%~dp0

REM Use baseDir to construct other absolute paths.

set vec=%baseDir%\binary_description
set info=%baseDir%\positive_description.txt
set bg=%baseDir%\negative_description.txt

REM Uncomment the next 4 variables for LBP training.
REM set featureType=LBP
REM set data=%baseDir%\lbpcascade_frontalcatface\\
REM set dst=%baseDir%\..\\cascades\\lbpcascade_frontalcatface.xml
REM set mode=BASIC

REM Uncomment the next 4 variables for Haar training with basic
REM features.
set featureType=HAAR
set data=%baseDir%\haarcascade_frontalcatface\\
set dst=%baseDir%\..\\cascades\\haarcascade_frontalcatface.xml
set mode=BASIC

REM Uncomment the next 4 variables for Haar training with
REM extended features.
REM set featureType=HAAR
REM set data=%baseDir%\haarcascade_frontalcatface_extended\\
REM set dst=%baseDir%\..\\cascades\\haarcascade_frontalcatface_extended.xml
REM set mode=ALL
```

```
REM Set numPosTotal to be the line count of info.
for /f %%c in ('find /c /v "" ^< "%info%"') do set numPosTotal=%%c

REM Set numNegTotal to be the line count of bg.
for /f %%c in ('find /c /v "" ^< "%bg%"') do set numNegTotal=%%c

set /a numPosPerStage=%numPosTotal%*9/10
set /a numNegPerStage=%numNegTotal%*9/10
set numStages=20
set minHitRate=0.995
set maxFalseAlarmRate=0.5

REM Ensure that the data directory exists and is empty.
if not exist "%data%" (mkdir "%data%") else del /f /q "%data%\*.xml"

opencv_createsamples -vec "%vec%" -info "%info%" -bg "%bg%" ^
        -num "%numPosTotal%"
opencv_traincascade -data "%data%" -vec "%vec%" -bg "%bg%" ^
        -numPos "%numPosPerStage%" -numNeg "%numNegPerStage%" ^
        -numStages "%numStages%" -minHitRate "%minHitRate%" ^
        -maxFalseAlarmRate "%maxFalseAlarmRate%" ^
        -featureType "%featureType%" -mode "%mode%"

copy /Y "%data%\cascade.xml" "%dst%"
```

On Mac or Linux, let's instead call our script `train.sh` and implement it as follows:

```
#!/bin/sh

vec=binary_description
info=positive_description.txt
bg=negative_description.txt

# Uncomment the next 4 variables for LBP training.
#featureType=LBP
#data=lbpcascade_frontalcatface/
#dst=../cascades/lbpcascade_frontalcatface.xml
#mode=BASIC

# Uncomment the next 4 variables for Haar training with basic
# features.
featureType=HAAR
data=haarcascade_frontalcatface/
dst=../cascades/haarcascade_frontalcatface.xml
mode=BASIC

# Uncomment the next 4 variables for Haar training with
# extended features.
```

```
#featureType=HAAR
#data=haarcascade_frontalcatface_extended/
#dst=../cascades/haarcascade_frontalcatface_extended.xml
#mode=ALL

# Set numPosTotal to be the line count of info.
numPosTotal=`wc -l < $info`

# Set numNegTotal to be the line count of bg.
numNegTotal=`wc -l < $bg`

numPosPerStage=$(($numPosTotal*9/10))
numNegPerStage=$(($numNegTotal*9/10))
numStages=20
minHitRate=0.995
maxFalseAlarmRate=0.5

# Ensure that the data directory exists and is empty.
if [ ! -d "$data" ]; then
    mkdir "$data"
else
    rm "$data/*.xml"
fi

opencv_createsamples -vec "$vec" -info "$info" -bg "$bg" \
        -num "$numPosTotal"
opencv_traincascade -data "$data" -vec "$vec" -bg "$bg" \
        -numPos "$numPosPerStage" -numNeg "$numNegPerStage" \
        -numStages "$numStages" -minHitRate "$minHitRate" \
        -maxFalseAlarmRate "$maxFalseAlarmRate" \
        -featureType "$featureType" -mode "$mode"

cp "$data/cascade.xml" "$dst"
```

The preceding versions of the training script are configured to use basic Haar features and will take a long, long time to run, perhaps more than a day. By commenting out the variables related to a basic Haar configuration and uncommenting the variables related to an LBP configuration, we can cut the training time down to several minutes. As a third alternative, variables for an extended Haar configuration (sensitive to diagonal patterns) are also present but currently commented out.

When the training is done, feel free to have a look at the generated files, including the following:

- For basic Haar features, cascades/haarcascade_frontalcatface.xml and cascade_training/haarcascade_frontalcatface/*

- For extended Haar features,
  `cascades/haarcascade_frontalcatface_extended.xml` and
  `cascade_training/haarcascade_frontalcatface_extended/*`
- For LBP, `cascades/lbpcascade_frontalcatface.xml` and
  `cascade_training/lbpcascade_frontalcatface/*`

Finally, let's run `InteractiveCatFaceRecognizer.py` to test our cascade!

> Remember that our detector is designed for frontal upright cat faces. The cat should be facing the camera and might need some incentive to hold that pose. For example, you could ask the cat to settle on a blanket or in your lap, and you could pat or comb the cat. See the following screenshot of my colleague, Chancellor Josephine (*Little Jo*) Antoinette Puddingcat, GRL (Grand Rock of Lambda), sitting for a test.
>
> If you do not have a cat (or even a human) who is willing to participate, then you can simply print a few images of a given cat (or human) from the web. Use heavy, matte paper and hold the print so that it faces the camera. Use prints of some images for training the recognizer and prints of other images for testing it:

Our detector is pretty good at finding frontal cat faces. However, I encourage you to experiment further, make it better, and share your results! The current version sometimes mistakes the center of a frontal human face for a frontal cat face. Perhaps we should have used more databases of human faces as negative training images. Alternatively, if we had used faces of several mammal species as positive training images, could we have created a more general mammal face detector? Let me know what you discover!

Planning the Angora Blue app

`Angora Blue` reuses the same detection and recognition models that we created earlier. It is a relatively linear and simple app because it has no GUI and does not modify any models. It just loads the detection and recognition models from file and then silently runs a camera until a face is recognized with a certain level of confidence. After recognizing a face, the app sends an email alert and exits. To elaborate, we may say the app has the following flow of execution:

1. Load face detection and face recognition models from file for both human and feline subjects.
2. Capture a live video from a camera. For each frame of video, it can do the following:
    - Detect all human faces in the frame. Perform recognition on each human face. If a face is recognized with a certain level of confidence, it sends an email alert and exits the app.
    - Detect all cat faces in the frame. Discard any cat faces that intersect with human faces. (We assume that such cat faces are false positives, since our cat detector sometimes mistakes human faces for cat faces.) For each remaining cat face, it performs recognition. If a face is recognized with a certain level of confidence, it sends an email alert and exits the app.

`Angora Blue` is capable of running on a Raspberry Pi. The Pi's small size makes it a nice platform for a hidden alarm system! Make sure that the Pi or other machine is connected to the internet in order to send email messages.

Training a Smart Alarm to Recognize the Villain and His Cat

Implementing the Angora Blue app

The `Angora Blue` app uses three new files—`GeomUtils.py`, `MailUtils.py`, and `AngoraBlue.py`, which should all be in our project's top folder. Given the app's dependencies on our previous work, the following files are relevant to `Angora Blue`:

- `cascades/haarcascade_frontalface_alt.xml`
- `cascades/haarcascade_frontalcatface.xml`
- `recognizers/lbph_human_faces.xml`
- `recognizers/lbph_cat_faces.xml`
- `ResizeUtils.py`: A utility function for resizing images, including camera capture dimensions
- `GeomUtils.py`: A utility function for geometric operations
- `MailUtils.py`: A utility function for sending emails
- `AngoraBlue.py`: The application that sends an email alert when a person or cat is recognized

First, let's create `GeomUtils.py`. It doesn't need any import statements. Let's add the following `intersects` function, which accepts two rectangles as arguments and returns either `True` (if they intersect) or `False` (otherwise), as shown in the following code:

```
def intersects(rect0, rect1):
    x0, y0, w0, h0 = rect0
    x1, y1, w1, h1 = rect1
    if x0 > x1 + w1: # rect0 is wholly to right of rect1
        return False
    if x1 > x0 + w0: # rect1 is wholly to right of rect0
        return False
    if y0 > y1 + h1: # rect0 is wholly below rect1
        return False
    if y1 > y0 + h0: # rect1 is wholly below rect0
        return False
    return True
```

Using the `intersects` function, let's write the following `difference` function, which accepts two lists of rectangles, `rects0` and `rects1`, and returns a new list containing the rectangles in `rects0` that don't intersect with any rectangle in `rects1`:

```
def difference(rects0, rects1):
    result = []
    for rect0 in rects0:
        anyIntersects = False
        for rect1 in rects1:
```

```
            if intersects(rect0, rect1):
                anyIntersects = True
                break
        if not anyIntersects:
            result += [rect0]
    return result
```

Later, we will use the `difference` function to filter out cat faces that intersect with human faces.

Now, let's create `MailUtils.py`. It needs the following `import` statement:

```
import smtplib
```

For the task of sending an email, let's copy the following function from Rosetta Code, a free wiki that offers utility functions in many programming languages, as shown in the following code:

```
def sendEmail(fromAddr, toAddrList, ccAddrList, subject, message,
              login, password, smtpServer='smtp.gmail.com:587'):

    # Taken from http://rosettacode.org/wiki/Send_an_email#Python

    header  = 'From: %s\n' % fromAddr
    header += 'To: %s\n' % ','.join(toAddrList)
    header += 'Cc: %s\n' % ','.join(ccAddrList)
    header += 'Subject: %s\n\n' % subject
    message = header + message

    server = smtplib.SMTP(smtpServer)
    server.starttls()
    server.login(login,password)
    problems = server.sendmail(fromAddr, toAddrList, message)
    server.quit()
    return problems
```

By default, the `sendEmail` function uses Gmail. By specifying the optional `smtpServer` argument, we can use a different service.

Since July 2014, the default security settings on Google accounts require apps to use not only SMTP authentication but also OAuth authentication in order to send an email through Gmail. Our `sendEmail` function uses a secure TLS connection but handles SMTP authentication only (as this is sufficient for most email services other than Gmail). To reconfigure your Google account for compatibility with our function, log in to your account, go to `https://www.google.com/settings/security/lesssecureapps`, select the **Enable** option, and click **Done**. For best security, you might wish to create a dummy Google account for this project and apply the custom security setting to this dummy account only. Alternatively, most email services besides Gmail should not require special configuration.

Now, we are ready to implement `AngoraBlue.py`. It starts with the following shebang line and imports:

```python
#!/usr/bin/env python


import numpy # Hint to PyInstaller
import cv2
import getpass
import os
import socket
import sys

import BinasciiUtils
import GeomUtils
import MailUtils
import PyInstallerUtils
import ResizeUtils
```

`Angora Blue` simply uses a `main` function and one helper function, `recognizeAndReport`. This helper function begins as follows, by iterating over a given list of face rectangles and using a given recognizer (be it a human recognizer or a cat recognizer) to get a label and distance (non-confidence) for each face, as shown in the following code:

```python
def recognizeAndReport(recognizer, grayImage, rects, maxDistance,
                       noun, smtpServer, login, password, fromAddr,
                       toAddrList, ccAddrList):
    for x, y, w, h in rects:
        crop = cv2.equalizeHist(grayImage[y:y+h, x:x+w])
        labelAsInt, distance = recognizer.predict(crop)
        labelAsStr = BinasciiUtils.intToFourChars(labelAsInt)
```

For testing, it is useful to log the recognition results here. However, we comment out the logging in the final version, as follows:

```
#print('%s %s %d' % (noun, labelAsStr, distance))
```

If any of the faces is recognized with a certain level of confidence (based on a `maxDistance` argument), we attempt to send an email alert. If the alert is sent successfully, the function returns `True`, meaning it did recognize and report a face. Otherwise, it returns `False`. Here is the remainder of the implementation:

```
        if distance <= maxDistance:
            subject = 'Angora Blue'
            message = 'We have sighted the %s known as %s.' % \
                    (noun, labelAsStr)
            try:
                problems = MailUtils.sendEmail(
                        fromAddr, toAddrList, ccAddrList, subject,
                        message, login, password, smtpServer)
                if problems:
                    sys.stderr.write(
                            'Email problems: {0}\n'.format(problems))
                else:
                    return True
            except socket.gaierror:
                sys.stderr.write('Unable to reach email server\n')
    return False
```

The `main` function starts by defining paths to the detection and recognition models. If either recognition model does not exist (because it has not been trained), we print an error and exit, as follows:

```
def main():

    humanCascadePath = PyInstallerUtils.resourcePath(
            # Uncomment the next argument for LBP.
            #'cascades/lbpcascade_frontalface.xml')
            # Uncomment the next argument for Haar.
            'cascades/haarcascade_frontalface_alt.xml')
    humanRecognizerPath = PyInstallerUtils.resourcePath(
            'recognizers/lbph_human_faces.xml')
    if not os.path.isfile(humanRecognizerPath):
        sys.stderr.write(
                'Human face recognizer not trained. Exiting.\n')
        return

    catCascadePath = PyInstallerUtils.resourcePath(
            # Uncomment the next argument for LBP.
```

```
        #'cascades/lbpcascade_frontalcatface.xml')
        # Uncomment the next argument for Haar with basic
        # features.
        #'cascades/haarcascade_frontalcatface.xml')
        # Uncomment the next argument for Haar with extended
        # features.
        'cascades/haarcascade_frontalcatface_extended.xml')
catRecognizerPath = PyInstallerUtils.resourcePath(
        'recognizers/lbph_cat_faces.xml')
if not os.path.isfile(catRecognizerPath):
    sys.stderr.write(
            'Cat face recognizer not trained. Exiting.\n')
    return
```

We prompt the user to enter email credentials and recipients, and we store the user responses in local variables, as shown in the following code:

```
print('What email settings shall we use to send alerts?')

defaultSMTPServer = 'smtp.gmail.com:587'
print('Enter SMTP server (default: %s):' % defaultSMTPServer)
smtpServer = sys.stdin.readline().rstrip()
if not smtpServer:
    smtpServer = defaultSMTPServer

print('Enter username:')
login = sys.stdin.readline().rstrip()

print('Enter password:')
password = getpass.getpass('')

defaultAddr = '%s@gmail.com' % login
print('Enter "from" email address (default: %s):' % defaultAddr)
fromAddr = sys.stdin.readline().rstrip()
if not fromAddr:
    fromAddr = defaultAddr

print('Enter comma-separated "to" email addresses (default: '
      '%s):' % defaultAddr)
toAddrList = sys.stdin.readline().rstrip().split(',')
if toAddrList == ['']:
    toAddrList = [defaultAddr]

print('Enter comma-separated "c.c." email addresses:')
ccAddrList = sys.stdin.readline().rstrip().split(',')
```

As in `Interactive Recognizer`, we start capturing video from a camera and we store the video's resolution in order to calculate the relative, minimum size of a face. Here is the relevant code:

```
capture = cv2.VideoCapture(0)
imageWidth, imageHeight = \
        ResizeUtils.cvResizeCapture(capture, (1280, 720))
minImageSize = min(imageWidth, imageHeight)
```

We load detectors and recognizers from file and set a minimum face size for detection and maximum distance (non-confidence) for recognition. We specify the values separately for human and feline subjects. You may need to tweak the values based on your particular camera setup and models. The code proceeds as follows:

```
humanDetector = cv2.CascadeClassifier(humanCascadePath)
humanRecognizer = cv2.face.LBPHFaceRecognizer_create()
humanRecognizer.read(humanRecognizerPath)
humanMinSize = (int(minImageSize * 0.25),
                int(minImageSize * 0.25))
humanMaxDistance = 25

catDetector = cv2.CascadeClassifier(catCascadePath)
catRecognizer = cv2.face.LBPHFaceRecognizer_create()
catRecognizer.read(catRecognizerPath)
catMinSize = (int(minImageSize * 0.125),
              int(minImageSize * 0.125))
catMaxDistance = 25
```

We read frames from the camera continuously until an email alert is sent as a result of face recognition. Each frame is converted into grayscale and equalized. Next, we detect and recognize human faces and possibly send an alert, as follows:

```
while True:
    success, image = capture.read()
    if image is not None:
        grayImage = cv2.cvtColor(image, cv2.COLOR_BGR2GRAY)
        equalizedGrayImage = cv2.equalizeHist(grayImage)

        humanRects = humanDetector.detectMultiScale(
            equalizedGrayImage, scaleFactor=1.3,
            minNeighbors=4, minSize=humanMinSize)
        if recognizeAndReport(
            humanRecognizer, grayImage, humanRects,
            humanMaxDistance, 'human', smtpServer, login,
            password, fromAddr, toAddrList, ccAddrList):
            break
```

If no alert has been sent, we continue to cat-detection and recognition. For cat-detection, we make extra efforts to eliminate false positives by specifying a higher `minNeighbors` value and by filtering out any cat faces that intersect human faces. Here is this final part of Angora Blue's implementation:

```
        catRects = catDetector.detectMultiScale(
                equalizedGrayImage, scaleFactor=1.2,
                minNeighbors=1, minSize=catMinSize)
        # Reject any cat faces that overlap with human faces.
        catRects = GeomUtils.difference(catRects, humanRects)
        if recognizeAndReport(
                catRecognizer, grayImage, catRects,
                catMaxDistance, 'cat', smtpServer, login,
                password, fromAddr, toAddrList, ccAddrList):
            break

if __name__ == '__main__':
    main()
```

Before testing `Angora Blue`, ensure that the two recognition models are trained using `Interactive Human Face Recognizer` and `Interactive Cat Face Recognizer`. Preferably, each model should contain two or more individuals. Then, set up a computer and webcam in a place where frontal human faces and frontal cat faces will be encountered. Try to get your friends and pets to participate in the following test cases:

- A human, who is unknown to the model, looks into the camera. Nothing should happen. If you get an email alert, increase `humanMaxDistance` and try again.
- A cat, who is unknown to the model, looks into the camera. Nothing should happen. If you get an email alert, increase `catMaxDistance` and try again.
- A human, who is known to the model, looks into the camera. You should get an email alert. If not, decrease `humanMaxDistance` or rerun `Interactive Human Face Recognizer` to add more samples of the given human face. Try `Angora Blue` again.
- A cat, who is known to the model, looks into the camera. You should get an email alert. If not, decrease `catMaxDistance` or rerun `Interactive Cat Face Recognizer` to add more samples of the given cat face. Try `Angora Blue` again.

Again, if you don't have enough human or feline volunteers, just get some heavy, matte paper and print faces from the web. Hold a print so that it is visible (and upright) from the camera's perspective, but ensure that you stay out of view so that the recognizer runs only on the print, not on you.

Once the recognition model and `Angora Blue` are tweaked, we are ready to deploy our alarm system to a vast network of webcam-enabled computers! Let the search for the blue-eyed Angora begin!

Building Angora Blue for distribution

We can use PyInstaller to bundle `Angora Blue`, along with detection and recognition models, for distribution. Since the build scripts should be quite similar to the ones we used for Luxocator (the `Chapter 2`, *Searching for Luxury Accommodations Worldwide*, project), we will not discuss their implementation here. However, they are included in this book's GitHub repository.

Further fun with finding felines

Kittydar (short for **kitty radar**), by Heather Arthur, is an open source, JavaScript library for detecting upright frontal cat faces. You can find its demo application at `http://harthur.github.io/kittydar/` and its source code at `https://github.com/harthur/kittydar`.

Another detector for upright frontal cat faces was developed by Microsoft Research using the Microsoft Cat Dataset 2008. The detector is described in the following research paper, but no demo application or source code has been released:

Weiwei Zhang, Jian Sun, and Xiaoou Tang. Cat Head Detection - How to Effectively Exploit Shape and Texture Features, *Proc. of European Conf. Computer Vision*, vol. 4, pp. 802-816, 2008.

If you know of other work on cat detectors, recognizers, or datasets, please write to tell me about it!

Summary

Like the previous chapter, this chapter has dealt with classification tasks, as well as interfaces among OpenCV, a source of images, and a GUI. This time, our classification labels have more objective meanings (a species or an individual's identity), so the classifier's success or failure is more obvious. To meet the challenge, we used much bigger sets of training images, we preprocessed the training images for greater consistency, and we applied two tried-and-true classification techniques in sequence (either Haar cascades or LBP cascades for detection and then LBPH for recognition).

The methodology presented in this chapter, as well as the entire `Interactive Recognizer` app and some of the other code, generalizes well to other original work in detection and recognition. With the right training images, you could detect and recognize many more animals in many poses. You could even detect an object such as a car and recognize the Batmobile!

For our next project, we turn our attention to a moving target, literally. We will try to detect a person who is in motion and then recognize particular gestures.

4
Controlling a Phone App with Your Suave Gestures

"You've got all the moves."
           - Lani Hall, Never Say Never Again (1983)

He raises an eyebrow; he lowers his chin; he twists the corners of his mouth; he folds one arm into the crook of the other as he points his pistol at the ceiling. It all looks very impressive, but is he simply wasting time while trying to remember people's names?

Agent 007 has a few old friends with normal names, such as Bill Tanner and Felix Leiter. Almost every other name is a number, a single letter, a mash-up of multiple languages, or a blindingly obvious double entendre. After a few vodka martinis and tranquilizer darts, any man would start to wonder whether his memory for names was playing tricks on him.

To put such doubts to rest, we will develop an Android app that determines a person's name based on a series of yes/no questions. To allow a secret agent to use it discretely, the app will rely on gesture controls and audio output, which can go to a Bluetooth headset so that others cannot hear.

The app's logic is like the game Twenty Questions. First, the app asks a question by playing an audio clip. Then, the user responds with a nod or a shake of the head. Each question is more specific than the last, until the app is ready to guess a name or give up. Recognizing the two possible head gestures—a nod or a shake—is our computer vision task for this chapter.

Specifically, this chapter covers the following programming topics:

- Using Android Studio and the Android SDK to build an Android app in Java
- Using OpenCV's Android camera functions to capture, process, and display images from the Android device's camera
- Tracking head gestures using OpenCV's functions for face detection, feature detection, and optical flow

The app's codename is `Goldgesture`.

Technical requirements

This chapter's project has the following software dependencies:

- Android Studio
- OpenCV Android pack

Setup instructions are covered in `Chapter 1`, *Preparing for the Mission*. Refer to the setup instructions for any version requirements. Instructions for building and running Android projects are covered in the current chapter.

The completed project for this chapter can be found in the book's GitHub repository, `https://github.com/PacktPublishing/OpenCV-4-for-Secret-Agents-Second-Edition`, in the `Chapter004` folder. If you want to open the completed project, just launch Android Studio, select **Open an existing Android Studio project**, and then select the `Chapter004/Goldgesture` folder.

Planning the Goldgesture app

`Goldgesture` is a GUI app built with the Android SDK and OpenCV's Java bindings for Android. It has just a single view, seen in the screenshot on the next page. The app has the following flow of execution:

1. Constantly display a live video feed from the front-facing (self-portrait) camera.
2. Perform human face detection using OpenCV's `CascadeClassifier` class.

3. When a human face is detected:
    1. Draw a blue rectangle around the face.
    2. Detect features of the face (points that should be easy to track in subsequent frames despite movement) using OpenCV's `goodFeaturesToTrack` function. Draw green circles around these features.
4. As the face moves, track the features in every frame using OpenCV's `calcOpticalFlowPyrLK` function. This function can continuously track the features even though `CascadeClassifier` is unlikely to continuously detect a face.
5. When the features' center point moves up and down by a certain amount and a certain number of times, deem that a nod has occurred.
6. When the features' center point moves left and right by a certain amount and a certain number of times, deem that a shake of the head has occurred.
7. Play a sequence of audio clips. At each juncture, choose the next clip depending (in part) on whether a nod or shake of the head has occurred.
8. Reset the tracking if its reliability deteriorates to a certain extent or if the user's head appears to be nodding and shaking at the same time:

The face-detection functionality in `Goldgesture` should already be familiar from the Angora Blue project in Chapter 3, *Training a Smart Alarm to Recognize the Villain and His Cat*. However, feature tracking, and specifically optical flow, is a new topic for us. Let's talk about the concepts a little before proceeding to set up our project.

Understanding optical flow

Optical flow is the pattern of apparent motion between two consecutive frames of video. We select feature points in the first frame and try to determine where those features have gone in the second frame. This search is subject to a few caveats:

- We make no attempt to distinguish between camera motion and subject motion.
- We assume that a feature's color or brightness remains similar between frames.
- We assume that neighboring pixels have similar motions.

OpenCV's `calcOpticalFlowPyrLK` function implements the Lucas-Kanade method of computing optical flow. Lucas-Kanade relies on a *3 x 3* neighborhood (that is, 9 pixels) around each feature. Taking each feature's neighborhood from the first frame, we try to find the best matching neighborhood in the second frame, based on least squares error. OpenCV's implementation of Lucas-Kanade uses an image pyramid, meaning it performs the search at various scales. Thus, it supports both large and small motions (`PyrLK` in the function name stands for *pyramidal Lucas-Kanade*). The following diagram is a visualization of a pyramid—a progression from low-resolution (or low-magnification) images to high-resolution (or high-magnification) images:

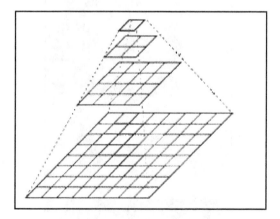

For more details on optical flow and the Lucas-Kanade method, see the official OpenCV documentation at http://docs.opencv.org/master/d7/d8b/tutorial_py_lucas_kanade.html.

OpenCV offers implementations of other optical flow algorithms as well. For example, the `calcOpticalFlowSF` function implements the SimpleFlow algorithm, which makes optimizations for high-resolution video by assuming that smooth (uniform) image regions move in unison. The `calcOpticalFlowFarneback` function implements Gunnar Farneback's algorithm, which posits that a neighborhood remains identifiable, even during motion, by the coefficients of a polynomial relationship among its pixel values. Both of these algorithms are forms of *dense* optical flow, meaning that they analyze every pixel in the image instead of just selected (*sparse*) features. More of OpenCV's optical flow functions are documented at https://docs.opencv.org/master/dc/d6b/group__video__track.html and https://docs.opencv.org/master/d2/d84/group__optflow.html.

Of the several options, why choose `calcOpticalFlowPyrLK`? *You see, it is a pyramid,* as Imhotep said to the Pharaoh Djoser, *and it has open spaces inside it.* A pyramidal, sparse technique is a good way for us to cheaply and robustly track a few features in a face, which may change scale as it moves nearer to or farther from the camera.

For our purposes, it is useful to select features inside a detected object, specifically a detected face. We choose an inner portion of the face (to avoid background regions) and then use an OpenCV function called `goodFeaturesToTrack`, which selects features based on the algorithm described in Jianbo Shi and Carlo Tomasi's paper, "Good Features to Track", *Proc. of IEEE Conf. on Computer Vision and Pattern Recognition*, pp. 593-600, June 1994.

As the name suggests, the **Good Features to Track** (**GFTT**) algorithm (also known as the **Shi-Tomasi algorithm**) takes into account the requirements of tracking algorithms and tracking use cases, and attempts to select features that work well with these algorithms and use cases. As described in detail in the paper, good features to track must have a stable appearance with respect to small changes in the camera's perspective. Examples of poor features to track are reflections (such as sunlight on a car's hood) and lines that cross at different depths (such as a tree's branches), since these features move quickly as the viewer or camera moves. The effects of a change in perspective can be simulated (albeit imperfectly) by warping a given image and moving its contents linearly. Based on such a simulation, the most stable features can be selected.

Controlling a Phone App with Your Suave Gestures

 OpenCV offers implementations of several feature-detection algorithms, besides Good Features to Track. For references to information about these other algorithms, please refer to `Appendix B`, *Learning More about Feature Detection in OpenCV*.

Setting up the project in Android Studio

For a refresher on setting up Android Studio and the OpenCV Android pack, refer to the *Setting up Android Studio and OpenCV* section in `Chapter 1`, *Preparing for the Mission*.

We will organize all the source code and resources for our Android app in an Android Studio project, as follows:

1. Open Android Studio and select **File** | **New** | **New Project...** from the menu. The **Create New Project** window should appear, and it should show the **Choose your project** form. Select **Empty Activity**, as shown in the following screenshot, and click **Next**:

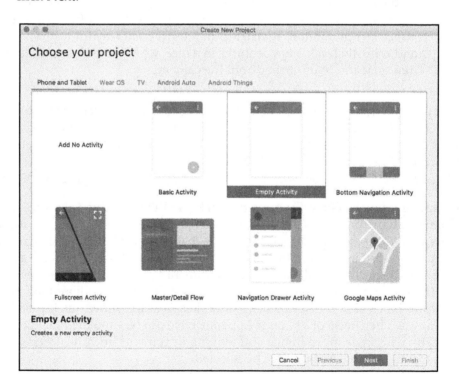

[132]

Chapter 4

2. The **Create New Project** window should show the **Configure your project** form. We want to specify that our app name is Goldgesture, its package name is com.nummist.goldgesture, it is a Java project, and its minimum Android SDK version is API level 21, which is Android 5.0. You may choose any new folder as the project's location. Fill out the form as shown in the following screenshot, and click **Finish**:

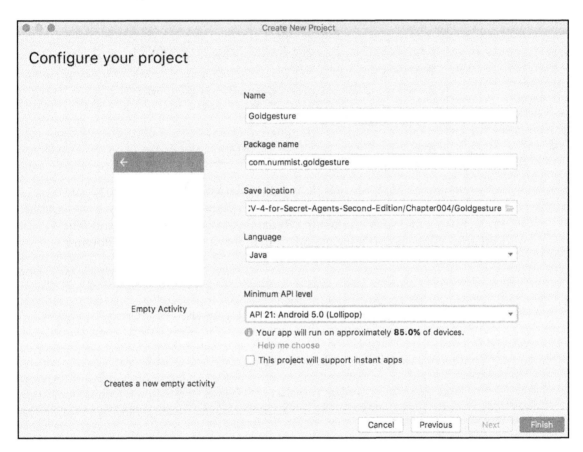

3. By default, Android Studio creates a main class, called **MainActivity**. Let's rename this to give it a more descriptive name, **CameraActivity**. Right-click on `app/src/main/java/com.nummist.goldgesture/MainActivity` (in the **Project** pane) and select **Refactor | Rename...** from the context menu. The **Rename** dialog should appear. Fill it out as shown in the following screenshot, and click **Refactor**:

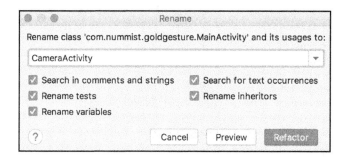

4. Let's rename the XML file that defines the GUI layout associated with the `main` class. Right-click on `app/src/main/res/layout/activity_main.xml` (in the **Project** pane) and select **Refactor | Rename...** from the context menu. The **Rename** dialog should appear again. Fill it out as shown in the following screenshot, and click **Refactor**:

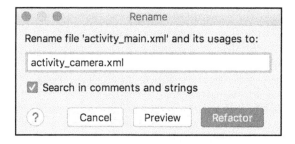

5. Since our app will depend on OpenCV, we need to import the OpenCV library module that we obtained as part of the OpenCV Android pack in `Chapter 1`, *Preparing for the Mission*. From Android Studio's menu, select **File** | **New** | **New Module...**. The **Create New Module** dialog should appear, and it should show the **New Module** form. Select **Import Gradle Project**, as shown in the following screenshot, and click **Next**:

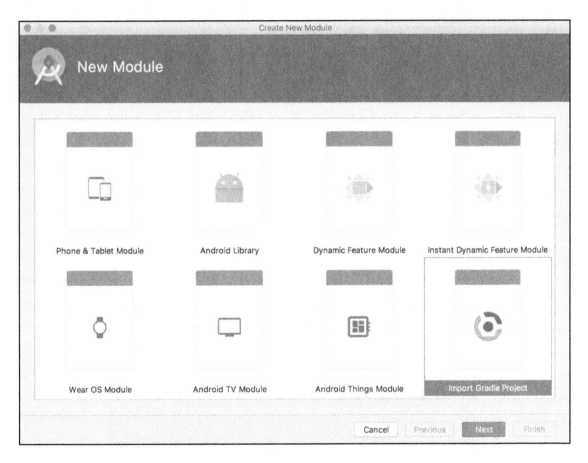

6. A file picker dialog should appear. Select the `sdk` subfolder of the OpenCV Android pack, as shown in the following screenshot, and confirm the choice by clicking the **Open** or **OK** button (whose name varies depending on the operating system):

7. The **Create New Module** dialog should show the **Import Module from Source** form. Enter `:OpenCV` in the **Module name** field, as shown in the following screenshot, and click **Finish**:

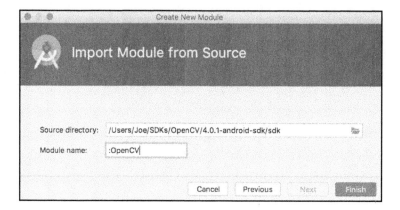

Chapter 4

At this point, Android Studio might prompt you to perform updates and accept license agreements so that you have all of OpenCV's dependencies. If you are prompted, agree.

8. We need to specify that the `Goldgesture` app module depends on the OpenCV library module. From Android Studio's menus, select **File** | **Project Structure...**. The **Project Structure** dialog should appear. Under **Modules**, select **app**. Then, select the **Dependencies** tab, as shown in the following screenshot:

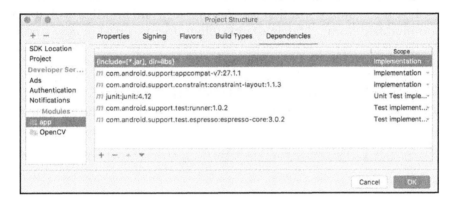

9. Hit the **+** button to add a dependency. A menu should appear. Select **Module dependency**. The **Choose Modules** dialog should appear. Select **:OpenCV**, as shown in the following screenshot, and click **OK**:

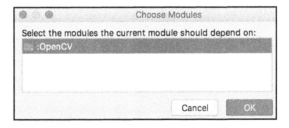

The OpenCV library is now linked into `Goldgesture`.

Getting a cascade file and audio files

Like parts of `Chapter 3`, *Training a Smart Alarm to Recognize the Villain and His Cat, Angora Blue project*, `Goldgesture` performs human face detection and requires one of the cascade files that comes with OpenCV. Also, `Goldgesture` uses audio clips. The cascade file and audio clips are located in the book's GitHub repository in the `Chapter004/Goldgesture/app/src/main/res/raw` subfolder. If you are recreating the project from scratch, you should copy these files to your own `app/src/main/res/raw` folder. This folder is a standard location for files that we want bundled with the Android app in raw (unmodified) form. By default, this folder does not exist in new Android Studio projects.

To create it in Android Studio, right-click on the `app/src/main/res` folder (in the **Project** pane) and select **New** | **Android Resource Directory** from the context menu. The **New Resource Directory** window should appear. Fill it out as shown in the following screenshot, and click **OK**:

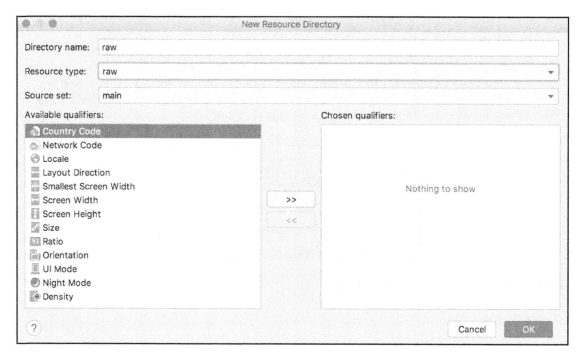

After you create the `app/src/main/res/raw` folder, you can drag and drop files into it in Android Studio.

Chapter 4

The audio clips are generated using the Vicki voice of the standard text-to-speech synthesizer on Mac. For example, one of the clips is created by running the following command in Terminal:

```
$ say 'You are 007! I win!' -v Vicki -o win_007.mp4
```

Speech synthesis is hours of fun for the whole family.

> The Mac speech synthesizer pronounces 007 as double-O seven. This is an anomaly. For example, 008 is pronounced as *zero, zero, eight*.

Specifying the app's requirements

`AndroidManifest.xml` (the Android Manifest) is the place where an app announces information that the system, Google Play, and other apps might need to know. For example, `Goldgesture` requires a front-facing camera and permission to use it (a license to shoot, one might say). `Goldgesture` also expects to run in landscape mode, regardless of the physical orientation of the phone, because OpenCV's camera preview always uses the camera's landscape dimensions (OpenCV's Android documentation does not indicate whether this behavior is intended. Perhaps future versions will provide better support for portrait orientation). To specify these requirements, edit `app/src/main/AndroidManifest.xml` to match the following sample:

```xml
<?xml version="1.0" encoding="utf-8"?>
<manifest xmlns:android="http://schemas.android.com/apk/res/android"
    package="com.nummist.goldgesture">

    <uses-permission android:name="android.permission.CAMERA" />

    <uses-feature android:name="android.hardware.camera.front" />

    <application
        android:allowBackup="true"
        android:icon="@mipmap/ic_launcher"
        android:label="@string/app_name"
        android:roundIcon="@mipmap/ic_launcher_round"
        android:supportsRtl="true"
        android:theme="@style/AppTheme">
<activity
android:name=".CameraActivity"
android:screenOrientation="landscape"
android:theme="@android:style/Theme.NoTitleBar.Fullscreen">
```

[139]

```xml
            <intent-filter>
            <action android:name="android.intent.action.MAIN" />

            <category android:name="android.intent.category.LAUNCHER" />
        </intent-filter>
        </activity>
            </application>

</manifest>
```

When you open `AndroidManifest.xml` in Android Studio, you might see two tabs, one labeled **Text** and another labeled **Merged Manifest**. Select the **Text** tab, which allows us to directly edit the source code of `AndroidManifest.xml` (by contrast, the **Merged Manifest** tab is not directly editable, and it shows a combination of settings from `AndroidManifest.xml` and the project properties).

Now, our app can use a camera and will remain in landscape mode. Also, if we publish it on Google Play, it will only be available to devices with a front-facing camera.

Laying out a camera preview as the main view

Android, like many systems, enables the programmer to specify GUI layouts in XML files. Our Java code can load an entire view, or pieces of it, from these XML files.

`Goldgesture` has a simple layout that contains only a camera preview, on which we draw some additional graphics using OpenCV. The camera preview is represented by an OpenCV class called `JavaCameraView`. Let's edit `app/src/main/res/layout/activity_camera.xml` to fill the layout with a `JavaCameraView`, using the front-facing camera, as follows:

```xml
<?xml version="1.0" encoding="utf-8"?>
<android.support.constraint.ConstraintLayout
    xmlns:android="http://schemas.android.com/apk/res/android"
    xmlns:app="http://schemas.android.com/apk/res-auto"
    xmlns:opencv="http://schemas.android.com/apk/res-auto"
    xmlns:tools="http://schemas.android.com/tools"
    android:layout_width="match_parent"
    android:layout_height="match_parent"
    tools:context=".CameraActivity">

    <org.opencv.android.JavaCameraView
```

```
            android:layout_width="fill_parent"
            android:layout_height="fill_parent"
            android:id="@+id/camera_view"
            app:layout_constraintBottom_toBottomOf="parent"
            app:layout_constraintLeft_toLeftOf="parent"
            app:layout_constraintRight_toRightOf="parent"
            app:layout_constraintTop_toTopOf="parent"
            opencv:camera_id="front" />

</android.support.constraint.ConstraintLayout>
```

Alternatively, OpenCV also provides a class called `JavaCamera2View`. Both `JavaCameraView` and `JavaCamera2View` are implementations of an interface called `CameraBridgeViewBase`. The difference is that `JavaCamera2View` builds atop a more recent version of Android's camera APIs, but currently it yields a lower frame rate on many devices. The performance of `JavaCamera2View` could improve in future versions of OpenCV or on future Android devices, so you might want to run your own performance tests on the particular Android devices you are targeting.

Tracking back-and-forth gestures

Several common gestures consist of a repetitive, back-and-forth movement. Consider the following examples of this type of gesture:

- Nodding (yes or I'm listening)
- Shaking one's head (no or dismay)
- Waving (a greeting)
- Shaking hands (a greeting)
- Shaking one's fist (a threat or a protest)
- Wagging a finger (scolding)
- Wiggling a finger or fingers (beckoning)
- Tapping one's foot against the ground (impatience)
- Tapping four fingers against a table (impatience)
- Tapping two fingers against a table (Thanks for the green tea)
- Pacing (anxiety)
- Jumping up and down (excitement, joy)

To help us recognize such gestures, let's write a class, `BackAndForthGesture`, which keeps track of the number of times that a value (such as an *x* coordinate or *y* coordinate) has oscillated between a low threshold and a high threshold. A certain number of oscillations can be considered a complete gesture.

Create a file, `app/src/main/java/com/nummist/goldgesture/BackAndForthGesture.java`. To do this in Android Studio, right-click on the `app/src/main/java/com.nummist.goldgesture` folder (in the **Project** pane) and select **New** | **Java Class** from the context menu. The **Create New Class** window should appear. Fill it out as shown in the following screenshot, and click **OK**:

As member variables, `BackAndForthGesture` will store the minimum distance or threshold that defines a back or forth motion, an initial position, the latest delta from this position, and the number of back movements and forth movements. Here is the first part of the class's code:

```
package com.nummist.goldgesture;

public final class BackAndForthGesture {

    private double mMinDistance;

    private double mStartPosition;
    private double mDelta;

    private int mBackCount;
    private int mForthCount;
```

The back-and-forth count (or number of oscillations) is the lesser of the back count and the forth count. Let's implement this rule in the following getter method:

```
public int getBackAndForthCount() {
    return Math.min(mBackCount, mForthCount);
}
```

The constructor takes one argument, the minimum distance or threshold of movement:

```
public BackAndForthGesture(final double minDistance) {
    mMinDistance = minDistance;
}
```

To begin tracking movement, we call a `start` method with an initial position as an argument. This method records the initial position and resets the delta and counts:

```
public void start(final double position) {
    mStartPosition = position;
    mDelta = 0.0;
    mBackCount = 0;
    mForthCount = 0;
}
```

We are considering position as a one-dimensional value because a head nodding (up and down) or shaking (left and right) is a linear gesture. For an upright head, only one of the image's two dimensions is relevant to a nod or shake gesture.

To continue tracking movement, we call an `update` method with the new position as an argument. This method recalculates the delta and if a threshold has just been passed, the back count or forth count is incremented:

```
public void update(final double position) {
    double lastDelta = mDelta;
    mDelta = position - mStartPosition;
    if (lastDelta < mMinDistance &&
            mDelta >= mMinDistance) {
        mForthCount++;
    } else if (lastDelta > -mMinDistance &&
            mDelta < -mMinDistance) {
        mBackCount++;
    }
}
```

If we consider the gesture complete, or for some other reason we believe the counts to be invalid, we call a `resetCounts` method:

```
public void resetCounts() {
    mBackCount = 0;
    mForthCount = 0;
}
```

Note that `BackAndForthGesture` contains no computer vision functionality of its own, but the position values we pass to it will be derived from computer vision.

Playing audio clips as questions and answers

The logic of the question-and-answer sequence is another component that has no computer vision functionality. We encapsulate it in a class called `YesNoAudioTree`, which is responsible for playing the next audio clip whenever the app's computer vision component notifies it of a yes or no answer.

Remember that the audio clips are part of the book's GitHub repository, and they belong in the project's `app/src/main/res/raw` folder. However, note that the audio clips in the repository are by no means an exhaustive set of questions and guesses about characters in the Bond franchise. Feel free to add your own clips and your own logic to play them.

Create a file, `app/src/main/java/com/nummist/goldgesture/YesNoAudioTree.java`. Our `YesNoAudioTree` class needs member variables to store a media player and a related context, an ID for the most-recently-played audio clip, and information gathered from the answers to previous questions. Specifically, the next question depends on whether the unknown person is already identified as a member of MI6, the CIA, the KGB, or a criminal organization. This information, along with the answer to the most recent question, will be enough for us to build a simple tree of questions to identify several characters from the Bond franchise. The class's implementation begins as follows:

```
package com.nummist.goldgesture;

import android.content.Context;
import android.media.MediaPlayer;
```

```
import android.media.MediaPlayer.OnCompletionListener;

public final class YesNoAudioTree {

    private enum Affiliation { UNKNOWN, MI6, CIA, KGB, CRIMINAL }

    private int mLastAudioResource;
    private Affiliation mAffiliation;

    private Context mContext;
    private MediaPlayer mMediaPlayer;
```

The class is instantiated with a `Context` object, which is a standard abstraction of the app's Android environment:

```
public YesNoAudioTree(final Context context) {
    mContext = context;
}
```

The `Context` object is needed to create a media player, as we will see later in this section of the chapter.

> For more information about the Android SDK's `MediaPlayer` class, see the official documentation at
> http://developer.android.com/reference/android/media/MediaPlayer.html.

To (re)start from the first question, we call a `start` method. It resets the data about the person and plays the first audio clip using a private helper method, `play`:

```
public void start() {
    mAffiliation = Affiliation.UNKNOWN;
    play(R.raw.intro);
}
```

To stop any current clip and clean up the audio player (for example, when the app pauses or finishes), we call a `stop` method:

```
public void stop() {
    if (mMediaPlayer != null) {
        mMediaPlayer.release();
    }
}
```

When the user has answered Yes to a question, we call the `takeYesBranch` method. It uses nested `switch` statements to pick the next audio clip based on previous answers and the most recent question:

```java
public void takeYesBranch() {

    if (mMediaPlayer != null && mMediaPlayer.isPlaying()) {
        // Do not interrupt the audio that is already playing.
        return;
    }

    switch (mAffiliation) {
        case UNKNOWN:
            switch (mLastAudioResource) {
                case R.raw.q_mi6:
                    mAffiliation = Affiliation.MI6;
                    play(R.raw.q_martinis);
                    break;
                case R.raw.q_cia:
                    mAffiliation = Affiliation.CIA;
                    play(R.raw.q_bond_friend);
                    break;
                case R.raw.q_kgb:
                    mAffiliation = Affiliation.KGB;
                    play(R.raw.q_chief);
                    break;
                case R.raw.q_criminal:
                    mAffiliation = Affiliation.CRIMINAL;
                    play(R.raw.q_chief);
                    break;
            }
            break;
        case MI6:
            // The person works for MI6.
            switch (mLastAudioResource) {
                case R.raw.q_martinis:
                    // The person drinks shaken martinis (007).
                    play(R.raw.win_007);
                    break;
                // ...
                // See the GitHub repository for more cases.
                // ...
                default:
                    // The person remains unknown.
                    play(R.raw.lose);
                    break;
            }
            break;
```

```
            // ...
            // See the GitHub repository for more cases.
            // ...
        }
    }
```

Similarly, when the user has answered No to a question, we call the `takeNoBranch` method, which also contains big, nested `switch` statements:

```
public void takeNoBranch() {

    if (mMediaPlayer != null && mMediaPlayer.isPlaying()) {
        // Do not interrupt the audio that is already playing.
        return;
    }

    switch (mAffiliation) {
        case UNKNOWN:
            switch (mLastAudioResource) {
                case R.raw.q_mi6:
                    // The person does not work for MI6.
                    // Ask whether the person works for a criminal
                    // organization.
                    play(R.raw.q_criminal);
                    break;
                // ...
                // See the GitHub repository for more cases.
                // ...
                default:
                    // The person remains unknown.
                    play(R.raw.lose);
                    break;
            }
        // ...
        // See the GitHub repository for more cases.
        // ...
    }
}
```

When certain clips finish, we want to automatically advance to another clip without requiring a Yes or No from the user. A private helper method, `takeAutoBranch`, implements the relevant logic in a `switch` statement:

```
private void takeAutoBranch() {
    switch (mLastAudioResource) {
        case R.raw.intro:
            play(R.raw.q_mi6);
            break;
```

```
            case R.raw.win_007:
            case R.raw.win_blofeld:
            case R.raw.win_gogol:
            case R.raw.win_jaws:
            case R.raw.win_leiter:
            case R.raw.win_m:
            case R.raw.win_moneypenny:
            case R.raw.win_q:
            case R.raw.win_rublevitch:
            case R.raw.win_tanner:
            case R.raw.lose:
                start();
                break;
        }
    }
```

Whenever we need to play an audio clip, we call the `play` private helper method. It creates an instance of `MediaPlayer` using the context and an audio clip's ID, which is given to `play` as an argument. The audio is played and a callback is set so that the media player will be cleaned up and `takeAutoBranch` will be called when the clip is done:

```
    private void play(final int audioResource) {
        mLastAudioResource = audioResource;
        mMediaPlayer = MediaPlayer.create(mContext, audioResource);
        mMediaPlayer.setOnCompletionListener(
                new OnCompletionListener() {
                    @Override
                    public void onCompletion(
                            final MediaPlayer mediaPlayer) {
                        mediaPlayer.release();
                        if (mMediaPlayer == mediaPlayer) {
                            mMediaPlayer = null;
                        }
                        takeAutoBranch();
                    }
                });
        mMediaPlayer.start();
    }
}
```

Now that we have written our supporting classes, we are ready to tackle the app's main class, including the computer vision functionality.

Capturing images and tracking faces in an activity

An Android app is a state machine in which each state is called an **activity**. An activity has a life cycle. For example, it can be created, paused, resumed, and finished. During a transition between activities, the paused or finished activity can send data to the created or resumed activity. An app can define many activities and transition between them in any order. It can even transition between activities defined by the Android SDK or by other apps.

> For more information about Android activities and their life cycles, see the official documentation at
> http://developer.android.com/guide/components/activities.html. For more information about OpenCV's Android and Java APIs (used throughout our activity class), see the official Javadocs at https://docs.opencv.org/master/javadoc/index.html.

OpenCV provides classes and interfaces that can be considered add-ons to an activity's life cycle. Specifically, we can use OpenCV callback methods to handle the following events:

- The camera preview starts
- The camera preview stops
- The camera preview captures a new frame

`Goldgesture` uses just one activity, called `CameraActivity`. `CameraActivity` uses a `CameraBridgeViewBase` object (more specifically, a `JavaCameraView` object) as its camera preview. (Recall that we saw this earlier, in the *Laying out a camera preview as the main view* section of this chapter, when we implemented `CameraActivity`'s layout in XML.) `CameraActivity` implements an interface called `CvCameraViewListener2`, which provides callbacks for this camera preview. (Alternatively, an interface called `CvCameraViewListener` can serve this purpose. The difference between the two interfaces is that `CvCameraViewListener2` allows us to specify a format for the captured image, whereas `CvCameraViewListener` does not.) The implementation of our class begins as follows:

```
package com.nummist.goldgesture;

// ...
// See the GitHub repository for imports
// ...

public final class CameraActivity extends Activity
```

```
    implements CvCameraViewListener2 {

// A tag for log output.
private static final String TAG = "CameraActivity";
```

For readability and easy editing, we use static final variables to store many parameters in our computer vision functions. You might wish to adjust these values based on experimentation. First, we have face-detection parameters that should be familiar to you from the Angora Blue project in Chapter 3, *Training a Smart Alarm to Recognize the Villain and His Cat*:

```
// Parameters for face detection.
private static final double SCALE_FACTOR = 1.2;
private static final int MIN_NEIGHBORS = 3;
private static final int FLAGS = Objdetect.CASCADE_SCALE_IMAGE;
private static final double MIN_SIZE_PROPORTIONAL = 0.25;
private static final double MAX_SIZE_PROPORTIONAL = 1.0;
```

For the purpose of selecting features, we do not use the entire detected face. Rather, we use an inner portion that is less likely to contain any non-face background. Thus, we define a proportion of the face that should be excluded from feature selection on each side:

```
// The portion of the face that is excluded from feature
// selection on each side.
// (We want to exclude boundary regions containing background.)
private static final double MASK_PADDING_PROPORTIONAL = 0.15;
```

For face tracking using optical flow, we define a minimum and maximum number of features. If we fail to track at least the minimum number of features, we deem that the face has been lost. We also define a minimum feature quality (relative to the quality of the best feature found), a minimum pixel distance between features, and a maximum acceptable error value when trying to match a new feature to an old feature. As we will see later in this section of the chapter, these parameters pertain to OpenCV's calcOpticalFlowPyrLK function and its return values. Here are the declarations:

```
// Parameters for face tracking.
private static final int MIN_FEATURES = 10;
private static final int MAX_FEATURES = 80;
private static final double MIN_FEATURE_QUALITY = 0.05;
private static final double MIN_FEATURE_DISTANCE = 4.0;
private static final float MAX_FEATURE_ERROR = 200f;
```

We also define how much movement (as a proportion of the image size) and how many back-and-forth cycles are required before we deem that a nod or shake has occurred:

```java
// Parameters for gesture detection
private static final double MIN_SHAKE_DIST_PROPORTIONAL = 0.01;
private static final double MIN_NOD_DIST_PROPORTIONAL = 0.0025;
private static final double MIN_BACK_AND_FORTH_COUNT = 2;
```

Our member variables include the camera view, the dimensions of captured images, and the images at various stages of processing. The images are stored in OpenCV Mat objects, which are analogous to the NumPy arrays that we saw in the Python bindings. OpenCV always captures the images in landscape format, but we reorient them to portrait format, which is a more common orientation for a picture of one's own face on a smartphone. Here are the relevant variable declarations:

```java
// The camera view.
private CameraBridgeViewBase mCameraView;

// The dimensions of the image before orientation.
private double mImageWidth;
private double mImageHeight;

// The current gray image before orientation.
private Mat mGrayUnoriented;

// The current and previous equalized gray images.
private Mat mEqualizedGray;
private Mat mLastEqualizedGray;
```

As seen in the following code and comments, we also declare several member variables related to face detection and tracking:

```java
// The mask, in which the face region is white and the
// background is black.
private Mat mMask;
private Scalar mMaskForegroundColor;
private Scalar mMaskBackgroundColor;

// The face detector, more detection parameters, and
// detected faces.
private CascadeClassifier mFaceDetector;
private Size mMinSize;
private Size mMaxSize;
private MatOfRect mFaces;

// The initial features before tracking.
private MatOfPoint mInitialFeatures;
```

```
// The current and previous features being tracked.
private MatOfPoint2f mFeatures;
private MatOfPoint2f mLastFeatures;

// The status codes and errors for the tracking.
private MatOfByte mFeatureStatuses;
private MatOfFloat mFeatureErrors;

// Whether a face was being tracked last frame.
private boolean mWasTrackingFace;

// Colors for drawing.
private Scalar mFaceRectColor;
private Scalar mFeatureColor;
```

Finally, we store instances of the classes that we defined earlier, namely `BackAndForthGesture` (in the *Tracking back-and-forth gestures* section of this chapter) and `YesNoAudioTree` (in the *Playing audio clips as questions and answers* section of this chapter):

```
// Gesture detectors.
private BackAndForthGesture mNodHeadGesture;
private BackAndForthGesture mShakeHeadGesture;

// The audio tree for the 20 questions game.
private YesNoAudioTree mAudioTree;
```

Now, let's implement the standard life cycle callbacks of an Android activity. First, when the activity is created, we try to load the OpenCV library (if for some reason this fails, we log an error message and exit). If OpenCV loads successfully, we specify that we want to keep the screen on even when there is no touch interaction (since all interaction is through the camera). Moreover, we need to load the layout from the XML file, get a reference to the camera preview, and set this activity as the handler for the camera preview's events. Here is the implementation:

```
@Override
protected void onCreate(final Bundle savedInstanceState) {
    super.onCreate(savedInstanceState);

    if (OpenCVLoader.initDebug()) {
        Log.i(TAG, "Initialized OpenCV");
    } else {
        Log.e(TAG, "Failed to initialize OpenCV");
        finish();
    }

    final Window window = getWindow();
    window.addFlags(
```

```
                WindowManager.LayoutParams.FLAG_KEEP_SCREEN_ON);

        setContentView(R.layout.activity_camera);
        mCameraView = (CameraBridgeViewBase)
                findViewById(R.id.camera_view);
        //mCameraView.enableFpsMeter();
        mCameraView.setCvCameraViewListener(this);
    }
```

Note that we have not yet initialized most of our member variables. Instead, we do so once the camera preview has started. When the activity is paused, we disable the camera preview, stop the audio, and reset the gesture recognition data, as seen in the following code:

```
    @Override
    public void onPause() {
        if (mCameraView != null) {
            mCameraView.disableView();
        }
        if (mAudioTree != null) {
            mAudioTree.stop();
        }
        resetGestures();
        super.onPause();
    }
```

When the activity resumes (including the first time it comes to the foreground, after being created), we check whether the user has granted permission for the app to use the camera. If permission has not yet been granted, we request it. (In some circumstances, Android requires us to display a rationale for the permission request. We do this through a private helper method called showRequestPermissionRationale.) If permission has already been granted, we enable the camera view. Here is the relevant code:

```
    @Override
    public void onResume() {
        super.onResume();
        if (ContextCompat.checkSelfPermission(this,
                Manifest.permission.CAMERA)
                != PackageManager.PERMISSION_GRANTED) {
            if (ActivityCompat.shouldShowRequestPermissionRationale(this,
                    Manifest.permission.CAMERA)) {
                showRequestPermissionRationale();
            } else {
                ActivityCompat.requestPermissions(this,
                        new String[] { Manifest.permission.CAMERA },
                        PERMISSIONS_REQUEST_CAMERA);
            }
```

```
        } else {
            Log.i(TAG, "Camera permissions were already granted");

            // Start the camera.
            mCameraView.enableView();
        }
    }
```

When the activity is destroyed, we clean things up in the same way as when the activity is paused:

```
@Override
public void onDestroy() {
    super.onDestroy();
    if (mCameraView != null) {
        // Stop the camera.
        mCameraView.disableView();
    }
    if (mAudioTree != null) {
        mAudioTree.stop();
    }
    resetGestures();
}
```

Our `showRequestPermissionRationale` helper method shows a dialog that explains why `Goldgesture` needs to use the camera. When the user clicks this dialog's `OK` button, we request permission to use the camera:

```
void showRequestPermissionRationale() {
    AlertDialog dialog = new AlertDialog.Builder(this).create();
    dialog.setTitle("Camera, please");
    dialog.setMessage(
            "Goldgesture uses the camera to see you nod or shake " +
            "your head. You will be asked for camera access.");
    dialog.setButton(AlertDialog.BUTTON_NEUTRAL, "OK",
            new DialogInterface.OnClickListener() {
                public void onClick(DialogInterface dialog,
                                    int which) {
                    dialog.dismiss();
                    ActivityCompat.requestPermissions(
                            CameraActivity.this,
                            new String[] {
                                    Manifest.permission.CAMERA },
                            PERMISSIONS_REQUEST_CAMERA);
                }
            });
    dialog.show();
}
```

We implement a callback to handle the result of the permission request. If the user granted permission to use the camera, we enable the camera view. Otherwise, we log an error and exit:

```java
@Override
public void onRequestPermissionsResult(final int requestCode,
        final String permissions[], final int[] grantResults) {
    switch (requestCode) {
        case PERMISSIONS_REQUEST_CAMERA: {
            if (grantResults.length > 0 &&
                    grantResults[0] == PackageManager.PERMISSION_GRANTED) {
                Log.i(TAG, "Camera permissions were granted just now");

                // Start the camera.
                mCameraView.enableView();
            } else {
                Log.e(TAG, "Camera permissions were denied");
                finish();
            }
            break;
        }
    }
}
```

Now, let's turn our attention to the camera callbacks. When the camera preview starts (after the OpenCV library is loaded and permission to use the camera is obtained), we initialize our remaining member variables. To begin, we store the pixel dimensions that the camera is using:

```java
@Override
public void onCameraViewStarted(final int width,
                                final int height) {

    mImageWidth = width;
    mImageHeight = height;
```

Next, we initialize our face-detection variables, mostly through a private helper method called `initFaceDetector`. The role of `initFaceDetector` includes loading the detector's cascade file, `app/main/res/raw/lbpcascade_frontalface.xml`. A lot of boilerplate code for file handling and error handling is involved in this task, so separating it into another function improves readability. We will examine the helper function's implementation later in this section of the chapter, but here is the call:

```java
        initFaceDetector();
        mFaces = new MatOfRect();
```

As we did in Chapter 3, *Training a Smart Alarm to Recognize the Villain and His Cat*, we determine the smaller of the two image dimensions and use it in proportional size calculations:

```
final int smallerSide;
if (height < width) {
    smallerSide = height;
} else {
    smallerSide = width;
}

final double minSizeSide =
        MIN_SIZE_PROPORTIONAL * smallerSide;
mMinSize = new Size(minSizeSide, minSizeSide);

final double maxSizeSide =
        MAX_SIZE_PROPORTIONAL * smallerSide;
mMaxSize = new Size(maxSizeSide, maxSizeSide);
```

We initialize matrices relating to the features:

```
mInitialFeatures = new MatOfPoint();
mFeatures = new MatOfPoint2f(new Point());
mLastFeatures = new MatOfPoint2f(new Point());
mFeatureStatuses = new MatOfByte();
mFeatureErrors = new MatOfFloat();
```

We specify colors (in **RGB (red, green, and blue)** format, not **BGR (blue, green, and red)**) for drawing a rectangle around the face and circles around the features:

```
mFaceRectColor = new Scalar(0.0, 0.0, 255.0);
mFeatureColor = new Scalar(0.0, 255.0, 0.0);
```

We initialize variables relating to nod and shake recognition:

```
final double minShakeDist =
        smallerSide * MIN_SHAKE_DIST_PROPORTIONAL;
mShakeHeadGesture = new BackAndForthGesture(minShakeDist);

final double minNodDist =
        smallerSide * MIN_NOD_DIST_PROPORTIONAL;
mNodHeadGesture = new BackAndForthGesture(minNodDist);
```

We initialize and start the audio sequence:

```
mAudioTree = new YesNoAudioTree(this);
mAudioTree.start();
```

Finally, we initialize the image matrices, most of which are transposed to be in portrait format:

```
mGrayUnoriented = new Mat(height, width, CvType.CV_8UC1);

// The rest of the matrices are transposed.

mEqualizedGray = new Mat(width, height, CvType.CV_8UC1);
mLastEqualizedGray = new Mat(width, height, CvType.CV_8UC1);

mMask = new Mat(width, height, CvType.CV_8UC1);
mMaskForegroundColor = new Scalar(255.0);
mMaskBackgroundColor = new Scalar(0.0);
}
```

When the camera view stops, we do not do anything. Here is the empty callback method:

```
@Override
public void onCameraViewStopped() {
}
```

When the camera captures a frame, we do all the real work, the computer vision. We start by getting the color image (in **red, green, blue, and alpha** (**RGBA**) format, not BGR), convert it to grayscale, and reorient it to portrait format. The reorientation from landscape to portrait format is equivalent to rotating the image's *content* 90 degrees *counterclockwise*, or rotating the image's *X and Y coordinate axes* 90 degrees *clockwise*. To accomplish this, we apply a transpose operation followed by a vertical flip. After reorienting the grayscale image to portrait format, we equalize it. Thus, the callback's implementation begins as follows:

```
@Override
public Mat onCameraFrame(final CvCameraViewFrame inputFrame) {
    final Mat rgba = inputFrame.rgba();

    // For processing, orient the image to portrait and equalize
    // it.
    Imgproc.cvtColor(rgba, mGrayUnoriented,
            Imgproc.COLOR_RGBA2GRAY);
    Core.transpose(mGrayUnoriented, mEqualizedGray);
    Core.flip(mEqualizedGray, mEqualizedGray, 0);
    Imgproc.equalizeHist(mEqualizedGray, mEqualizedGray);
```

We get the RGBA image by calling `inputFrame.rgba()` and then we convert it to grayscale. Alternatively, we could get the grayscale image directly by calling `inputFrame.gray()`. In our case, we want both the RGBA and grayscale images because we use the RGBA image for display and the grayscale image for detection and tracking.

Next, we declare a list of features. A standard Java `List` allows for fast insertion and removal of elements, whereas an OpenCV `Mat` does not, so we are going to need a `List` when we filter out features that did not track well. Here is the declaration:

```
final List<Point> featuresList;
```

We detect faces—a familiar task from the Angora Blue project in Chapter 3, *Training a Smart Alarm to Recognize the Villain and His Cat*. Unlike in OpenCV's Python bindings, the structure to store the face rectangles is provided as an argument:

```
mFaceDetector.detectMultiScale(
        mEqualizedGray, mFaces, SCALE_FACTOR, MIN_NEIGHBORS,
        FLAGS, mMinSize, mMaxSize);
```

If at least one face is detected, we take the first detected face and draw a rectangle around it. We are performing face detection on an image in portrait orientation, but we are drawing the original image in landscape orientation, so some conversion of coordinates is necessary. Note that the origin (the upper-left corner) of the portrait image corresponds to the upper-right corner of the landscape image. Here is the code:

```
if (mFaces.rows() > 0) { // Detected at least one face

    // Get the first detected face.
    final double[] face = mFaces.get(0, 0);

    double minX = face[0];
    double minY = face[1];
    double width = face[2];
    double height = face[3];
    double maxX = minX + width;
    double maxY = minY + height;

    // Draw the face.
    Imgproc.rectangle(
            rgba, new Point(mImageWidth - maxY, minX),
            new Point(mImageWidth - minY, maxX),
            mFaceRectColor);
```

Next, we select features within the inner part of the detected face. We specify the region of interest by passing a mask to OpenCV's `goodFeaturesToTrack` function. A mask is an image that is white in the foreground (the inner part of the face) and black in the background. The following code finds the region of interest, creates the mask, and calls `goodFeaturesToTrack` with all relevant parameters:

```java
// Create a mask for the face region.
double smallerSide;
if (height < width) {
    smallerSide = height;
} else {
    smallerSide = width;
}
double maskPadding =
        smallerSide * MASK_PADDING_PROPORTIONAL;
mMask.setTo(mMaskBackgroundColor);
Imgproc.rectangle(
        mMask,
        new Point(minX + maskPadding,
                minY + maskPadding),
        new Point(maxX - maskPadding,
                maxY - maskPadding),
        mMaskForegroundColor, -1);

// Find features in the face region.
Imgproc.goodFeaturesToTrack(
        mEqualizedGray, mInitialFeatures, MAX_FEATURES,
        MIN_FEATURE_QUALITY, MIN_FEATURE_DISTANCE,
        mMask, 3, false, 0.04);
mFeatures.fromArray(mInitialFeatures.toArray());
featuresList = mFeatures.toList();
```

Note that we copy the features into several variables: a matrix of initial features, a matrix of current features, and a mutable list of features that we will filter later.

Depending on whether we were already tracking a face, we call a helper function to either initialize our data on gestures or update our data on gestures. We also record that we are now tracking a face:

```java
if (mWasTrackingFace) {
    updateGestureDetection();
} else {
    startGestureDetection();
}
mWasTrackingFace = true;
```

Controlling a Phone App with Your Suave Gestures

Alternatively, we might not have detected any face in this frame. Then, we update any previously-selected features using OpenCV's `calcOpticalFlowPyrLK` function to give us a matrix of new features, a matrix of error values, and a matrix of status values (`0` for an invalid feature, `1` for a valid feature). Being invalid typically means that the new feature is estimated to be outside the frame and thus it can no longer be tracked by optical flow. We convert the new features to a list and filter out the ones that are invalid or have a high error, as seen in the following code:

```
// if (mFaces.rows > 0) { ... See above ... }
} else { // Did not detect any face
    Video.calcOpticalFlowPyrLK(
            mLastEqualizedGray, mEqualizedGray, mLastFeatures,
            mFeatures, mFeatureStatuses, mFeatureErrors);

    // Filter out features that are not found or have high
    // error.
    featuresList = new LinkedList<Point>(mFeatures.toList());
    final LinkedList<Byte> featureStatusesList =
            new LinkedList<Byte>(mFeatureStatuses.toList());
    final LinkedList<Float> featureErrorsList =
            new LinkedList<Float>(mFeatureErrors.toList());
    for (int i = 0; i < featuresList.size();) {
        if (featureStatusesList.get(i) == 0 ||
                featureErrorsList.get(i) > MAX_FEATURE_ERROR) {
            featuresList.remove(i);
            featureStatusesList.remove(i);
            featureErrorsList.remove(i);
        } else {
            i++;
        }
    }
}
```

If too few features remain after filtering, we deem that the face is no longer tracked and we discard all features. Otherwise, we put the accepted features back in the matrix of current features and we update our data on gestures:

```
if (featuresList.size() < MIN_FEATURES) {
    // The number of remaining features is too low; we have
    // probably lost the target completely.

    // Discard the remaining features.
    featuresList.clear();
    mFeatures.fromList(featuresList);

    mWasTrackingFace = false;
} else {
    mFeatures.fromList(featuresList);
```

```
            updateGestureDetection();
        }
    }
```

We draw green circles around the current features. Again, we must convert coordinates from portrait format back to landscape format in order to draw on the original image:

```
    // Draw the current features.
    for (int i = 0; i< featuresList.size(); i++) {
        final Point p = featuresList.get(i);
        final Point pTrans = new Point(
                mImageWidth - p.y,
                p.x);
        Imgproc.circle(rgba, pTrans, 8, mFeatureColor);
    }
```

At the end of the frame, the current equalized gray image and current features become the previous equalized gray image and previous features. Rather than copying these matrices, we swap references:

```
    // Swap the references to the current and previous images.
    final Mat swapEqualizedGray = mLastEqualizedGray;
    mLastEqualizedGray = mEqualizedGray;
    mEqualizedGray = swapEqualizedGray;

    // Swap the references to the current and previous features.
    final MatOfPoint2f swapFeatures = mLastFeatures;
    mLastFeatures = mFeatures;
    mFeatures = swapFeatures;
```

We horizontally flip the preview image to make it look like a mirror. Then, we return it so that OpenCV can display it:

```
    // Mirror (horizontally flip) the preview.
    Core.flip(rgba, rgba, 1);

    return rgba;
}
```

We have mentioned several helper functions, which we will examine now. When we start analyzing face motion, we find the geometric mean of the features and use the mean's x and y coordinates, respectively, as the starting coordinates for shake and nod gestures:

```
    private void startGestureDetection() {

        double[] featuresCenter = Core.mean(mFeatures).val;

        // Motion in x may indicate a shake of the head.
```

Controlling a Phone App with Your Suave Gestures

```
        mShakeHeadGesture.start(featuresCenter[0]);

        // Motion in y may indicate a nod of the head.
        mNodHeadGesture.start(featuresCenter[1]);
    }
```

Recall that our `BackAndForthGesture` class uses one-dimensional positions. For an upright head, only the x coordinate is relevant to a shake gesture and only the y coordinate is relevant to a nod gesture.

Similarly, as we continue to analyze face motion, we find the features' new geometric mean and use the mean's coordinates to update the shake and nod data. Based on the number of back-and-forth shaking or nodding motions, we may take a yes branch or a no branch in the question-and-answer tree. Alternatively, we may decide that the user's current gesture is ambiguous (both a yes and a no), in which case we reset the data:

```
    private void updateGestureDetection() {

        final double[] featuresCenter = Core.mean(mFeatures).val;

        // Motion in x may indicate a shake of the head.
        mShakeHeadGesture.update(featuresCenter[0]);
        final int shakeBackAndForthCount =
                mShakeHeadGesture.getBackAndForthCount();
        //Log.i(TAG, "shakeBackAndForthCount=" +
        //        shakeBackAndForthCount);
        final boolean shakingHead =
                (shakeBackAndForthCount >=
                        MIN_BACK_AND_FORTH_COUNT);

        // Motion in y may indicate a nod of the head.
        mNodHeadGesture.update(featuresCenter[1]);
        final int nodBackAndForthCount =
                mNodHeadGesture.getBackAndForthCount();
        //Log.i(TAG, "nodBackAndForthCount=" +
        //        nodBackAndForthCount);
        final boolean noddingHead =
                (nodBackAndForthCount >=
                        MIN_BACK_AND_FORTH_COUNT);

        if (shakingHead && noddingHead) {
            // The gesture is ambiguous. Ignore it.
            resetGestures();
        } else if (shakingHead) {
            mAudioTree.takeNoBranch();
            resetGestures();
```

```
        } else if (noddingHead) {
            mAudioTree.takeYesBranch();
            resetGestures();
        }
    }
```

We always reset the nod gesture data and the shake gesture data at the same time:

```
    private void resetGestures() {
        if (mNodHeadGesture != null) {
            mNodHeadGesture.resetCounts();
        }
        if (mShakeHeadGesture != null) {
            mShakeHeadGesture.resetCounts();
        }
    }
```

Our helper method for initializing the face detector is very similar to the method found in an official OpenCV sample project that performs face detection on Android. We copy the cascade's raw data from the app bundle to a new file that is more accessible. Then, we initialize a `CascadeClassifier` object using this file's path. If an error is encountered at any point, we log it and close the app. Here is the method's implementation:

```
    private void initFaceDetector() {
        try {
            // Load cascade file from application resources.

            InputStream is = getResources().openRawResource(
                    R.raw.lbpcascade_frontalface);
            File cascadeDir = getDir(
                    "cascade", Context.MODE_PRIVATE);
            File cascadeFile = new File(
                    cascadeDir, "lbpcascade_frontalface.xml");
            FileOutputStream os = new FileOutputStream(cascadeFile);

            byte[] buffer = new byte[4096];
            int bytesRead;
            while ((bytesRead = is.read(buffer)) != -1) {
                os.write(buffer, 0, bytesRead);
            }
            is.close();
            os.close();

            mFaceDetector = new CascadeClassifier(
                    cascadeFile.getAbsolutePath());
            if (mFaceDetector.empty()) {
                Log.e(TAG, "Failed to load cascade");
                finish();
```

```
        } else {
            Log.i(TAG, "Loaded cascade from " +
                    cascadeFile.getAbsolutePath());
        }

        cascadeDir.delete();

    } catch (IOException e) {
        e.printStackTrace();
        Log.e(TAG, "Failed to load cascade. Exception caught: "
                + e);
        finish();
    }
  }
}
```

That's all the code! We are ready to test. Make sure your Android device has its sound turned on. Plug the device into a USB port and press the run button (the play icon in green). The first time you run the project, you might see the **Select Deployment Target** window:

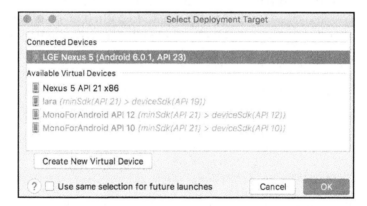

If you see this window, select your Android device and hit the **OK** button.

Soon, you should see the app's camera preview appear on your device. Nod or shake your head knowingly as the questions are asked:

Chapter 4

You should see a blue rectangle around your face, and green dots that remain (more or less) anchored to some features of your face as you move. Refer to the previous screenshot as an example.

To improve the gesture detection results for your particular camera and environment, you may want to experiment with adjusting the parameters that we defined as constants in the code. Moreover, try to keep the camera still. Camera motion will interfere with our gesture detection algorithm because we rely on optical flow, which does not differentiate between camera motion and subject motion.

Summary

Silence is golden—or perhaps gestures are. At least, gestures can fill an awkward silence and control an app that whispers reminders in your earphones.

In this chapter, we built our first Android app with OpenCV's Java bindings. We also learned to use optical flow to track the movement of an object after detection. Thus, we are able to recognize a gesture, such as a head moving up and down in a nod.

In the next chapter, our project deals with motion in three dimensions. We will build a system that estimates changes in distance in order to alert a driver when the car is being followed.

5
Equipping Your Car with a Rearview Camera and Hazard Detection

"Comes the morning and the headlights fade away."
– The Living Daylights (1987)

James Bond is a car thief. The movies show that he has stolen many automobiles, often from innocent bystanders. We do not know whether these unfortunate people ever recovered their property but, even if they did, the damages from collisions, submersions, bullets, and rockets would have had a lasting impact on their insurance premiums. Bond has also stolen a propeller plane, a tank, and a moon buggy.

The man has been driving since the 1950s, and perhaps it is time that he stopped.

Be that as it may, we can break away from the old Cold War days of indifference to collateral damage. With modern technology, we can provide a driver with timely information about others who are sharing the road. This information may make it easier to avoid collisions and to properly aim the vehicle's rocket launchers so that a chase scene can be conducted in an orderly manner, without flattening whole city blocks. Secret agents will not lose so many cars and, thus, will not feel compelled to steal so many.

Since driver assistance is a broad topic, let's focus on one scenario. Twilight and nighttime are difficult times for drivers, including secret agents. We might be blinded by the lack of natural light or the glare of headlights. However, we can make a computer vision system that sees headlights (or rear lights) clearly and can estimate their distance from them. This system can also distinguish between lights of different colors, a feature which is relevant to identifying signals and types of vehicles.

We will choose computationally inexpensive techniques, suitable for a low-powered computer—namely, Raspberry Pi—which we can plug into a car's cigarette lighter through an adapter. An LCD panel can display the relevant information, along with a live, rearview video feed that is less glaring than real headlights.

This project presents us with several new topics and challenges, such as the following:

- How to detect blobs of light and classify their color
- How to estimate the distance from the camera to a detected object whose realworld size is known
- How to set up a low-budget lab where we can experiment with lights of many colors
- How to set up a Raspberry Pi and peripherals in a car

Realistically, our quick, homemade project is not sufficiently robust to be relied upon as an automotive safety tool, so take it with a grain of salt. However, it is a fun introduction to analyzing signal lights and wiring up a custom in-car computer. The choice of Raspberry Pi as a platform challenges us to think about the car as an environment for rapid prototyping. We can plug in any standard peripherals, including a webcam, keyboard, mouse, and even a monitor, giving us a complete desktop Linux system with Python—on wheels! (Snakes in a car!) For more exotic projects, the Pi is compatible with many electronics kits, too! A smartphone or tablet is also a good alternative for use in a car, and is easier to power than a Pi with a monitor, but the Pi excels as a well-rounded prototyping tool.

All we need now is a name for our project. So, let the app be known as `The Living Headlights`.

Technical requirements

This chapter's project has the following software dependencies:

- **A Python environment with the following modules**: OpenCV, NumPy, SciPy, wxPython

Setup instructions are covered in `Chapter 1`, *Preparing for the Mission*. Refer to the setup instructions for any version requirements. Basic instructions for running Python code are covered in `Appendix C`, *Running with Snakes (or, First Steps with Python)*.

The completed project for this chapter can be found in this book's GitHub repository, `https://github.com/PacktPublishing/OpenCV-4-for-Secret-Agents-Second-Edition`, in the `Chapter005` folder.

Planning The Living Headlights app

For this app, we need to return to the cross-platform wxPython framework. Optionally, we can also develop and test our wxPython application on a Windows, Mac, or Linux desktop or laptop before deploying it to our Raspberry Pi computer. With the Raspbian operating system, the Pi can run wxPython, just as any Linux desktop could.

The GUI for `The Living Headlights` includes a live video feed, a set of controls where the user can enter their true distance from headlights, and a label that initially displays a set of instructions, as seen in the following screenshot:

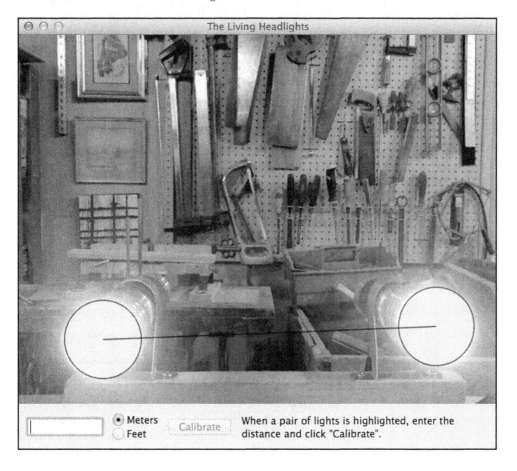

When a pair of headlights is detected, the user must perform a one-time calibration step. This step consists of entering the true distance between the camera and headlights (specifically, the midpoint between the headlights) and then clicking on the **Calibrate** button. Thereafter, the app continuously updates and displays an estimate of the headlights' distance and color, as seen in the label at the bottom of the following screenshot:

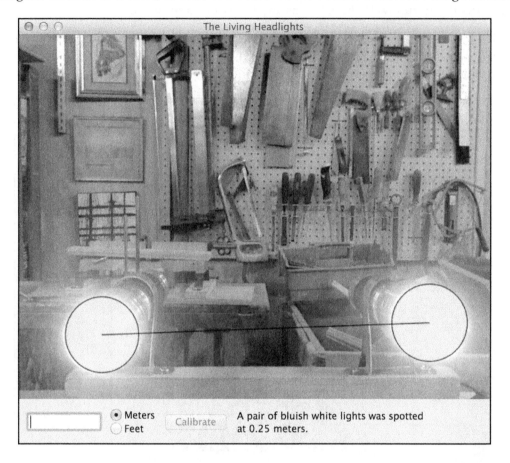

The calibration and the selected unit (**Meters** or **Feet**) are stored in a configuration file when the app closes. They are reloaded from this file when the app reopens. The calibration remains valid as long as the same camera and lens are used, the lens does not zoom, and the spacing between two headlights in a pair remains approximately constant for all pairs of headlights.

Atop the video feed, colored circles are drawn to mark detected lights, and lines are drawn between pairs of detected lights whose colors match. Such a pair is considered to be a set of headlights.

Next, let's consider techniques for detecting lights and classifying their colors.

Detecting lights as blobs

To the human eye, light can appear both very bright and very colorful. Imagine a sunny landscape or a storefront lit by a neon sign; they are bright and colorful! However, a camera captures a range of contrast that is much narrower and not as intelligently selected, so that the sunny landscape or neon-lit storefront can look washed out. This problem of poorly controlled contrast is especially bad in cheap cameras or cameras that have small sensors, such as webcams. As a result, bright light sources tend to be imaged as big white blobs with thin rims of color. These blobs also tend to mimic a lens's iris—typically, a polygon approximating a circle.

The thought of all lights becoming white and circular makes the world seem like a poorer place, if you ask me. Nonetheless, in computer vision, we can take advantage of such a predictable pattern. We can look for white blobs that are nearly circular and we can infer their human-perceptible color from a sample that includes extra pixels around the rim.

Blob detection is actually a major branch of computer vision. Unlike the face detectors (or other object detectors) that we discussed in previous chapters, a blob detector is not trained. There is no concept of a reference image, so meaningful classifications such as *This blob is a light* or *This blob is skin* are more complicated to produce. Classification goes beyond the ken of the blob detector itself. We explicitly define thresholds between non-lights and lights, and between different human-perceptible colors of lights, based on *a priori* knowledge about typical shapes and colors of light sources, as imaged by a webcam.

Other terms for a blob include a *connected component* and a *region*. However, in this book, we just say *blob*.

At its simplest, blob detection consists of the five following steps:

1. Partition the image into two or more colors. For example, this can be accomplished by *binary thresholding* (also called **binarization**), whereby all grayscale values above a threshold are converted into white and all grayscale values below the threshold are converted into black.

2. Find the *contour* of each contiguously colored region, that is, each blob. The contour is a set of points describing the region's outline.
3. Merge blobs that are deemed to be neighbors.
4. Optionally, determine each blob's *features*. These are higher-level measurements such as the center point, radius, and circularity. The usefulness of these features lies in their simplicity. For further blob-related computations and logic, it may be best to avoid complex representation, such as a contour's many points.
5. Reject blobs that fail to meet certain measurable criteria.

OpenCV implements a simple blob detector in a class called `cv2.SimpleBlobDetector` (appropriately enough). This class's constructor takes an instance of a helper class called `cv2.SimpleBlobDetector_Params`, which describes the criteria for accepting or rejecting a candidate blob. `SimpleBlobDetector_Params` has the following member variables:

- `thresholdStep`, `minThreshold`, and `maxThreshold`: The search for blobs is based on a series of binarized images (analogous to the series of scaled images that are searched by a Haar cascade detector, as described in Chapter 3, *Training a Smart Alarm to Recognize the Villain and His Cat*). The thresholds for binarization are based on the range and step size given by these variables. We use 8, 191, and 255.
- `minRepeatability`: This variable minus one is the minimum number of neighbors that a blob must have. We use 2, meaning that a blob must have at least one neighbor. If we did not require at least one neighbor, the detector would tend to report a large number of blobs, with a lot of overlap between blobs.
- `minDistBetweenBlobs`: Blobs must be at least this many pixels apart. Blobs that are closer than the minimum distance from each other are counted as neighbors. We use a minimum distance calculated as two percent of the image's larger dimension (typically width).
- `filterByColor` (True or False) and `blobColor`: If `filterByColor` is True, a blob's central pixel must exactly match `blobColor`. We use True and 255 (white), based on our assumption that light sources are white blobs.
- `filterByArea` (True or False), `minArea`, and `maxArea`: If `filterByArea` is True, a blob's area in pixels must fall within the given range. We use True and a range calculated as 0.5 percent to 10 percent of the image's larger dimension (typically width).

- `filterByCircularity` (`True` or `False`), `minCircularity`, and `maxCircularity`: If `filterByCircularity` is `True`, a blob's circularity must fall within the given range, where circularity is defined as `4 * PI * area / (perimeter ^ 2)`. A circle's circularity is 1.0 and a line's circularity is 0.0. For our approximately circular light sources, we use `True` and the range 0.7 to 1.0.
- `filterByInertia` (`True` or `False`), `minInertiaRatio`, and `maxInertiaRatio`: If `filterByInertia` is `True`, a blob's inertia ratio must fall within the given range. A relatively high inertia ratio implies that the blob is relatively elongated (and would thus require more torque to rotate along its longest axis). A circle's inertia ratio is 1.0 and a line's inertia ratio is 0.0. We use `filterByInertia=False` (no filtering by inertia) because the circularity test already gives sufficient control over the shape for our purposes.
- `filterByConvexity` (`True` or `False`), `minConvexity`, and `maxConvexity`: If `filterByConvexity` is `True`, a blob's convexity must fall within the given range, where convexity is defined as `area/hullArea`. Here, `hullArea` refers to the area of the convex hull—the convex polygon surrounding all the points of a contour with the minimum area. Convexity is always more than 0.0 and less than 1.0. A relatively high convexity implies that the contour is relatively smooth. We use `filterByConvexity=False` (no filtering by convexity) because the circularity test already gives sufficient control over the shape for our purposes.

Although these parameters cover many useful criteria, they are designed for grayscale images and do not provide a practical means of filtering or classifying blobs based on separate criteria for hue, saturation, and luminosity. The suggested values in the preceding list are tuned to extract bright blobs of light. However, we may want to classify such blobs by subtle variations in color, especially around the blob's edge.

Hue refers to a color's angle on the color wheel, where *0* degrees is red, *120* is green, and *240* is blue. The hue in degrees can be calculated from RGB values with the following formula:

$hue = (180/PI) * atan2(sqrt(3) * (g - b), 2 * r - g - b)$

Saturation refers to a color's distance from grayscale. There are several alternative formulations of an RGB color's saturation. We use the following formulation, which some authors call **chroma** instead of saturation:

$saturation = max(r, g, b) - min(r, g, b)$

We can classify a light source's human-perceptible color based on the average hue and saturation of the blob and some surrounding pixels. The combination of a low saturation and a blue or yellow hue tends to suggest that the light will appear white to human vision. Other light sources may appear (in order of ascending hue) as red, orange/amber/yellow, green (a wide range from spring green to emerald), blue/purple (another wide range), or pink, to give just a few examples. Threshold values can be chosen based on trial and error.

Using the techniques we've mentioned, we can detect the location, pixel radius, and perceptual color of light sources. However, we need additional techniques to get an estimate of the real distance between the camera and a pair of headlights. Let's turn our attention to this problem now.

Estimating distances (a cheap approach)

Suppose we have an object sitting in front of a pinhole camera. Regardless of the distance between the camera and the object, the following equation holds true:

$objectSizeInImage/focalLength = objectSizeInReality/distance$

We may use any unit (such as pixels) in the equation's left-hand side and any unit (such as meters) in its right-hand side (on each side of the equation, the division cancels the unit). Moreover, we may define the object's size based on anything linear that we can detect in the image, such as the diameter of a detected blob or the width of a detected face rectangle.

Let's rearrange the equation to illustrate that the distance to the object is inversely proportional to the object's size in the image:

$distance = focalLength * objectSizeInReality/objectSizeInImage$

Let's assume that the object's real size and the camera's focal length are constant (a constant focal length means that the lens does not zoom and we do not swap the lens for a different lens). Consider the following arrangement, which isolates this pair of constants on the right-hand side of the equation:

$distance * objectSizeInImage = focalLength * objectSizeInReality$

As the right-hand side of the equation is constant, so is the left. We may conclude that the following relationship holds true over time:

$newDist * newObjectSizeInImage = oldDist * oldObjectSizeInImage$

Let's solve the following equation for the new distance:

$newDist = oldDist * oldObjectSizeInImage/newObjectSizeInImage$

Now, let's think about applying this equation in software. To provide a ground truth, the user must take a single, true measurement of the distance to use as the *old* distance in all future calculations. As well as this, we must know the object's old pixel size and its subsequent new size so that we can compute the new distance any time there is a detection result. Let's review the following assumptions:

- There is no lens distortion; the pinhole camera model applies
- Focal length is constant; no zoom is applied and the lens is not swapped for a different lens
- The object is rigid; its real-world measurements do not change
- The camera is always viewing the same side of the object; the relative rotation of the camera and object does not change

You might wonder whether the first assumption is problematic, as webcams often have cheap wide angle lenses with significant distortion. Despite lens distortion, does the object's size in the image remain inversely proportional to the real distance between the camera and object? The following paper reports experimental results for a lens that appears to distort badly and an object that is located off-center (in an image region where distortion is likely to be especially bad)—M. N. A. Wahab, N. Sivadev, and K. Sundaraj. *Target distance estimation using monocular vision system for mobile robot*. **IEEE Conference on Open Systems (ICOS)** 2011 Proceedings, vol. 11, no. 15, p. 25-28. September 2011.

Using exponential regression, the authors show that the following model is a good fit for experimental data ($R^2=0.995$):

```
distanceInCentimeters = 4042 * (objectSizeInPixels ^ -1.2)
```

Note that the exponent is close to *-1*, and thus the statistical model is not far from the ideal inverse relationship. (Even the poor-quality lens and off-center subject did not disprove our assumptions!)

We can also ensure that the second assumption (no zooming and no swapping of the lens) holds true.

Let's consider the third and fourth assumptions (rigidity and constant rotation) in the case of a camera and object—one in each car on a highway. Except in a crash, most of a car's exterior parts are rigid. Except when passing or pulling over, one car travels directly behind the other on a surface that is mostly flat and mostly straight. However, on a road that is hilly or has many turns, these assumptions start to fall apart. It becomes more difficult to predict which side of the object is currently being viewed; thus, it is more difficult to say whether our reference measurements apply to a particular side.

Of course, we need to define a generic car part to be our *object*. The headlights (and the space between them) are a decent choice, since we have a method for detecting them and the distance between headlights is consistent across many cars—although not all.

All distance estimation techniques in computer vision rely on some assumptions or calibration steps that relate to the camera, the object, the relationship between camera and object, or lighting. For comparison, let's consider some of the following common distance estimation techniques:

- A **time-of-flight** (**ToF**) camera shines a light on objects and measures the intensity of any reflected light. This intensity is used to estimate the distance at each pixel based on the known fall-off characteristics of the light source. Some ToF cameras, such as Microsoft Kinect, use an infrared light source. Other, more expensive ToF cameras scan a scene with a laser or even use a grid of lasers. ToF cameras may suffer from interference if other bright lights are being imaged, so they are poorly suited to our application.
- A **stereo camera** consists of two parallel cameras with a known, fixed distance between them. In each frame, a pair of images is captured, features are identified, and a *disparity* or pixel distance is calculated for each pair of corresponding features. We can convert disparity into real distance based on the cameras' known field of view and the distance between them. For our application, stereo techniques would be feasible, but they are also computationally expensive and use a lot of input bus bandwidth. Optimizing these techniques for Raspberry Pi would be a big challenge.
- **Structure from Motion** (**SfM**) techniques only need a single, regular camera, but rely on moving the camera by known distances over time. For each pair of images taken from neighboring locations, disparities are calculated, as with a stereo camera. In this scenario, as well as knowing the camera's movements, we must know the object's movements or lack thereof. Due to these limitations, SfM techniques are poorly suited to our application, as our camera and object are mounted on two freely moving vehicles.

- Various **3D feature tracking** techniques entail estimating the rotation of an object, as well as its distance and other coordinates. Edges and texture details are also considered. The differences between models of cars make it difficult to define one set of features that are suitable for 3D tracking, and so 3D feature tracking is not well-suited to our application. Moreover, 3D tracking is computationally expensive, especially by the standards of a low-powered computer such as Raspberry Pi.

> For more information on these techniques, refer to the following books, available from Packt Publishing:
>
> - Kinect and other ToF cameras are covered in the first edition of my book, *OpenCV Computer Vision with Python*, specifically *Chapter 5, Detecting Foreground/Background Regions and Depth*.
> - 3D feature tracking and SfM are covered in *Mastering OpenCV with Practical Computer Vision Projects*, specifically *Chapter 3, Markerless Augmented Reality*, and *Chapter 4, Exploring Structure from Motion Using OpenCV*.
> - Stereo vision and 3D feature tracking are covered in Robert Laganière's *OpenCV 3 Computer Vision Application Programming Cookbook*, specifically *Chapter 10, Estimating Projective Relations in Images*.
> - Stereo vision and 3D pose estimation are also covered in Alexey Spizhevoy and Aleksandr Rybnikov's *OpenCV 3 Computer Vision with Python Cookbook*, specifically *Chapter 9, Multiple View Geometry*.

On balance, the simplistic approach—based on pixel distances being inversely proportional to real distances—is a justifiable choice given our application and our intent to support the Pi.

Implementing The Living Headlights app

The `Living Headlights` app will use the following files:

- `LivingHeadlights.py`: This is a new file that contains our application class and its `main` function.

- `ColorUtils.py`: This is a new file that contains the utility functions required to convert colors into different representations.
- `GeomUtils.py`: This contains utility functions for geometric calculations. Copy or link to the version that we used in Chapter 3, *Training a Smart Alarm to Recognize the Villain and His Cat*.
- `PyInstallerUtils.py`: This contains utility functions for accessing resources in a PyInstaller application bundle. Copy or link to the version that we used in Chapter 3, *Training a Smart Alarm to Recognize the Villain and His Cat*.
- `ResizeUtils.py`: This contains utility functions for resizing images, including camera capture dimensions. Copy or link to the version that we used in Chapter 3, *Training a Smart Alarm to Recognize the Villain and His Cat*.
- `WxUtils.py`: This contains utility functions for using OpenCV images in wxPython apps. Copy or link to the version that we used in Chapter 3, *Training a Smart Alarm to Recognize the Villain and His Cat*.

Let's get started with the creation of `ColorUtils.py`. Here, we need functions to calculate a color's hue and saturation according to the formulae mentioned in the *Detecting lights as blobs* section. The module's implementation is shown in the following code:

```
import math


def hueFromBGR(color):
    b, g, r = color
    # Note: sqrt(3) = 1.7320508075688772
    hue = math.degrees(math.atan2(
        1.7320508075688772 * (g - b), 2 * r - g - b))
    if hue < 0.0:
        hue += 360.0
    return hue

def saturationFromBGR(color):
    return max(color) - min(color)
```

If we want to convert an entire image (that is, every pixel) to hue, saturation, and either luminosity or value, we can use the following OpenCV method, `cvtColor`:

```
hslImage = cv2.cvtColor(bgrImage, cv2.COLOR_BGR2HLS)

hsvImage = cv2.cvtColor(bgrImage, cv2.COLOR_BGR2HSV)
```

See the following Wikipedia article for definitions of saturation, luminosity, and value in HSV and HSL color models at https://en.wikipedia.org/wiki/HSL_and_HSV. Our definition of saturation is called **chroma** in the Wikipedia article, which differs from HSL saturation, and in turn differs again from HSV saturation. Moreover, OpenCV represents hue in units of two degrees (a range of 0 to 180) so that the hue channel fits inside a byte.

For some types of image segmentation problems, it is useful to convert the entire image into HSV, HSL, or another color model. For example, see Rebecca Stone's blog post about segmenting images of clown fish at https://realpython.com/python-opencv-color-spaces/, or Vikas Gupta's blog post about segmenting images of Rubik's cubes at https://www.learnopencv.com/color-spaces-in-opencv-cpp-python/.

We have written our own conversion functions because, for our purposes, converting an entire image is unnecessary; we just need to convert a sample from each blob. We also prefer a more accurate floating-point representation instead of the byte-sized integer representation that OpenCV imposes.

We also need to modify `GeomUtils.py` by adding a function to calculate the Euclidean distance between two 2D points, such as the pixel coordinates of two headlights in an image. At the top of the file, let's add an import statement and implement the function, as shown in the following code:

```
import math


def dist2D(p0, p1):
    deltaX = p1[0] - p0[0]
    deltaY = p1[1] - p0[1]
    return math.sqrt(deltaX * deltaX +
                     deltaY * deltaY)
```

Distances (and other magnitudes) can also be calculated using NumPy's `linalg.norm` function, as seen in the following code:

```
dist = numpy.linalg.norm(a1 - a0)
```

Here, `a0` and `a1` can be any size and shape. However, for a low-dimensional space such as 2D or 3D coordinate vectors, the overhead of using NumPy arrays is probably not worthwhile, so a utility function such as ours is a reasonable alternative.

The preceding code contains all the new utility functions. Now, let's create a file, `LivingHeadlights.py`, for the app's `main` class, `LivingHeadlights`. Like `InteractiveRecognizer` in Chapter 3, *Training a Smart Alarm to Recognize the Villain and His Cat*, `LivingHeadlights` is a class for a wxPython app that captures and processes images on a background thread (to avoid blocking the GUI on the main thread), allows a user to enter reference data, serializes its reference data when exiting, and deserializes its reference data when starting up again. This time, serialization and deserialization is accomplished using Python's `cPickle` module or, if `cPickle` is unavailable for any reason, the less-optimized `pickle` module. Let's add the following import statements to the start of `LivingHeadlights.py`:

```
#!/usr/bin/env python


import numpy
import cv2
import os
import threading
import wx

try:
    import cPickle as pickle
except:
    import pickle

import ColorUtils
import GeomUtils
import PyInstallerUtils
import ResizeUtils
import WxUtils
```

Let's also define some BGR color values and names at the start of the module. We will classify each blob as one of the following colors, depending on its hue and saturation:

```
COLOR_Red         = ((  0,   0, 255), 'red')
COLOR_YellowWhite = ((223, 247, 255), 'yellowish white')
COLOR_AmberYellow = ((  0, 191, 255), 'amber or yellow')
COLOR_Green       = ((128, 255, 128), 'green')
COLOR_BlueWhite   = ((255, 231, 223), 'bluish white')
COLOR_BluePurple  = ((255,  64,   0), 'blue or purple')
COLOR_Pink        = ((240, 128, 255), 'pink')
```

Now, let's begin implementing the class. The initializer takes several arguments relating to the configuration of the blob detector and the camera. Refer back to the *Detecting lights as blobs* section for explanations of the blob detection parameters supported by OpenCV's `SimpleBlobDetector` and `SimpleBlobDetector_Params` classes. The class declaration and initializer declaration is as follows:

```
class LivingHeadlights(wx.Frame):

    def __init__(self, configPath, thresholdStep=8.0,
                 minThreshold=191.0, maxThreshold=255.0,
                 minRepeatability=2,
                 minDistBetweenBlobsProportional=0.02,
                 minBlobAreaProportional=0.005,
                 maxBlobAreaProportional=0.1,
                 minBlobCircularity=0.7, cameraDeviceID=0,
                 imageSize=(640, 480),
                 title='The Living Headlights'):
```

We start the initializer's implementation by setting a public Boolean variable that indicates to the app to display a mirrored image and a protected Boolean variable that ensures the app is running, as follows:

```
self.mirrored = True

self._running = True
```

If there is any configuration file saved from a previous run of the app, we deserialize the reference measurements (the pixel distance between lights and the real distance in meters between lights and the camera), as well as the user's preferred unit of measurement (`meters` or `feet`), as follows:

```
self._configPath = configPath
self._pixelDistBetweenLights = None
if os.path.isfile(configPath):
    with open(self._configPath, 'rb') as file:
        self._referencePixelDistBetweenLights = \
                pickle.load(file)
        self._referenceMetersToCamera = \
                pickle.load(file)
        self._convertMetersToFeet = pickle.load(file)
else:
    self._referencePixelDistBetweenLights = None
    self._referenceMetersToCamera = None
    self._convertMetersToFeet = False
```

Now, we initialize a `VideoCapture` object and try to configure the size of the captured images. If the requested size is unsupported, we fall back to the default size, as shown in the following code:

```
self._capture = cv2.VideoCapture(cameraDeviceID)
size = ResizeUtils.cvResizeCapture(
        self._capture, imageSize)
w, h = size
self._imageWidth, self._imageHeight = w, h
```

We also need to declare variables for the images we will capture, process, and display. Initially, these are `None`. We also need to create a lock to manage thread-safe access to an image that will be captured and processed on one thread, and then drawn to the screen on another thread. The relevant declarations are as follows:

```
self._image = None
self._grayImage = None

self._imageFrontBuffer = None
self._imageFrontBufferLock = threading.Lock()
```

Now, we create a `SimpleBlobDetector_Params` object and a `SimpleBlobDetector` object based on the arguments passed to the app's initializer, as follows:

```
minDistBetweenBlobs = \
        min(w, h) * \
        minDistBetweenBlobsProportional

area = w * h
minBlobArea = area * minBlobAreaProportional
maxBlobArea = area * maxBlobAreaProportional

detectorParams = cv2.SimpleBlobDetector_Params()

detectorParams.minDistBetweenBlobs = \
        minDistBetweenBlobs

detectorParams.thresholdStep = thresholdStep
detectorParams.minThreshold = minThreshold
detectorParams.maxThreshold = maxThreshold

detectorParams.minRepeatability = minRepeatability

detectorParams.filterByArea = True
detectorParams.minArea = minBlobArea
detectorParams.maxArea = maxBlobArea
```

```
detectorParams.filterByColor = True
detectorParams.blobColor = 255

detectorParams.filterByCircularity = True
detectorParams.minCircularity = minBlobCircularity

detectorParams.filterByInertia = False

detectorParams.filterByConvexity = False

self._detector = cv2.SimpleBlobDetector_create(
    detectorParams)
```

Here, we specify the style of the app's window and we initialize the following base class, wx.Frame:

```
style = wx.CLOSE_BOX | wx.MINIMIZE_BOX | \
        wx.CAPTION | wx.SYSTEM_MENU | \
        wx.CLIP_CHILDREN
wx.Frame.__init__(self, None, title=title,
                  style=style, size=size)
self.SetBackgroundColour(wx.Colour(232, 232, 232))
```

We now need to bind the *Esc* key to a callback that closes the app, as follows:

```
self.Bind(wx.EVT_CLOSE, self._onCloseWindow)

quitCommandID = wx.NewId()
self.Bind(wx.EVT_MENU, self._onQuitCommand,
          id=quitCommandID)
acceleratorTable = wx.AcceleratorTable([
    (wx.ACCEL_NORMAL, wx.WXK_ESCAPE,
     quitCommandID)
])
self.SetAcceleratorTable(acceleratorTable)
```

Now, let's create the GUI elements, including the bitmap, the text field for the reference distance, radio buttons for the unit (meters or feet), and the **Calibrate** button. We also need to bind callbacks for various input events, as shown in the following code:

```
self._videoPanel = wx.Panel(self, size=size)
self._videoPanel.Bind(
    wx.EVT_ERASE_BACKGROUND,
    self._onVideoPanelEraseBackground)
self._videoPanel.Bind(
    wx.EVT_PAINT, self._onVideoPanelPaint)

self._videoBitmap = None
```

```python
self._calibrationTextCtrl = wx.TextCtrl(
        self, style=wx.TE_PROCESS_ENTER)
self._calibrationTextCtrl.Bind(
        wx.EVT_KEY_UP,
        self._onCalibrationTextCtrlKeyUp)

self._distanceStaticText = wx.StaticText(self)
if self._referencePixelDistBetweenLights is None:
    self._showInstructions()
else:
    self._clearMessage()

self._calibrationButton = wx.Button(
        self, label='Calibrate')
self._calibrationButton.Bind(
        wx.EVT_BUTTON, self._calibrate)
self._calibrationButton.Disable()

border = 12

metersButton = wx.RadioButton(self,
                              label='Meters')
metersButton.Bind(wx.EVT_RADIOBUTTON,
                  self._onSelectMeters)

feetButton = wx.RadioButton(self, label='Feet')
feetButton.Bind(wx.EVT_RADIOBUTTON,
                self._onSelectFeet)
```

We need to ensure that the proper radio buttons start in the selected state, depending on the configuration data that we deserialized earlier, as follows:

```python
if self._convertMetersToFeet:
    feetButton.SetValue(True)
else:
    metersButton.SetValue(True)
```

Next, we stack the radio buttons vertically using a `BoxSizer`, as follows:

```python
unitButtonsSizer = wx.BoxSizer(wx.VERTICAL)
unitButtonsSizer.Add(metersButton)
unitButtonsSizer.Add(feetButton)
```

We then line up all of our controls horizontally, again using a `BoxSizer`, as follows:

```python
controlsSizer = wx.BoxSizer(wx.HORIZONTAL)
style = wx.ALIGN_CENTER_VERTICAL | wx.RIGHT
controlsSizer.Add(self._calibrationTextCtrl, 0,
```

```
                    style, border)
controlsSizer.Add(unitButtonsSizer, 0, style,
                    border)
controlsSizer.Add(self._calibrationButton, 0,
                    style, border)
controlsSizer.Add(self._distanceStaticText, 0,
                    wx.ALIGN_CENTER_VERTICAL)
```

To finish our layout, we place the controls below the image, as shown in the following code:

```
rootSizer = wx.BoxSizer(wx.VERTICAL)
rootSizer.Add(self._videoPanel)
rootSizer.Add(controlsSizer, 0,
            wx.EXPAND | wx.ALL, border)
self.SetSizerAndFit(rootSizer)
```

The last thing we do in the initializer is start a background thread to capture and process images from the camera using the following code:

```
self._captureThread = threading.Thread(
        target=self._runCaptureLoop)
self._captureThread.start()
```

When closing the app, we first ensure that the capture thread terminates, just as we did for the InteractiveRecognizer in Chapter 3, *Training a Smart Alarm to Recognize the Villain and His Cat*. We also use pickle or cPickle to serialize the reference measurements and preferred unit (meters or feet) to a file. The implementation of the relevant callback is as follows:

```
def _onCloseWindow(self, event):
    self._running = False
    self._captureThread.join()
    configDir = os.path.dirname(self._configPath)
    if not os.path.isdir(configDir):
        os.makedirs(configDir)
    with open(self._configPath, 'wb') as file:
        pickle.dump(self._referencePixelDistBetweenLights,
                    file)
        pickle.dump(self._referenceMetersToCamera, file)
        pickle.dump(self._convertMetersToFeet, file)
    self.Destroy()
```

The callback associated with the *Esc* button just closes the app, as follows:

```
def _onQuitCommand(self, event):
    self.Close()
```

Equipping Your Car with a Rearview Camera and Hazard Detection

The video panel's erase and paint events are bound to callbacks, `_onVideoPanelEraseBackground` and `_onVideoPanelPaint`, which have the same implementations as `InteractiveRecognizer` in Chapter 3, *Training a Smart Alarm to Recognize the Villain and His Cat*, as follows:

```python
def _onVideoPanelEraseBackground(self, event):
    pass

def _onVideoPanelPaint(self, event):

    self._imageFrontBufferLock.acquire()

    if self._imageFrontBuffer is None:
        self._imageFrontBufferLock.release()
        return

    # Convert the image to bitmap format.
    self._videoBitmap = \
            WxUtils.wxBitmapFromCvImage(self._imageFrontBuffer)

    self._imageFrontBufferLock.release()

    # Show the bitmap.
    dc = wx.BufferedPaintDC(self._videoPanel)
    dc.DrawBitmap(self._videoBitmap, 0, 0)
```

When either of the radio buttons are selected, we need to record the newly selected unit of measurement, as seen in the following two callback methods:

```python
def _onSelectMeters(self, event):
    self._convertMetersToFeet = False

def _onSelectFeet(self, event):
    self._convertMetersToFeet = True
```

Whenever a new character is entered in the text field, we need to call a helper method to validate the text as potential input, as follows:

```python
def _onCalibrationTextCtrlKeyUp(self, event):
    self._enableOrDisableCalibrationButton()
```

When the **Calibrate** button is clicked, we parse the measurement from the text field, clear the text field, convert the measurement into `meters` if necessary, and store it. The button's callback is implemented as follows:

```python
def _calibrate(self, event):
    self._referencePixelDistBetweenLights = \
```

[186]

```
            self._pixelDistBetweenLights
    s = self._calibrationTextCtrl.GetValue()
    self._calibrationTextCtrl.SetValue('')
    self._referenceMetersToCamera = float(s)
    if self._convertMetersToFeet:
        self._referenceMetersToCamera *= 0.3048
```

As in Chapter 3, *Training a Smart Alarm to Recognize the Villain and His Cat*, the background thread runs a loop, which includes capturing an image, calling a helper method to process the image, and then handing the image to another thread for display. Optionally, the image may be mirrored (flipped horizontally) before being displayed. The loop's implementation is as follows:

```
def _runCaptureLoop(self):
    while self._running:
        success, self._image = self._capture.read(
                self._image)
        if self._image is not None:
            self._detectAndEstimateDistance()
            if (self.mirrored):
                self._image[:] = numpy.fliplr(self._image)

            # Perform a thread-safe swap of the front and
            # back image buffers.
            self._imageFrontBufferLock.acquire()
            self._imageFrontBuffer, self._image = \
                    self._image, self._imageFrontBuffer
            self._imageFrontBufferLock.release()

            # Send a refresh event to the video panel so
            # that it will draw the image from the front
            # buffer.
            self._videoPanel.Refresh()
```

The helper method for processing the image is quite long, so let's look at it in several chunks. First, we detect blobs in a gray version of the image and then initialize a dictionary to sort the blobs by color, as follows:

```
def _detectAndEstimateDistance(self):

    self._grayImage = cv2.cvtColor(
            self._image, cv2.COLOR_BGR2GRAY,
            self._grayImage)
    blobs = self._detector.detect(self._grayImage)
    blobsForColors = {}
```

For each blob, we crop out a square region that is likely to include a white circle of light, plus some more saturated pixels around the edge, as shown in the following code:

```
for blob in blobs:

    centerXAsInt, centerYAsInt = \
            (int(n) for n in blob.pt)
    radiusAsInt = int(blob.size)

    minX = max(0, centerXAsInt - radiusAsInt)
    maxX = min(self._imageWidth,
               centerXAsInt + radiusAsInt)
    minY = max(0, centerYAsInt - radiusAsInt)
    maxY = min(self._imageHeight,
               centerYAsInt + radiusAsInt)

    region = self._image[minY:maxY, minX:maxX]
```

Next, we find the average hue and saturation of the region and, using those values, we classify the blob as one of the colors we defined at the top of this module, as follows:

```
# Get the region's dimensions, which may
# differ from the blob's diameter if the blob
# extends past the edge of the image.
h, w = region.shape[:2]

meanColor = region.reshape(w * h, 3).mean(0)
meanHue = ColorUtils.hueFromBGR(meanColor)
meanSaturation = ColorUtils.saturationFromBGR(
        meanColor)

if meanHue < 22.5 or meanHue > 337.5:
    color = COLOR_Red
elif meanHue < 67.5:
    if meanSaturation < 25.0:
        color = COLOR_YellowWhite
    else:
        color = COLOR_AmberYellow
elif meanHue < 172.5:
    color = COLOR_Green
elif meanHue < 277.5:
    if meanSaturation < 25.0:
        color = COLOR_BlueWhite
    else:
        color = COLOR_BluePurple
else:
    color = COLOR_Pink
```

```
            if color in blobsForColors:
                blobsForColors[color] += [blob]
            else:
                blobsForColors[color] = [blob]
```

Depending on your camera's color rendition, you may need to tweak some of the hue and saturation thresholds.

Note that our color-matching logic is based on perceptual (subjective) similarity and not on the geometric distance in any color model, such as RGB, HSV, or HSL. Perceptually, a *green* light could be emerald green (geometrically close to cyan), neon green, or even spring green (geometrically close to yellow), but most people would never mistake a spring green light for an *amber* light, nor a yellowish-orange light for a *red* light. Within the reddish and yellowish ranges, most people perceive more abrupt distinctions between colors.

Finally, after classifying all blobs, we call a helper method that handles the classification results and a helper method that may enable or disable the **Calibrate** button, as follows:

```
        self._processBlobsForColors(blobsForColors)
        self._enableOrDisableCalibrationButton()
```

Based on the color classification results, we want to highlight the blobs in certain colors, draw lines that connect pairs of like-colored blobs (if any), and display a message about the estimated distance to the first such pair of blobs. We use the BGR color values and human-readable color names that we defined at the top of this module. The relevant code is as follows:

```
    def _processBlobsForColors(self, blobsForColors):

        self._pixelDistBetweenLights = None

        for color in blobsForColors:

            prevBlob = None

            for blob in blobsForColors[color]:

                colorBGR, colorName = color

                centerAsInts = \
                        tuple(int(n) for n in blob.pt)
                radiusAsInt = int(blob.size)
```

```
            # Fill the circle with the selected color.
            cv2.circle(self._image, centerAsInts,
                       radiusAsInt, colorBGR,
                       cv2.FILLED, cv2.LINE_AA)
            # Outline the circle in black.
            cv2.circle(self._image, centerAsInts,
                       radiusAsInt, (0, 0, 0), 1,
                       cv2.LINE_AA)

            if prevBlob is not None:

                if self._pixelDistBetweenLights is \
                        None:
                    self._pixelDistBetweenLights = \
                        GeomUtils.dist2D(blob.pt,
                                         prevBlob.pt)
                    wx.CallAfter(self._showDistance,
                                 colorName)

                prevCenterAsInts = \
                    tuple(int(n) for n in prevBlob.pt)

                # Connect the current and previous
                # circle with a black line.
                cv2.line(self._image, prevCenterAsInts,
                         centerAsInts, (0, 0, 0), 1,
                         cv2.LINE_AA)

            prevBlob = blob
```

Next, let's look at the helper method that enables or disables the **Calibrate** button. The button should be enabled only when a pixel distance between two lights is being measured and a number (the real distance between the lights and camera) is in the text field. The following code illustrates the tests for these conditions:

```
    def _enableOrDisableCalibrationButton(self):
        s = self._calibrationTextCtrl.GetValue()
        if len(s) < 1 or \
                self._pixelDistBetweenLights is None:
            self._calibrationButton.Disable()
        else:
            # Validate that the input is a number.
            try:
                float(s)
                self._calibrationButton.Enable()
            except:
                self._calibrationButton.Disable()
```

The helper method that shows the instructional message is as follows:

```
def _showInstructions(self):
    self._showMessage(
            'When a pair of lights is highlighted, '
            'enter the\ndistance and click '
            '"Calibrate".')
```

The helper method that shows the estimated distance in either `meters` or `feet` is as follows:

```
def _showDistance(self, colorName):
    if self._referenceMetersToCamera is None:
        return
    value = self._referenceMetersToCamera * \
            self._referencePixelDistBetweenLights / \
            self._pixelDistBetweenLights
    if self._convertMetersToFeet:
        value /= 0.3048
        unit = 'feet'
    else:
        unit = 'meters'
    self._showMessage(
            'A pair of %s lights was spotted\nat '
            '%.2f %s.' % \
            (colorName, value, unit))
```

Once the message is cleared, we need to leave an endline character so that the label still has the same height as when it is populated, as follows:

```
def _clearMessage(self):
    # Insert an endline for consistent spacing.
    self._showMessage('\n')
```

Showing a message simply entails changing the text of the `StaticText` object, as seen in the following helper method:

```
def _showMessage(self, message):
    self._distanceStaticText.SetLabel(message)
```

The class is complete. Now, we just need the following `main` function (similar to our `main` functions for previous wxPython apps) to specify a file path for serialization and deserialization and to launch the app, as shown in the following code:

```
def main():
    app = wx.App()
    configPath = PyInstallerUtils.resourcePath(
            'config.dat')
```

```
        livingHeadlights = LivingHeadlights(configPath)
        livingHeadlights.Show()
        app.MainLoop()

    if __name__ == '__main__':
        main()
```

There we have it! That's the whole implementation of `The Living Headlights` app! This project's code is short, but it does include some unusual requirements for setup and testing. Let's turn to these tasks now.

Testing The Living Headlights app at home

Do not run out onto the highway at night to point your laptop's webcam into the headlights! We can devise more convenient and safer ways to test `The Living Headlights`, even if you don't own a car or don't drive.

A pair of LED flashlights is a good proxy for a pair of headlights. A flashlight with many LEDs (for example, 19) is preferable because it creates a denser circle of light that is more likely to be detected as exactly one blob. To ensure that the distance between the two flashlights remains constant, we can attach them to a rigid object, such as a board, using brackets, clamps, or tape. My father Bob Howse is great at constructing such things. Take a look at my flashlight holder in the following image:

The following image shows a frontal view of the flashlight holder, including a decorative grill:

Set up the lights in front of the webcam (parallel to the webcam's lens), run the app, and make sure that the lights are being detected. Then, using a tape measure, find the distance between the webcam and the center point between the front of the lights, as seen in the following image:

Type the distance into the text field and click **Calibrate**. Then, move the lights either closer to or further away from the camera, ensuring they are parallel to the camera's lens. Check that the app is updating the distance estimate appropriately.

To simulate colored car lights, place a thick piece of colored glass in front of the flashlights, as close to the light source as possible. Stained glass (the kind used in church windows) works well, and you may find it in craft supply stores. Colored lens filters for photography or videography should also work. They are widely available, new or used, from camera stores. Colored acetate or other thin materials do not work as well, as the LED lights are very intense. The following image shows an existing light setup using an orange or amber-colored stained glass filter:

The following screenshot shows the app's analysis of the lighting setup:

Check that the app is reporting the appropriate color for the detected lights. Depending on your particular camera's color rendition, you may find that you'll need to adjust some of the hue and saturation thresholds in the `detectAndEstimateDistance` method. You might also want to experiment with adjusting the attributes of
the `SimpleBlobDetector_Params` object in the initializer to see their effects on the detection of lights and other blobs.

Once we are satisfied that the app is working well with our homemade apparatus, we can step up to a more realistic level of testing!

Testing The Living Headlights app in a car

When choosing the hardware for a car-based setup, it's important to consider the following questions:

- Can the car's outlets power the hardware?
- Can the hardware fit conveniently in the car?

A Raspberry Pi draws power from a 5V supply through its micro USB port. We can satisfy this power requirement by plugging a USB adapter into the car's cigarette lighter and then connecting it to the Pi through a USB to micro USB cable. Make sure that your adapter's voltage is exactly 5V and that its amperage is equal to or greater than the recommended amperage for your Pi model. For example, the official documentation at https://www.raspberrypi.org/documentation/faqs/ recommends a 5V, 2.5A power supply for Raspberry Pi 3 Model B. The following image shows a setup using a first-generation Raspberry Pi Model A:

Normally, the cigarette lighter is a 12V power source, so it can power a variety of devices through an adapter. You could even power a chain of devices, and the Pi need not be the first device in the chain. Later in this section, we will discuss the example of a Pi drawing power from a USB port on a SunFounder LCD display, which in turn draws power from a cigarette lighter receptacle through an adapter.

Standard USB peripherals, such as a webcam, mouse, and keyboard, can draw enough power from Pi's USB ports. Although the Pi only has two USB ports, we can use a USB splitter to power to a webcam, mouse, and keyboard simultaneously. Alternatively, some keyboards have a built-in touchpad that can be used as a mouse. Another option is to simply make do with only using two peripherals at a time and swapping one of them for the third peripheral as needed. In any case, once our app has been started and calibrated (and once we are driving!), we no longer need the keyboard or mouse input.

The webcam should sit against the inside of the car's rear window. The webcam's lens should be as close to the window as possible to reduce the visibility of grime, moisture, and reflections (for example, the reflection of the webcam's *on* light). If the Raspberry Pi lies just behind the car's front seats, the webcam cable should be able to reach the back window, while the power cable should still reach the USB adapter in the cigarette lighter receptacle. If not, use a longer USB to micro USB cable for the power and, if necessary, position the Pi farther back in the car. Alternatively, use a webcam with a longer cable. The following image shows the suggested positioning of the Pi:

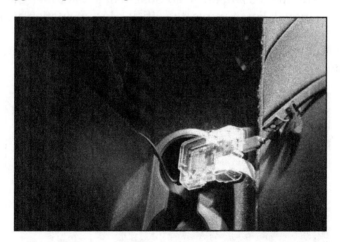

Similarly, the following image shows the suggested positioning of the camera:

Now, it's time for the hard part—the display. For video output, the Pi supports HDMI (as found in new TVs and many new monitors). Some older Pi models also support composite RCA (as found in old TVs). For other common connectors, we can use an adapter, such as HDMI to DVI or HDMI to VGA. The Pi also has limited support (through third-party kernel extensions) for video output through DSI or SPI (as found in cellphone displays and prototyping kits).

 Do not use a CRT television or monitor in a vehicle or in any environment where it is liable to be bumped. A CRT may implode if the glass is damaged. Instead, use an LCD television or monitor.

A small display is desirable because it can be more conveniently mounted on the dashboard and it consumes less power. For example, the SunFounder Raspberry Pi 10.1 HDMI IPS LCD Monitor requires a 12V, 1A power source. This display includes a USB port that can deliver 5V, 2A of power, which satisfies the recommended power specs for most Pi versions, including Raspberry Pi 2 Model B, but not quite Raspberry Pi 3 Model B. For more information, see the product's page on the SunFounder website, `https://www.sunfounder.com/10-1-inch-hdmi-lcd.html`.

Typically, though, a display needs a much higher voltage and wattage than the cigarette lighter can supply. Conveniently, some cars have an electrical outlet that resembles a wall socket, with the standard voltage for the type of socket but a lower maximum wattage. My car has a 110V, 150W, outlet for two-pronged North American plugs (NEMA 1-15P). As seen in the following image, I used an extension cord to convert the two-pronged connection into a three-pronged connection (NEMA 5-15P) that my monitor cables use:

I tried plugging in three different monitors (one at a time, of course), with the following results:

- **HP Pavilion 25xi (25"**, *1920 x 1080)*: Does not turn on. Presumably requires a higher wattage.
- **HP w2207 (22"**, *1680 x 1050,* **19.8 lbs)**: Does not turn on, but its weight and sturdy hinge make it useful as a flail to beat off hijackers—just in case the rocket launchers fail.
- **Xplio XP22WD (22"**, *1440 x 900)*: Turns on and works!

If you are unable to power a monitor from any of your car's outlets, an alternative is to use a battery block to power the monitor. Another alternative is to use a laptop or netbook as a substitute for the entire Pi-based system.

The XP22WD's ports are seen in the following image. To connect the Pi, I am using an HDMI to DVI cable because the monitor does not have an HDMI port:

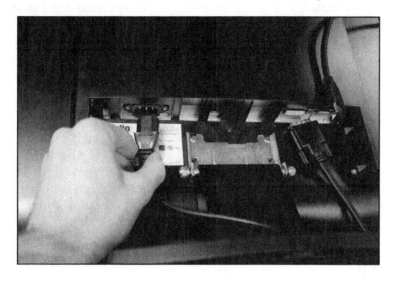

Unfortunately, my monitors are too big to mount on a dashboard! However, for the purpose of testing the system on my driveway, placing the monitor in the passenger seat is fine, as follows:

Voilà! We've proved that a car can power a Pi, peripherals, and a desktop monitor! As soon as the car is turned on, our system boots and runs in exactly the same way as a Linux desktop. We can now launch `The Living Headlights` app from the command line, or from an IDE such as Geany. Our app's behavior on Pi should be identical to its behavior on a conventional desktop system, except that on Pi, we will experience a lower frame rate (less *frequent* frame updates) and greater lag (less *timely* frame updates). Raspberry Pi has relatively limited processing power; therefore, it will need more time to process each frame, and a greater number of camera frames will be dropped while the software processes an old frame.

Once you get your app running in a car, remember to recalibrate it so that it estimates distances based on the size of real headlights and not the size of a flashlight rig! The most practical way to perform this recalibration would be with two parked cars. One parked car should have its headlights on, and it should be behind the car that contains the Pi. Measure the distance between the parked cars, and use this as the calibration value.

Summary

This chapter gave us the opportunity to scale down the complexity of our algorithms to support low-powered hardware. We also played with colorful lights, a homemade toy car, a puzzle of adapters, and a real car!

There is plenty of scope for extending the functionality of `The Living Headlights`. For example, we could take an average of multiple reference measurements or store different reference measurements for different colors of lights. We could analyze patterns of flashing, colored lights across multiple frames to judge whether the vehicle behind us is a police car or a road maintenance truck, or is even signaling to turn. We could try to detect the flash of rocket launchers, though testing might be problematic.

The next chapter's project is not something a driver should use, though! In the next chapter, we are going to take a pen-and-paper sketch in one hand and a smartphone in the other as we turn a geometric drawing into a physics simulation!

6
Creating a Physics Simulation Based on a Pen and Paper Sketch

"James Bond lives in a nightmarish world where laws are written at the point of a gun."
– Yuri Zhukov, Pravda, 30 September 1965

"Just a moment. Three measures of Gordon's, one of vodka, half a measure of Kina Lillet. Shake it very well until it's ice-cold, then add a large thin slice of lemon peel. Got it?"
– Casino Royale, Chapter 7, Rouge et Noir (1953)

James Bond is a precise man. Like a physicist, he seems to see order in a world where others see chaos. Another mission, another romance, another shaken drink, another crashing car or helicopter or skier, and another gunshot, do not change the way the world works—the way the Cold War works. He seems to take comfort in this consistency.

A psychologist might say that Bond is reenacting an unhappy childhood, which the novels reveal to us in brief glimpses. The boy lacked a permanent home. His father was an international arms dealer for the Vickers company, so the family moved often for work. When James was 11, his parents died in a mountain climbing accident, the first of many dramatic, untimely deaths in the Bond saga. An aunt in Kent took in the orphaned James, but the next year he was sent to boarding at Eton College. There, the lonesome boy became infatuated with a maid, got into trouble over it, and was expelled, the first of his many short-lived and fraught romances. Next, he was sent even further from family, to Fettes College in Scotland. The pattern of displacement and trouble was set. By 16, he was trying to live the life of a playboy in Paris. By 20, he was a dropout from the University of Geneva and he was off to join the Royal Navy at the height of the Second World War.

Amid all that upheaval, Bond did manage to learn a thing or two. He is clever—not just with his eyebrow-raising witty remarks, but also with his fast solutions to puzzles that involve mechanics, kinematics, or physics. He is never caught flat-footed (although he is sometimes caught in other ways).

The moral of the story is that a secret agent must practice his physics, even under the most trying of circumstances. An app can help with that.

When I think about problems of geometry or physics, I like to draw them with a pen and paper. However, I also like to see animations. Our app, `Rollingball`, will allow us to combine these two media. It will use computer vision to detect simple geometric shapes that the user can draw on paper. Then, based on the detected shapes, the app will create a physics simulation that the user can watch. The user can also influence the simulation by tilting the device to alter the simulated direction of gravity. The experience is like designing and playing with one's own version of a ball-in-a-maze puzzle, a fine toy for aspiring secret agents.

Building games is fun, but it is not all fun and games! We have a new list of skills to master in this chapter:

- Detecting linear and circular edges with the Hough transform
- Using OpenCV in the Unity game engine
- Building a Unity game for Android
- Converting coordinates from OpenCV's space to Unity's space and creating three-dimensional objects in Unity based on our detection results in OpenCV
- Customizing the appearance and physics behavior of three-dimensional objects in Unity, using shaders, materials, and physics materials
- Drawing lines and rectangles using OpenGL calls from Unity

With these goals in mind, let's get ready to play ball!

Technical requirements

This chapter's project has the following software dependencies:

- Unity—a cross-platform game engine that supports Windows and Mac as development platforms. Development on Linux is not supported in this chapter.
- OpenCV for Unity.
- Android SDK, which comes with Android Studio.

Where not otherwise noted, setup instructions are covered in Chapter 1, *Preparing for the Mission*. You might want to build and run the project in Chapter 4, *Controlling a Phone App with Your Suave Gestures*, to ensure that Android SDK is properly set up as part of Android Studio. Setup instructions for OpenCV for Unity are covered in the current chapter, in the section *Setting up OpenCV for Unity*. Always refer to the setup instructions for any version requirements. Instructions for building and running Unity projects are covered in the current chapter.

The completed project from this chapter can be found in this book's GitHub repository, at https://github.com/PacktPublishing/OpenCV-4-for-Secret-Agents-Second-Edition, in the Chapter006 folder. The repository doesn't contain the OpenCV for Unity plugin, which must be licensed and added to the project, as described in the *Setting up OpenCV for Unity* section in this chapter.

Planning the Rollingball app

Rollingball will be a mobile app. We will develop it in the Unity game engine by using a third-party plugin called **OpenCV for Unity**. The app will be compatible with both Android and iOS. Our build instructions will focus on Android, but we will also provide a few notes for readers who are experienced with the iOS build process (on Mac).

 For instructions on setting up Unity and finding relevant documentation and tutorials, please refer back to the *Setting up Unity and OpenCV* section in Chapter 1, *Preparing for the Mission*. At the time of writing this book, Unity's officially supported development environments are Windows and Mac, although there is ongoing beta development toward Linux support.

Using the mobile device's camera, Rollingball will scan two types of primitive shapes—circles and lines. The user will start by drawing any combination of these primitive shapes, or by setting up linear or circular objects on a plain background. For example, refer to the following image:

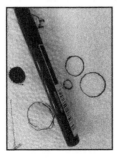

Here, we have several circles drawn on a paper napkin. Our detector will work best with outlines, rather than solid circles, and particularly with smoothly drawn outlines, rather than lumpy or broken outlines. For this image, our detector will work best on the two rightmost circles. We also have a pen with edges that look like straight lines against the background of the paper. Our detector will work well with these linear edges.

`Rollingball` is a simple app in which the user primarily interacts with one Android activity or one iOS view controller. A live video feed fills most of the background. When circles or lines are detected, they are highlighted in red, as shown in the following screenshot:

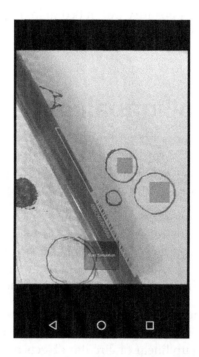

Note that some linear edges are detected multiple times. Lighting effects and discontinuities in the pen's color create ambiguities about where its edges are located.

Chapter 6

The user can press a button to start the physics simulation. During the simulation, the video pauses, the detector stops running, and the red-highlighted areas are replaced with cyan balls and lines. The lines are stationary, but the balls fall freely and may bounce off each other and off the lines. Real-world gravity, as measured by the mobile device's gravity sensor, is used to control the simulated direction of gravity. However, the simulation is two-dimensional, and gravity is flattened so that it points toward an edge of the screen. The following screenshot shows the simulated balls after they have fallen partway down the page, bounced apart, and rolled along the lines:

The user can press the button again to clear all the simulated objects and resume the live video and detection. The cycle can continue indefinitely, with the user choosing to simulate different drawings or different views of the same drawing.

Now, let's consider the techniques for detecting circles and lines.

Detecting circles and lines

From `The Living Headlights` (our project in `Chapter 5`, *Equipping Your Car with a Rearview Camera and Hazard Detection*), we are already familiar with one technique for detecting circles. We treated the problem as a special case of blob detection, and we used an OpenCV class, `SimpleBlobDetector`, which allows us to specify many detection criteria, such as a blob's size, color, and circularity (or non-circularity, that is, linearity).

A **blob** is a shape filled with a solid (or nearly solid) color. This definition implies that many circular or linear objects are not detectable as blobs. In the following screenshot, we can see a sunlit desk with a china teapot, china bowl, and pewter bowl:

The bowls and the lid of the teapot have approximately circular outlines in this top-down view. However, they are unlikely to pass detection as blobs, because the interior of each shape is multicolored, especially in uneven light.

Blob detection starts with a simple threshold filter (marking bright regions as white and dark regions as black); a more general approach to shape detection should start with an edge-finding filter (marking edge regions as white and interior regions as black) and then a thresholding process. We define an edge as the discontinuity between neighboring regions of different brightness. Thus, an edge pixel has darker neighbors on one side and brighter neighbors on the opposite side. An edge-finding filter subtracts neighbor values from one side and adds them from the opposite side, in order to measure how strongly a pixel exhibits this edge-like contrast in a given direction. To achieve a measurement that is independent of edges' directions, we can apply multiple filters (each oriented for edges of a different direction) and treat each filter's output as a dimension of a vector whose magnitude represents the overall **edginess** of the pixel. A set of such measurements for all pixels is sometimes called the **derivative** of the image. Having computed the image's derivative, we select a threshold value based on the minimum contrast that we require in an edge. A high threshold accepts only high-contrast edges, while a lower threshold also accepts lower-contrast edges.

A popular edge-finding technique is the **Canny algorithm**. OpenCV's implementation, the `Imgproc.Canny` function, performs both filtering and thresholding. As arguments, it takes a grayscale image, an output image, a low threshold value, and a high threshold value. The low threshold should accept all pixels that might be part of a good edge. The high threshold should only accept pixels that are definitely part of a good edge. From the set whose members might be edge pixels, the Canny algorithm only accepts the members that connect to definite edge pixels. The double criteria help to ensure that we can accept thin extremities of a major edge, while rejecting edges that are altogether faint. For example, a pen stroke or the curb of a road extending into the distance may be a major edge with thin extremities.

Having identified edge pixels, we can count how many of them are intersected by a given primitive shape. The greater the number of intersections, the more confident we can be that the given primitive shape correctly represents an edge in the image. Each intersection is called a **vote**, and a shape needs a specified number of votes to be accepted as a real edge's shape. Out of all possible primitive shapes (of a given kind) in the image, we consider an evenly spaced, representative sample. We do so by specifying a step size for the shapes' geometric parameters. (For example, a line's parameters are a point and angle, while a circle's parameters are a center point and radius.) This sample of possible shapes is called a **grid**, the individual shapes in it are called **cells**, and votes are said to be cast in cells. This process (tallying the matches between actual edge pixels and a sample of possible shapes) is the core of a technique called the **Hough transform**, which has various specializations, such as **Hough line detection** and **Hough circle detection**.

Hough line detection has two implementations in OpenCV—`Imgproc.HoughLines`, which is based on the original Hough transform, and `Imgproc.HoughLinesP`, which is based on a probabilistic variant of the Hough transform. `Imgproc.HoughLines` does an exhaustive count of intersections for all possible lines for a given pair of step sizes, in pixels and in radians. `Imgproc.HoughLinesP` is usually faster (particularly in images with a few long line segments), as it takes possible lines in a random order and discards some of the possible lines after finding a good line in a region. `Imgproc.HoughLines` expresses each line as a distance from the origin and an angle, whereas `Imgproc.HoughLinesP` expresses each line as two points, the endpoints of a detected segment of the line, which is a more useful representation, since it gives us the option to treat the detection results as line segments, rather than indefinitely long lines. For both functions, the arguments include the image (which should be preprocessed with Canny, or a similar algorithm), the step sizes in pixels and radians, and the minimum number of intersections required to accept a line. The arguments to `Imgproc.HoughLinesP` also include a minimum length between endpoints and a maximum gap, where a gap consists of non-edge pixels between edge pixels that intersect the line.

Hough circle detection has one implementation in OpenCV, `Imgproc.HoughCircles`, which is based on a variant of the Hough transform that makes use of gradient information at edges. This function's arguments include the image (not preprocessed with Canny or a similar algorithm, as `Imgproc.HoughCircles` applies the Canny algorithm internally), a downsampling factor (which acts somewhat like a blur factor to smooth the edges of potential circles), a minimum distance between detected circles' centers, a Canny edge detection threshold, a minimum number of intersections required to accept a circle, and minimum and maximum radii. The specified Canny threshold is the upper threshold; internally, the lower threshold is hardcoded as half of the upper threshold.

For more details on the Canny algorithm, the Hough transform, and OpenCV's implementations of them, refer to *Chapter 7, Extracting Lines, Contours, and Components,* in Robert Laganière's book, *OpenCV 3 Computer Vision Application Programming Cookbook* (*Packt Publishing, 2017*).

Despite using a more efficient algorithm than the original Hough transform, `Imgproc.HoughCircles` is a computationally expensive function. Nonetheless, we use it in `Rollingball`, since many of today's mobile devices can handle the cost. For low-powered devices, such as Raspberry Pi, we would consider blob detection as a cheaper alternative. `Imgproc.HoughCircles` tends to work best with outlines of circles, whereas blob detection only works on solid circles. For line detection, we use the `Imgproc.HoughLinesP` function, which is not as expensive as OpenCV's other Hough detectors.

Having chosen the algorithms and their OpenCV implementations, let's set up the plugin that will let us easily access this functionality in Unity.

Setting up OpenCV for Unity

Unity provides a cross-platform framework for scripting games in C#. However, it also supports platform-specific plugins in languages such as C, C++, Objective-C (for Mac and iOS), and Java (for Android). Developers may publish these plugins (and other assets) on the Unity Asset Store. Many published plugins represent a large amount of high-quality work, and buying one may be more economical than writing your own.

OpenCV for Unity, by ENOX SOFTWARE (https://enoxsoftware.com), is a $95 plugin (at the time of writing this book). It offers a C# API that is closely based on OpenCV's official Java (Android) bindings. However, the plugin wraps OpenCV's C++ libraries and is compatible with Android, iOS, Windows Phone, Windows, Mac, Linux, and WebGL. It is reliable in my experience, and it saves us a lot of work that we would otherwise put into custom C++ code and C# wrappers. Moreover, it comes with several valuable samples.

> OpenCV for Unity is not the only set of third-party C# bindings for OpenCV. Alternatives include OpenCvSharp (https://github.com/shimat/opencvsharp) and Emgu CV (http://www.emgu.com). However, in this book, we use OpenCV for Unity because it offers easy integration with Unity and it tends to be updated quickly when new OpenCV versions are released.

Creating a Physics Simulation Based on a Pen and Paper Sketch

Let's go shopping. Open Unity and create a new project. From the menu bar, select **Window | Asset Store**. If you haven't already created a Unity account, follow the prompts to create one. Once you have logged into the store, you should see the **Asset Store** window. Enter `OpenCV for Unity` in the search bar in the upper-right corner. Click on the **OpenCV for Unity** link among the search results. You should see something similar to the following screenshot:

Click on the **Add to Cart** button and complete the transaction, as directed. Click on the **Download** button and wait for the download to complete. Click on the **Import** button. You should now see the **Import Unity Package** window, as shown in the following screenshot:

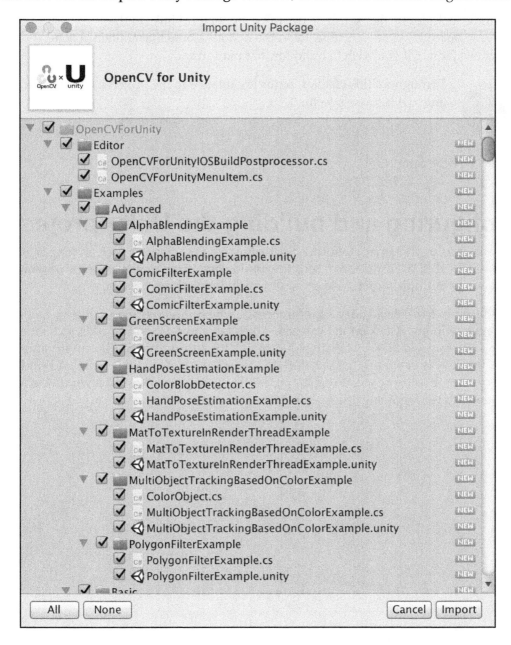

This is a list of all of the files in the bundle that we just purchased. Ensure that all of their checkboxes are checked, and then click on the **Import** button. Soon, you should see all of the files in the **Project** pane of the Unity editor.

The bundle includes further setup instructions and helpful links in the `OpenCVForUnity/ReadMe.pdf` file. Read the `ReadMe!` note that contains useful instructions for iOS if you wish to build for that platform.

> Throughout this chapter, paths are relative to the project's `Assets` folder, unless otherwise specified.

Next, let's try the samples.

Configuring and building the Unity project

Unity supports many target platforms. Switching to a new target is easy, as long as our plugins support it. We just need to set a few build configuration values, some of which are shared across multiple targets, and some of which are platform-specific.

From the menu bar, select **Unity | Preferences...**, which should bring up the **Preferences** window. Click on the **External Tools** tab and set **Android SDK** to be the base path to your Android SDK installation. Normally, for an Android Studio environment, the path to the SDK is `C:\Users\username\AppData\Local\Android\sdk\` on Windows or `Users/<your_username>/Library/Android/sdk/` on Mac. Now, the window should look similar to the following screenshot:

Chapter 6

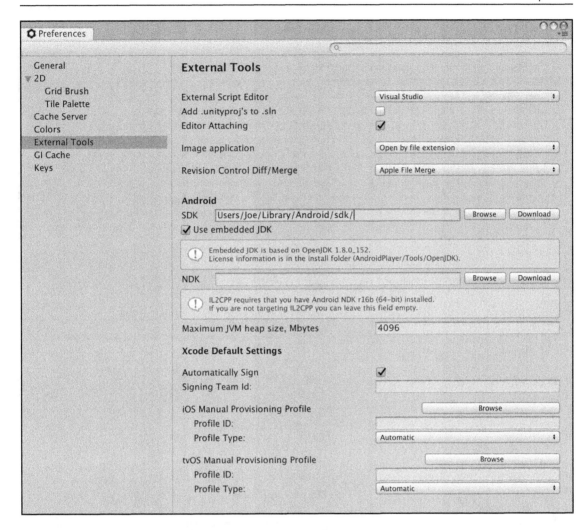

Now, from the menu bar, select **File** | **Build Settings**. The **Build Settings** window should appear. Drag all of the sample scene files, such as `OpenCVForUnity/Examples/OpenCVForUnityExample.unity` and `OpenCVForUnity/Examples/Advanced/ComicFilterExample/ComicFilterExample.unity`, from the **Project** pane to the **Scenes In Build** list in the **Build Settings** window. The first scene in the list is the start-up scene. Ensure that `OpenCVForUnityExample` is the first in the list. (Drag and drop the list items to reorder them.) Also, ensure that all of the scenes' checkboxes are checked. Click on the **Android** platform, and then the **Switch Platform** button. The window should now look like the following screenshot:

Creating a Physics Simulation Based on a Pen and Paper Sketch

Click on the **Player Settings...** button. A list of settings should appear in the **Inspector** pane of the Unity editor. Fill in a **Company Name**, such as `Nummist Media Corporation Limited`, and a **Product Name**, such as `Rollingball`. Optionally, select a **Default Icon** (which must be an image file that you have added somewhere in the **Project** pane). Click on **Resolution and Presentation** to expand it, and then, for **Default Orientation**, select **Portrait**. So far, the **PlayerSettings** options should look similar to the following screenshot:

Chapter 6

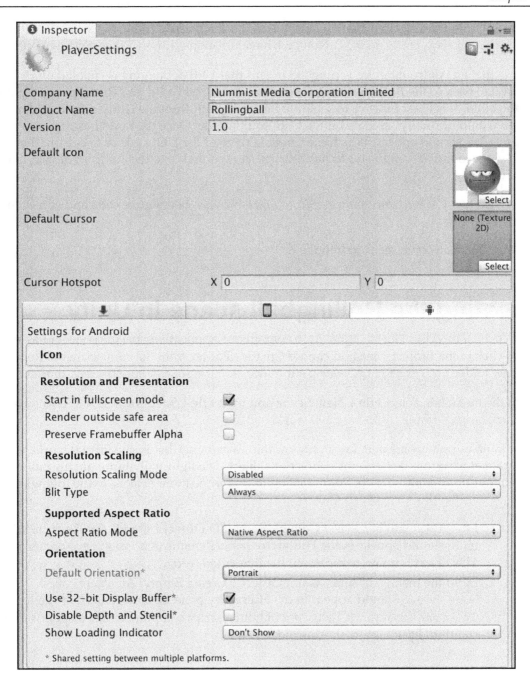

Click on **Other Settings** to expand it, and then fill out a **Bundle Identifier** with something like com.nummist.rollingball. Now, we have finished with the **PlayerSettings** options.

Ensure that an Android device is plugged in and that USB debugging is enabled on the device. Go back to the **Build Settings** window and click on **Build and Run**. Specify a path for the build. It is good practice to separate the build path from the Unity project folder, just as you would normally separate builds from source code. Once the build has begun, a progress bar should appear. Watch the **Console** pane of the Unity editor to be sure that no build errors occur. When the build has finished, it is copied onto the Android device, and then it runs.

Enjoy the OpenCV for Unity samples! If you like, browse their source code and scenes in the Unity editor.

Next, we have our own scene to build!

Creating the Rollingball scene in Unity

Let's create a directory, Rollingball, to contain our application-specific code and assets. Right-click in the **Project** pane and choose **Create | Folder** from the context menu. Rename the new folder Rollingball. Create a subfolder, Rollingball/Scenes, in a similar way.

From the menu bar, select **File | New Scene** and then **File | Save As...**. Save the scene as Rollingball/Scenes/Rollingball.unity.

By default, our newly created scene only contains a camera (that is, the virtual world's camera, not a capture device) and a directional light. The light will illuminate the balls and lines in our physics simulation. We are going to add three more objects, in the following way:

1. From the menu bar, select **GameObject | 3D Object | Quad**. An object called Quad should appear in the **Hierarchy** pane. Rename Quad to VideoRenderer. This object is going to represent the live video feed.
2. From the menu bar, select **GameObject | Create Empty**. An object called GameObject should appear in the **Hierarchy** pane. Rename GameObject to QuitOnAndroidBack. Later, it will hold a script component that responds to the standard back button on Android.

Objects in the **Hierarchy** are called **game objects**, and the sections that are visible in their **Inspector** panes are called **components**.

Drag the **Main Camera** onto the **VideoRenderer** to make the former a child of the latter. A child moves, rotates, and scales up or down when its parent does. The relevance is that we want our camera to maintain a predictable relationship with the live video background.

Parent-child relationships in the **Hierarchy** do not represent object-oriented inheritance; in other words, a child does not have an **is a** relationship with its parent. Rather, a parent who has a one-to-many **has a** relationship with its children.

With the new objects created and the **Main Camera** reparented, the **Hierarchy** should look like the following screenshot:

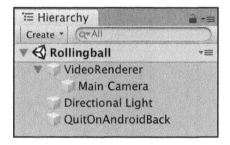

The **VideoRenderer** and **Main Camera** will be configured in code, based on the properties of the mobile device's video camera. However, let's set some reasonable defaults. Select the **VideoRenderer** in the **Hierarchy**, and then, in the **Inspector** pane, edit its **Transform** properties to match the following screenshot:

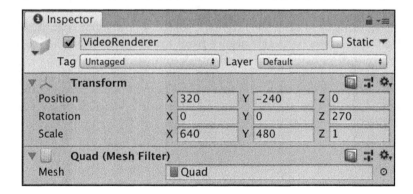

Creating a Physics Simulation Based on a Pen and Paper Sketch

Similarly, select **Main Camera** and edit its **Transform** and **Camera** properties to match the following screenshot:

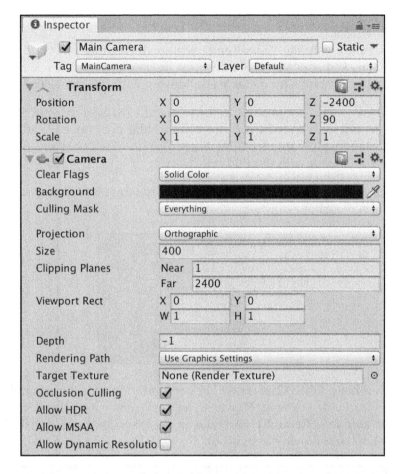

Note that we have configured an orthographic projection, meaning that the objects' pixel sizes are constant, regardless of their distance from the camera. This configuration is appropriate for a two-dimensional game or simulation, such as Rollingball.

These four objects are the foundation of our scene. The rest of the project involves attaching custom properties to these objects and using C# scripts to control them and create new objects around them.

Creating Unity assets and adding them to the scene

The custom properties and behaviors in a Unity project are defined through various types of files that are generically called **assets**. Our project has four remaining questions and requirements that we must address by creating and configuring assets:

- What is the appearance of the surfaces in the scene—namely, the video feed, the detected circles and lines, and the simulated balls and lines? We need to write *shader* code and create *Material* configurations to define the appearance of these surfaces.
- How bouncy are the balls? We need to create a *Physics Material* configuration to answer this all-important question.
- What objects represent a simulated ball and a simulated line? We need to create and configure *Prefab* objects that the simulation can instantiate.
- How does it all behave? We need to write Unity *scripts*—specifically, code that subclasses a Unity class called `MonoBehaviour`—in order to control objects in the scene at various stages in their life cycles.

The following subsections will tackle these requirements one by one.

Writing shaders and creating materials

A **shader** is a set of functions that run on the GPU. Although such functions can be applied to general-purpose computing, typically, they are used for graphics rendering—that is, to define the color of output pixels on the screen based on input that describes the lighting, geometry, surface texture, and perhaps other variables, such as time. Unity comes with many shaders for common styles of three-dimensional and two-dimensional rendering. We can also write our own shaders.

 For in-depth tutorials on shader scripting in Unity, see the *Unity 2018 Shaders and Effects Cookbook*, by John P. Doran and Alan Zucconi (*Packt Publishing, 2018*).

Let's create a folder, `Rollingball/Shaders`, and then create a shader in it (by clicking on **Create** | **Shader** | **Standard Surface Shader** in the **Project** pane's context menu). Rename the shader `DrawSolidColor`. Double-click on it to edit it, and replace the contents with the following code:

```
Shader "Draw/Solid Color" {
  Properties {
    _Color ("Main Color", Color) = (1.0, 1.0, 1.0, 1.0)
  }
  SubShader {
    Pass { Color [_Color] }
  }
}
```

This humble shader has one parameter—a color. The shader renders pixels in this color regardless of conditions, such as lighting. For the purposes of the **Inspector** GUI, the shader's name is **Draw** | **Solid Color**, and its parameter's name is **Main Color**.

A material has a shader and a set of parameter values for the shader. The same shader may be used by multiple materials, which may use different parameter values. Let's create a material that draws solid red. We will use this material to highlight detected circles and lines.

Create a new folder, `Rollingball/Materials`, and then create a material in it (by clicking on **Create** | **Material** in the context menu). Rename the material `DrawSolidRed`. Select it, and in the **Inspector**, set its shader to **Draw** | **Solid Color** and its **Main Color** to the RGBA value for red (255, 0, 0, 255). The **Inspector** should now look as follows:

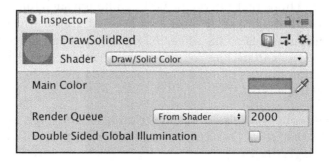

We are going to create two more materials using shaders that come with Unity. First, create a material, name it `Cyan`, and configure it so that its shader is **Legacy Shaders** | **Diffuse** and its **Main Color** is cyan (0, 255, 255, 255). Leave the **Base (RBG)** texture as **None**. We will apply this material to the simulated balls and lines. Its **Inspector** should look as follows:

Chapter 6

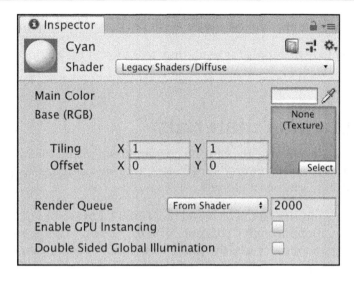

Now, create a material named **Video** and configure it so that its shader is **Unlit | Texture**. Leave the **Base (RBG)** texture as **None**. Later, through code, we will assign the video texture to this material. Drag the **Video** material (from the **Project** pane) to **VideoRenderer** (in the **Hierarchy** pane) in order to assign the material to the quad. Select **VideoRenderer** and confirm that its **Inspector** includes the following items:

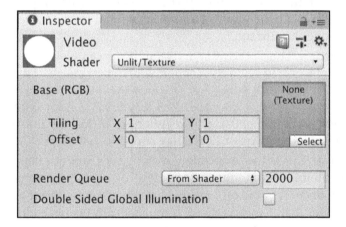

[221]

We will assign the remaining materials once we have created prefabs and scripts.

Now that we have made materials for rendering, let's look at the analogous concept of physics materials.

Creating physics materials

Although Unity's rendering pipeline can run custom functions that we write in shaders, its physics pipeline runs fixed functions. Nonetheless, we can configure the parameters of those functions through physics materials.

 Unity's physics engine is based on NVIDIA PhysX. PhysX supports acceleration through CUDA on NVIDIA GeForce GPUs. However, on typical mobile devices, the physics calculations will run on the CPU.

Let's create a folder, `Rollingball/Physics Materials`, and in it, create a physics material (by clicking on **Create** | **Physics Material** in the context menu). Rename the physics material `Bouncy`. Select it, and note that it has the following properties in the **Inspector**:

- **Dynamic Friction**: This is the ratio between the force that presses two objects together (for example, gravity) and the frictional force that resists continued motion along the surface.
- **Static Friction**: This is the ratio between the force pressing two objects together (for example, gravity) and the frictional force that resists initial motion along the surface. Refer to Wikipedia (`https://en.wikipedia.org/wiki/Friction#Approximate_coefficients_of_friction`) for sample values. For static friction, a value of 0.04 is like Teflon on Teflon, a value of 1.0 is like rubber on concrete, and a value of 1.05 is like copper on cast iron.
- **Bounciness**: This is the proportion of an object's kinetic energy that it retains when it bounces off another surface. Here, a value of `0` means that the object doesn't bounce. A value of `1` means that it bounces without a loss of energy. A value greater than 1 means that it (unrealistically) gains energy when it bounces.
- **Friction Combine**: When objects collide, which object's friction value affects this object? The options are **Average**, **Minimum**, **Multiply**, and **Maximum**.
- **Bounce Combine**: When objects collide, which object's bounciness value affects this object? The options are **Average**, **Minimum**, **Multiply**, and **Maximum**.

Careful! Are those physics materials explosive?
A physics simulation is said to explode when the values grow continually and overflow the system's floating-point numeric limits. For example, if a collision's combined bounciness is greater than 1 and the collision occurs repeatedly, then over time, the forces tend toward infinity. Kaboom! We broke the physics engine.

Even without weird physics materials, numeric problems arise in scenes of an extremely large or small scale. For example, consider a multiplayer game that uses input from the **Global Positioning System** (**GPS**) so that objects in a Unity scene are positioned according to the players' real-world longitude and latitude. The physics simulation cannot handle a human-sized object in this scene, because the object and the forces acting on it are so small that they vanish inside the margin of floating-point error! This is a case where the simulation implodes (rather than explodes).

Let's set the **Bounciness** to 1 (very bouncy!) and leave the other values at their defaults. Later, you can adjust everything to your tastes, if you wish. The **Inspector** should look as follows:

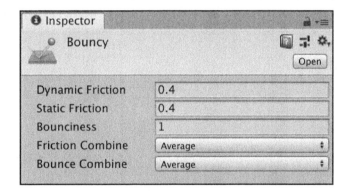

Our simulated lines will use default physics parameters, so they don't need a physics material.

Now that we have our rendering materials and physics materials, let's create prefabs for an entire simulated ball and an entire simulated line.

Creating prefabs

A **prefab** is an object that isn't a part of a scene itself, but is designed to be copied into scenes during editing or at runtime. It can be copied many times to make many objects in the scene. At runtime, the copies have no special connection to the prefab or each other, and all copies can behave independently. Although the role of a prefab is sometimes likened to the role of a class, a prefab is not a type.

Even though prefabs are not part of a scene, they are created and typically edited through a scene. Let's create a sphere in the scene by selecting **GameObject | 3D Object | Sphere** from the menu bar. An object named **Sphere** should appear in the **Hierarchy**. Rename it `SimulatedCircle`. Drag each of the following assets from the **Project** pane onto `SimulatedCircle` in the **Hierarchy**:

- **Cyan** (in `Rollingball/Materials`)
- **Bouncy** (in `Rollingball/PhysicsMaterials`)

Now, select **SimulatedCircle**. In the **Inspector**, click on **Add Component** and select **Physics | Rigidbody**. A **Rigidbody** section should appear in the **Inspector**. In this section, expand the **Constraints** field and check **Freeze Position | Z**. The effect of this change is to constrain the sphere's motion to two dimensions. Confirm that the **Inspector** looks like this:

Chapter 6

Create a folder, Rollingball/Prefabs, and drag SimulatedCircle from the **Hierarchy** into the folder in the **Project** pane. A prefab, also named SimulatedCircle, should appear in the folder. Meanwhile, the name of the SimulatedCircle object in the **Hierarchy** should turn blue to indicate that the object has a prefab connection. Changes to the object in the scene may be applied back to the prefab by clicking on the **Apply** button in the scene object's **Inspector**. Conversely, changes to the prefab (at edit time, not at runtime) are automatically applied to instances in scenes, except for properties in which an instance has unapplied changes.

Now, let's follow similar steps to create a prefab of a simulated line. Create a cube in the scene by selecting **GameObject | 3D Object | Cube** from the menu bar. An object named **Cube** should appear in the **Hierarchy**. Rename it SimulatedLine. Drag **Cyan** from the **Project** pane onto **SimulatedLine** in the **Hierarchy**. Select **SimulatedLine**, add a **Rigidbody** component, and, in the **Rigidbody** section of its **Inspector**, check **Is Kinematic**, which means that the object is not moved by the physics simulation (even though it is a part of the simulation for the purpose of other objects colliding with it). Recall that we want the lines to be stationary. They are just obstacles for the falling balls. The **Inspector** should now look like this:

Chapter 6

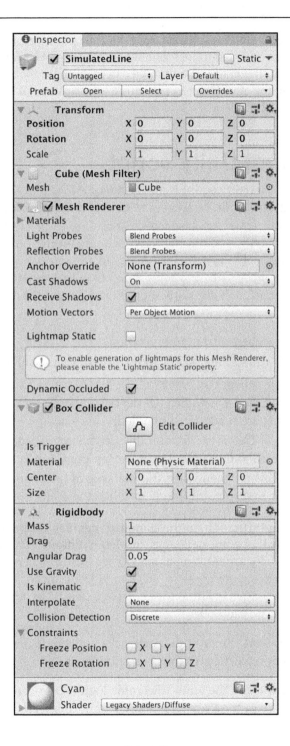

[227]

Let's clean up our scene by deleting the instances of the prefabs from the **Hierarchy** so that we don't have any circles or lines in the scene when it opens. (However, we want to keep the prefabs themselves in the **Project** so that we can instantiate them later through our scripts.) Now, let's turn our attention to the writing of scripts, which, among other things, are able to copy prefabs at runtime.

Writing our first Unity script

As we mentioned earlier, a Unity script is a subclass of MonoBehaviour. A MonoBehaviour object can obtain references to objects in the **Hierarchy** and components that we attach to these objects in the **Inspector**. A MonoBehaviour object also has its own **Inspector**, where we can assign additional references, including references to **Project** assets, such as prefabs. At runtime, Unity sends messages to all MonoBehaviour objects when certain events occur. A subclass of MonoBehaviour may implement callbacks for any of these messages. MonoBehaviour supports more than 60 standard message callbacks. Here are some examples:

- Awake: This is called during initialization.
- Start: This is called after Awake, but before the first call to Update.
- Update: This is called every frame.
- OnGUI: This is called when the GUI overlay is ready for rendering instructions and GUI events are ready to be handled.
- OnPostRender: This is called after the scene is rendered. This is an appropriate callback in which to implement post-processing effects.
- OnDestroy: This is called when this instance of the script is about to be destroyed. For example, this happens when the scene is about to end.

For more information on the standard message callbacks and the arguments that some callbacks' implementations may optionally take, see the official documentation at http://docs.unity3d.com/ScriptReference/MonoBehaviour.html. Also, note that we can send custom messages to all MonoBehaviour objects by using the SendMessage method.

Implementations of these and Unity's other callbacks may be private, protected, or public. Unity calls them regardless of the protection level.

To summarize, then, scripts are the glue—the game logic—connecting runtime events to various objects that we see in the **Project**, **Hierarchy**, and **Inspector**.

Let's create a folder, `Rollingball/Scripts`, and in that, create a script (by clicking on **Create** | **C# Script** in the context menu). Rename the script `QuitOnAndroidBack` and double-click on it to edit it. Replace its contents with the following code:

```
using UnityEngine;

namespace com.nummist.rollingball {

    public sealed class QuitOnAndroidBack : MonoBehaviour {

        void Start() {
            // Show the standard Android navigation bar.
            Screen.fullScreen = false;
        }

        void Update() {
            if (Input.GetKeyUp(KeyCode.Escape)) {
                Application.Quit();
            }
        }
    }
}
```

We are using a namespace, `com.nummist.rollingball`, to keep our code organized and to avoid potential conflicts between our type names and type names in other parties' code. Namespaces in C# are like packages in Java. Our class is called `QuitOnAndroidBack`. It extends Unity's `MonoBehaviour` class. We use the `sealed` modifier (similar to Java's `final` modifier) to indicate that we don't intend to create subclasses of `QuitOnAndroidBack`.

> Note that `MonoBehaviour` uses the UK English spelling of behavior.

Thanks to Unity's callback system, the script's `Start` method is called after the object is initialized—in this case, at the start of the scene. Our `Start` method ensures that the standard Android navigation bar is visible. After `Start`, the script's `Update` method gets called every frame. It checks whether the user has pressed a key (or button) that is mapped to the `Escape` keycode. On Android, the standard back button is mapped to `Escape`. When the key (or button) is pressed, the application quits.

Save the script and drag it from the **Project** pane to the `QuitOnAndroidBack` object in the **Hierarchy**. Click on the `QuitOnAndroidBack` object and confirm that its **Inspector** looks like the following screenshot:

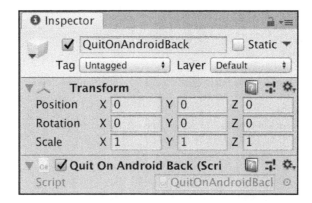

That was an easy script, right? The next one is a bit trickier, but more fun, because it handles everything except quitting.

Writing the main Rollingball script

Let's create a folder, `Rollingball/Scripts`, and in it, create a script (by clicking on **Create** | **C# Script** in the context menu). Rename the script `DetectAndSimulate` and double-click on it to edit it. Delete its default contents and begin the code with the following `import` statements:

```
using UnityEngine;
using System.Collections;
using System.Collections.Generic;
using System.IO;

using OpenCVForUnity.CoreModule;
using OpenCVForUnity.ImgprocModule;
using OpenCVForUnity.UnityUtils;
```

Next, let's declare our namespace and class with the following code:

```
namespace com.nummist.rollingball {

    [RequireComponent (typeof(Camera))]
    public sealed class DetectAndSimulate : MonoBehaviour {
```

Note that the class has an attribute, `[RequireComponent (typeof(Camera))]`, which means that the script can only be attached to a game object that has a camera (not a video camera, but rather, a game-world camera representing the player's virtual eye in the scene). We specify this requirement because we are going to highlight the detected shapes through an implementation of the standard `OnPostRender` callback, and this callback only gets called for scripts attached to a game object with a camera.

`DetectAndSimulate` needs to store representations of circles and lines in both two-dimensional screen space and three-dimensional world space. Coordinates in screen space (that is, on the user's screen) are measured in pixels, with the screen's top-left pixel pixel being the origin. Coordinates in world space (that is, in the game scene where we recently positioned `VideoRenderer` and `Main Camera`) are measured in arbitrary units with an arbitrary origin. The representations of circles and lines don't need to be visible to any other class in our application, so it is appropriate to define their types as private inner structs. Our `Circle` type stores two-dimensional coordinates representing the circle's center in screen space, a float representing its radius in screen space, and three-dimensional coordinates representing the circle's center in world space. A constructor accepts all of these values as arguments. Here is the `Circle` implementation:

```
struct Circle {

    public Vector2 screenPosition;
    public float screenDiameter;
    public Vector3 worldPosition;

    public Circle(Vector2 screenPosition,
                  float screenDiameter,
                  Vector3 worldPosition) {
        this.screenPosition = screenPosition;
        this.screenDiameter = screenDiameter;
        this.worldPosition = worldPosition;
    }
}
```

We define another inner struct, `Line`, to store two sets of two-dimensional coordinates representing endpoints in screen space and two sets of three-dimensional coordinates representing the same endpoints in world space. A constructor accepts all of these values as arguments. Here is the implementation of `Line`:

```
struct Line {
    public Vector2 screenPoint0;
    public Vector2 screenPoint1;
    public Vector3 worldPoint0;
    public Vector3 worldPoint1;
    public Line(Vector2 screenPoint0,
```

```
                    Vector2 screenPoint1,
                    Vector3 worldPoint0,
                    Vector3 worldPoint1) {
    this.screenPoint0 = screenPoint0;
    this.screenPoint1 = screenPoint1;
    this.worldPoint0 = worldPoint0;
    this.worldPoint1 = worldPoint1;
  }
}
```

Next, we define member variables that are editable in the **Inspector**. Such a variable is marked with the `[SerializeField]` attribute, which means that Unity serializes the variable, despite it being non-public. (Alternatively, public variables are also editable in the **Inspector**.) The following four variables describe our preferences for camera input, including the direction the camera faces, its resolution, and its frame rate:

```
[SerializeField] bool useFrontFacingCamera = false;
[SerializeField] int preferredCaptureWidth = 640;
[SerializeField] int preferredCaptureHeight = 480;
[SerializeField] int preferredFPS = 15;
```

At runtime, the camera devices and modes available to us may differ from these preferences.

We will also make several more variables editable in the **Inspector**—namely, a reference to the video background's renderer, a reference to the material for highlighting detected shapes, a factor for adjusting the scale of the simulation's gravity, references to the simulated shapes' prefabs, and a font size for the button:

```
[SerializeField] Renderer videoRenderer;

[SerializeField] Material drawPreviewMaterial;

[SerializeField] float gravityScale = 8f;

[SerializeField] GameObject simulatedCirclePrefab;
[SerializeField] GameObject simulatedLinePrefab;

[SerializeField] int buttonFontSize = 24;
```

We also have a number of member variables that don't need to be editable in the **Inspector**. Among them are references to the game world's camera, a reference to the real-world camera's video texture, matrices to store images and intermediate processing results, and measurements relating to camera images, the screen, simulated objects, and the button:

```
Camera _camera;

WebCamTexture webCamTexture;
Color32[] colors;
Mat rgbaMat;
Mat grayMat;
Mat cannyMat;

float screenWidth;
float screenHeight;
float screenPixelsPerImagePixel;
float screenPixelsYOffset;

float raycastDistance;
float lineThickness;
UnityEngine.Rect buttonRect;
```

We store a matrix of Hough circle representations in OpenCV's format (which has image coordinates for a landscape image, in this case) and a list of circle representations in our own `Circle` format (which has screen coordinates for a portrait screen, as well as three-dimensional coordinates for a game world):

```
Mat houghCircles;
List<Circle> circles = new List<Circle>();
```

Similarly, we store a matrix of Hough line representations in OpenCV's format and a list of line representations in our own `Line` format:

```
Mat houghLines;
List<Line> lines = new List<Line>();
```

We hold a reference to the gyroscope input device and we store the magnitude of gravity to be used in our physics simulation:

```
Gyroscope gyro;
float gravityMagnitude;
```

We (and the Unity API) are using the terms **gyroscope** and **gyro** loosely. We are referring to a fusion of motion sensors that may or may not include a real gyroscope. A gyroscope can be simulated, albeit poorly, by using other real sensors, such as an accelerometer or gravity sensor.

Unity provides a property, `SystemInfo.supportsGyroscope`, to indicate whether the device has a real gyroscope. However, this information doesn't concern us. We just use Unity's `Gyroscope.gravity` property, which might be derived from a real gravity sensor or might be simulated by using other real sensors, such as an accelerometer and/or gyroscope. Unity Android apps are configured to require an accelerometer by default, so we can safely assume that at least a simulated gravity sensor is available.

We keep track of a list of simulated objects, and we provide a property, `simulating`, that is `true` when the list is non-empty:

```
List<GameObject> simulatedObjects =
        new List<GameObject>();
bool simulating {
    get {
        return simulatedObjects.Count > 0;
    }
}
```

Now, let's turn our attention to methods. We implement the standard `Start` callback. The implementation begins by getting a reference to the attached camera, initializing matrices, getting a reference to the gyro, and computing the magnitude of the game world's gravity, as seen in the following code:

```
void Start() {

    // Cache the reference to the game world's
    // camera.
    _camera = GetComponent<Camera>();

    houghCircles = new Mat();
    houghLines = new Mat();

    gyro = Input.gyro;
    gravityMagnitude = Physics.gravity.magnitude *
                       gravityScale;
```

The `MonoBehaviour` object provides getters for many components that may be attached to the same game object as the script. Such components would appear alongside the script in the Inspector. For example, the `camera` getter returns a `Camera` object (or `null`, if none are present). These getters are expensive because they use introspection. Thus, if you need to refer to a component repeatedly, it is more efficient to store the reference in a member variable by using a statement such as `_camera = camera;`.

You might be wondering why we initialize `Mat` objects in the `Start` method, instead of initializing them when we declare them or in a constructor for `DetectAndSimulate`. The reason is that the OpenCV libraries are not necessarily loaded until after scripts such as `DetectAndSimulate` have been constructed.

The implementation of `Start` proceeds by finding a camera that faces the required direction (either front or rear, depending on the value of the preceding `useFrontFacingCamera` field). If we are playing the scene in the Unity editor (in order to debug the script and scene during development), we hardcode the camera direction to be front-facing, in order to support typical webcams. If no suitable camera is found, the method returns early, as seen in the following code:

```
#if UNITY_EDITOR
            useFrontFacingCamera = true;
#endif

            // Try to find a (physical) camera that faces
            // the required direction.
            WebCamDevice[] devices = WebCamTexture.devices;
            int numDevices = devices.Length;
            for (int i = 0; i < numDevices; i++) {
                WebCamDevice device = devices[i];
                if (device.isFrontFacing ==
                        useFrontFacingCamera) {
                    string name = device.name;
                    Debug.Log("Selecting camera with " +
                            "index " + i + " and name " +
                            name);
                    webCamTexture = new WebCamTexture(
                            name, preferredCaptureWidth,
                            preferredCaptureHeight,
                            preferredFPS);
                    break;
                }
            }
```

```
        if (webCamTexture == null) {
            // No camera faces the required direction.
            // Give up.
            Debug.LogError("No suitable camera found");
            Destroy(this);
            return;
        }
```

Throughout our implementation of DetectAndSimulate, when we encounter an unrecoverable runtime problem, we call Destroy(this);, thereby deleting the instance of the script and preventing further messages from reaching its callbacks.

The Start callback concludes by activating the camera and gyroscope (including the gravity sensor) and launching a helper coroutine called Init:

```
        // Ask the camera to start capturing.
        webCamTexture.Play();

        if (gyro != null) {
            gyro.enabled = true;
        }

        // Wait for the camera to start capturing.
        // Then, initialize everything else.
        StartCoroutine(Init());
    }
```

A **coroutine** is a method that doesn't necessarily run to completion in one frame. Rather, it can yield for one or more frames, in order to wait for a certain condition to be fulfilled or to make something happen after a defined delay. Note that a coroutine runs on the main thread.

Our Init coroutine begins by waiting for the camera to capture the first frame. Then, we determine the frame's dimensions and we create OpenCV matrices to match these dimensions. Here is the first part of the method's implementation:

```
    IEnumerator Init() {
        // Wait for the camera to start capturing.
        while (!webCamTexture.didUpdateThisFrame) {
            yield return null;
        }
        int captureWidth = webCamTexture.width;
        int captureHeight = webCamTexture.height;
        float captureDiagonal = Mathf.Sqrt(
                captureWidth * captureWidth +
```

```
                captureHeight * captureHeight);
        Debug.Log("Started capturing frames at " +
                captureWidth + "x" + captureHeight);
        colors = new Color32[
                captureWidth * captureHeight];
        rgbaMat = new Mat(captureHeight, captureWidth,
                CvType.CV_8UC4);
        grayMat = new Mat(captureHeight, captureWidth,
                CvType.CV_8UC1);
        cannyMat = new Mat(captureHeight, captureWidth,
                CvType.CV_8UC1);
```

The coroutine proceeds by configuring the game world's orthographic camera and video quad to match the capture resolution and to render the video texture:

```
        transform.localPosition =
                new Vector3(0f, 0f, -captureWidth);
        _camera.nearClipPlane = 1;
        _camera.farClipPlane = captureWidth + 1;
        _camera.orthographicSize =
                0.5f * captureDiagonal;
        raycastDistance = 0.5f * captureWidth;

        Transform videoRendererTransform =
                videoRenderer.transform;
        videoRendererTransform.localPosition =
                new Vector3(captureWidth / 2,
                        -captureHeight / 2, 0f);
        videoRendererTransform.localScale =
                new Vector3(captureWidth,
                        captureHeight, 1f);

        videoRenderer.material.mainTexture =
                webCamTexture;
```

The device's screen and captured camera images likely have different resolutions. Moreover, recall that our application is configured for portrait orientation (in **PlayerSettings**). This orientation affects screen coordinates, but not the coordinates in camera images, which will remain in landscape orientation. Thus, we need to calculate the conversion factors between image coordinates and screen coordinates, as seen in the following code:

```
        // Calculate the conversion factors between
        // image and screen coordinates.
        // Note that the image is landscape but the
        // screen is portrait.
        screenWidth = (float)Screen.width;
```

```
screenHeight = (float)Screen.height;
screenPixelsPerImagePixel =
        screenWidth / captureHeight;
screenPixelsYOffset =
        0.5f * (screenHeight - (screenWidth *
        captureWidth / captureHeight));
```

Our conversions will be based on fitting the video background to the width of the portrait screen, while either letterboxing or cropping the video at the top and bottom, if necessary.

The thickness of the simulated lines and the dimensions of the button are based on the screen resolution, as seen in the following code, which concludes the `Init` coroutine:

```
lineThickness = 0.01f * screenWidth;

buttonRect = new UnityEngine.Rect(
        0.4f * screenWidth,
        0.75f * screenHeight,
        0.2f * screenWidth,
        0.1f * screenHeight);
}
```

We implement the standard `Update` callback by processing gravity sensor input and processing camera input, provided that certain conditions are met. At the beginning of the method, if OpenCV objects are not yet initialized, the method returns early. Otherwise, the game world's direction of gravity is updated based on the real-world direction of gravity, as detected by the device's gravity sensor. Here is the first part of the method's implementation:

```
void Update() {

    if (rgbaMat == null) {
        // Initialization is not yet complete.
        return;
    }

    if (gyro != null) {
        // Align the game-world gravity to real-world
        // gravity.
        Vector3 gravity = gyro.gravity;
        gravity.z = 0f;
        gravity = gravityMagnitude *
                gravity.normalized;
        Physics.gravity = gravity;
    }
```

Next, if there is no new camera frame ready or if the simulation is currently running, the method returns early. Otherwise, we convert the frame into OpenCV's format, convert it into gray, find the edges, and call two helper methods, `UpdateCircles` and `UpdateLines`, to perform shape detection. Here is the relevant code, which concludes the `Update` method:

```
    if (!webCamTexture.didUpdateThisFrame) {
        // No new frame is ready.
        return;
    }

    if (simulating) {
        // No new detection results are needed.
        return;
    }

    // Convert the RGBA image to OpenCV's format using
    // a utility function from OpenCV for Unity.
    Utils.webCamTextureToMat(webCamTexture,
                    rgbaMat, colors);

    // Convert the OpenCV image to gray and
    // equalize it.
    Imgproc.cvtColor(rgbaMat, grayMat,
                    Imgproc.COLOR_RGBA2GRAY);
    Imgproc.Canny(grayMat, cannyMat, 50.0, 200.0);

    UpdateCircles();
    UpdateLines();
}
```

Our `UpdateCircles` helper method begins by performing Hough circle detection. We are looking for circles at least `10.0` pixels apart, with a radius of at least `5.0` pixels, and at most, `60` pixels. We specify that internally, `HoughCircles` should use a Canny upper threshold of `200`, down sample by a factor of `2`, and require `150.0` intersections to accept a circle. We clear the list of any previously detected circles. Then, we iterate over the results of the Hough circle detection. Here is the opening of the method's implementation:

```
void UpdateCircles() {

    // Detect blobs.
    Imgproc.HoughCircles(grayMat, houghCircles,
                    Imgproc.HOUGH_GRADIENT, 2.0,
                    10.0, 200.0, 150.0, 5, 60);

    //
    // Calculate the circles' screen coordinates
```

[239]

```
        // and world coordinates.
        //

        // Clear the previous coordinates.
        circles.Clear();

        // Count the elements in the matrix of Hough circles.
        // Each circle should have 3 elements:
        // { x, y, radius }
        int numHoughCircleElems = houghCircles.cols() *
                                  houghCircles.rows() *
                                  houghCircles.channels();

        if (numHoughCircleElems == 0) {
            return;
        }

        // Convert the matrix of Hough circles to a 1D array:
        // { x_0, y_0, radius_0, ..., x_n, y_n, radius_n }
        float[] houghCirclesArray = new float[numHoughCircleElems];
        houghCircles.get(0, 0, houghCirclesArray);

        // Iterate over the circles.
        for (int i = 0; i < numHoughCircleElems; i += 3) {
```

We use a helper method, `ConvertToScreenPosition`, to convert each circle's center point from the image space to the screen space. We also convert its diameter:

```
            // Convert circles' image coordinates to
            // screen coordinates.
            Vector2 screenPosition =
                    ConvertToScreenPosition(
                            houghCirclesArray[i],
                            houghCirclesArray[i + 1]);
            float screenDiameter =
                    houghCirclesArray[i + 2] *
                    screenPixelsPerImagePixel;
```

We use another helper method, `ConvertToWorldPosition`, to convert the circle's center point from the screen space to the world space. We also convert its diameter. Having done our conversions, we instantiate a `Circle` and add it to the list. Here is the code, which completes the `UpdateCircles` method:

```
            // Convert screen coordinates to world
            // coordinates based on raycasting.
            Vector3 worldPosition =
                    ConvertToWorldPosition(
```

```
                screenPosition);

        Circle circle = new Circle(
                screenPosition, screenDiameter,
                worldPosition);
        circles.Add(circle);
    }
}
```

Our `UpdateLines` helper method begins by performing probabilistic Hough line detection with step sizes of one pixel and one degree. For each line, we require at least 50 detected intersections with edge pixels, a length of at least 50 pixels, and no gaps of more than 10.0 pixels. We clear the list of any previously detected lines. Then, we iterate over the results of the Hough line detection. Here is the first part of the method's implementation:

```
void UpdateLines() {

    // Detect lines.
    Imgproc.HoughLinesP(cannyMat, houghLines, 1.0,
                        Mathf.PI / 180.0, 50,
                        50.0, 10.0);

    //
    // Calculate the lines' screen coordinates and
    // world coordinates.
    //

    // Clear the previous coordinates.
    lines.Clear();

    // Count the elements in the matrix of Hough lines.
    // Each line should have 4 elements:
    // { x_start, y_start, x_end, y_end }
    int numHoughLineElems = houghLines.cols() *
                            houghLines.rows() *
                            houghLines.channels();

    if (numHoughLineElems == 0) {
        return;
    }

    // Convert the matrix of Hough circles to a 1D array:
    // { x_start_0, y_start_0, x_end_0, y_end_0, ...,
    //   x_start_n, y_start_n, x_end_n, y_end_n }
    int[] houghLinesArray = new int[numHoughLineElems];
    houghLines.get(0, 0, houghLinesArray);
```

Creating a Physics Simulation Based on a Pen and Paper Sketch

```
// Iterate over the lines.
for (int i = 0; i < numHoughLineElems; i += 4) {
```

We use our `ConvertToScreenPosition` helper method to convert each line's endpoints from the image space to the screen space:

```
// Convert lines' image coordinates to
// screen coordinates.
Vector2 screenPoint0 =
        ConvertToScreenPosition(
                houghLinesArray[i],
                houghLinesArray[i + 1]);
Vector2 screenPoint1 =
        ConvertToScreenPosition(
                houghLinesArray[i + 2],
                houghLinesArray[i + 3]);
```

Similarly, we use our `ConvertToWorldPosition` helper method to convert the line's endpoints from the screen space to the world space. Having done our conversions, we instantiate a `Line` and add it to the list. Here is the code, which completes the `UpdateLines` method:

```
// Convert screen coordinates to world
// coordinates based on raycasting.
Vector3 worldPoint0 =
        ConvertToWorldPosition(
                screenPoint0);
Vector3 worldPoint1 =
        ConvertToWorldPosition(
                screenPoint1);

Line line = new Line(
        screenPoint0, screenPoint1,
        worldPoint0, worldPoint1);
lines.Add(line);
    }
}
```

Our `ConvertToScreenPosition` helper method takes into account the fact that our screen coordinates are in portrait format, whereas our image coordinates are in landscape format. The conversion from image space to screen space is implemented as follows:

```
Vector2 ConvertToScreenPosition(float imageX,
                                float imageY) {
    float screenX = screenWidth - imageY *
            screenPixelsPerImagePixel;
    float screenY = screenHeight - imageX *
```

```
                    screenPixelsPerImagePixel -
                    screenPixelsYOffset;
        return new Vector2(screenX, screenY);
    }
```

Our `ConvertToWorldPosition` helper method uses Unity's built-in raycasting functionality and our specified target distance, `raycastDistance`, to convert the given two-dimensional screen coordinates into three-dimensional world coordinates:

```
    Vector3 ConvertToWorldPosition(
            Vector2 screenPosition) {
        Ray ray = _camera.ScreenPointToRay(
                screenPosition);
        return ray.GetPoint(raycastDistance);
    }
```

We implement the standard `OnPostRender` callback by checking whether any simulated balls or lines are present, and, if not, by calling a helper method, `DrawPreview`. Here is the code:

```
    void OnPostRender() {
        if (!simulating) {
            DrawPreview();
        }
    }
```

The `DrawPreview` helper method serves to show the positions and dimensions of detected circles and lines, if any. To avoid unnecessary draw calls, the method returns early if there are no objects to draw, as seen in the following code:

```
    void DrawPreview() {

        // Draw 2D representations of the detected
        // circles and lines, if any.

        int numCircles = circles.Count;
        int numLines = lines.Count;
        if (numCircles < 1 && numLines < 1) {
            return;
        }
```

Having determined that there are detected shapes to draw, the method proceeds by configuring the OpenGL context to draw in the screen space by using `drawPreviewMaterial`. This setup is seen in the following code:

```
GL.PushMatrix();
if (drawPreviewMaterial != null) {
    drawPreviewMaterial.SetPass(0);
}
GL.LoadPixelMatrix();
```

If there are any detected circles, we do one draw call to highlight them all. Specifically, we tell OpenGL to begin drawing quads, we feed it the screen coordinates of squares that approximate the circles, and then we tell it to stop drawing quads. Here is the code:

```
if (numCircles > 0) {
    // Draw the circles.
    GL.Begin(GL.QUADS);
    for (int i = 0; i < numCircles; i++) {
        Circle circle = circles[i];
        float centerX =
                circle.screenPosition.x;
        float centerY =
                circle.screenPosition.y;
        float radius =
                0.5f * circle.screenDiameter;
        float minX = centerX - radius;
        float maxX = centerX + radius;
        float minY = centerY - radius;
        float maxY = centerY + radius;
        GL.Vertex3(minX, minY, 0f);
        GL.Vertex3(minX, maxY, 0f);
        GL.Vertex3(maxX, maxY, 0f);
        GL.Vertex3(maxX, minY, 0f);
    }
    GL.End();
}
```

Similarly, if there are any detected lines, we do one draw call to highlight them all. Specifically, we tell OpenGL to begin drawing lines, we feed it the lines' screen coordinates, and then we tell it to stop drawing lines. Here is the code, which completes the `DrawPreview` method:

```
if (numLines > 0) {
    // Draw the lines.
    GL.Begin(GL.LINES);
    for (int i = 0; i < numLines; i++) {
        Line line = lines[i];
```

```
                GL.Vertex(line.screenPoint0);
                GL.Vertex(line.screenPoint1);
            }
            GL.End();
        }

        GL.PopMatrix();
    }
```

We implement the standard `OnGUI` callback by drawing a button. Depending on whether simulated balls and lines are already present, the button says either **Stop Simulation** or **Start Simulation**. (However, if there are no simulated balls or lines, and there are also no detected balls or lines, then the button is not shown at all.) When the button is clicked, a helper method is called (either `StopSimulation` or `StartSimulation`). Here is the code for `OnGUI`:

```
void OnGUI() {
    GUI.skin.button.fontSize = buttonFontSize;
    if (simulating) {
        if (GUI.Button(buttonRect,
                       "Stop Simulation")) {
            StopSimulation();
        }
    } else if (circles.Count > 0 || lines.Count > 0) {
        if (GUI.Button(buttonRect,
                       "Start Simulation")) {
            StartSimulation();
        }
    }
}
```

The `StartSimulation` helper method begins by pausing the video feed and placing copies of the `simulatedCirclePrefab` atop the detected circles. Each instance is scaled to match a detected circle's diameter. Here is the first part of the method:

```
void StartSimulation() {

    // Freeze the video background
    webCamTexture.Pause();

    // Create the circles' representation in the
    // physics simulation.
    int numCircles = circles.Count;
    for (int i = 0; i < numCircles; i++) {
        Circle circle = circles[i];
        GameObject simulatedCircle =
                (GameObject)Instantiate(
```

Creating a Physics Simulation Based on a Pen and Paper Sketch

```
            simulatedCirclePrefab);
    Transform simulatedCircleTransform =
            simulatedCircle.transform;
    simulatedCircleTransform.position =
            circle.worldPosition;
    simulatedCircleTransform.localScale =
            circle.screenDiameter *
            Vector3.one;
    simulatedObjects.Add(simulatedCircle);
}
```

The method finishes by placing copies of `simulatedLinePrefab` atop the detected lines. Each instance is scaled to match a detected line's length. Here is the rest of the method:

```
// Create the lines' representation in the
// physics simulation.
int numLines = lines.Count;
for (int i = 0; i < numLines; i++) {
    Line line = lines[i];
    GameObject simulatedLine =
            (GameObject)Instantiate(
                    simulatedLinePrefab);
    Transform simulatedLineTransform =
            simulatedLine.transform;
    float angle = -Vector2.Angle(
            Vector2.right, line.screenPoint1 -
                    line.screenPoint0);
    Vector3 worldPoint0 = line.worldPoint0;
    Vector3 worldPoint1 = line.worldPoint1;
    simulatedLineTransform.position =
            0.5f * (worldPoint0 + worldPoint1);
    simulatedLineTransform.eulerAngles =
            new Vector3(0f, 0f, angle);
    simulatedLineTransform.localScale =
            new Vector3(
                    Vector3.Distance(
                            worldPoint0,
                            worldPoint1),
                    lineThickness,
                    lineThickness);
    simulatedObjects.Add(simulatedLine);
    }
}
```

The `StopSimulation` helper method simply serves to resume the video feed, delete all simulated balls and lines, and clear the list that contained these simulated objects. With the list empty, the conditions for the detectors to run (in the `Update` method) are fulfilled again. `StopSimulation` is implemented like this:

```
void StopSimulation() {

    // Unfreeze the video background.
    webCamTexture.Play();

    // Destroy all objects in the physics simulation.
    int numSimulatedObjects =
            simulatedObjects.Count;
    for (int i = 0; i < numSimulatedObjects; i++) {
        GameObject simulatedObject =
                simulatedObjects[i];
        Destroy(simulatedObject);
    }
    simulatedObjects.Clear();
}
```

When the script's instance is destroyed (at the end of the scene), we ensure that the webcam and gyroscope are released, as seen in the following code:

```
    void OnDestroy() {
        if (webCamTexture != null) {
            webCamTexture.Stop();
        }
        if (gyro != null) {
            gyro.enabled = false;
        }
    }
  }
}
```

Save the script and drag it from the **Project** pane to the **Main Camera** object in the **Hierarchy**. Click on the **Main Camera** object, and, in the **Detect And Simulate (Script)** section of its **Inspector**, drag the following objects to the following fields:

- Drag `VideoRenderer` (from the **Hierarchy**) to the **Video Renderer** field (in the **Inspector**)
- Drag `DrawSolidRed` (from `Rollingball/Materials` in the **Project** pane) to the **Draw Preview Material** field (in the **Inspector**)

- Drag `SimulatedCircle` (from `Rollingball/Prefabs` in the **Project** pane) to the **Simulated Circle Prefab** field (in the **Inspector**)
- Drag `SimulatedLine` (from `Rollingball/Prefabs` in the **Project** pane) to the **Simulated Line Prefab** field (in the **Inspector**)

After these changes, the script's section in the **Inspector** should look like the following screenshot:

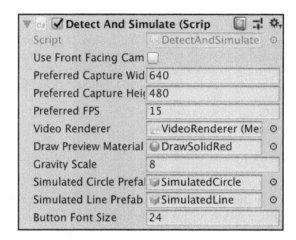

Our main scene is complete! Now, we need a simple launcher scene that is responsible for obtaining the user's permission to access the camera and for launching the main scene.

Creating the launcher scene in Unity

Our `Rollingball` scene, and specifically the `DetectAndSimulate` script, attempts to access a camera through Unity's `WebCamDevice` and `WebCamTexture` classes. Unity is somewhat smart about camera permissions on Android. At the start of the `Rollingball` scene (or any scene that requires camera access), Unity will automatically check whether the user has granted permission for camera access; if not, Unity will request permission. Unfortunately, this automatic request comes too late for `DetectAndSimulate` to properly access the camera in its `Start` and `Init` methods. To avoid this kind of problem, it is better to write a launcher scene with a script that explicitly requests camera access.

Create a new scene and save it as `Launcher` in the `Rollingball/Scenes` folder. Delete the **Directional Light** from the scene. Add an empty object and name it `Launcher`. Now, the scene's **Hierarchy** should look like this:

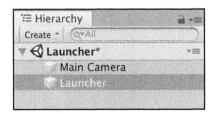

Edit the **Main Camera** in the **Inspector** to give it a solid black background, as shown in the following screenshot:

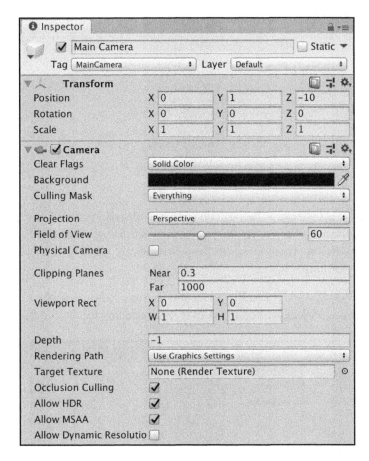

In `Rollingball/Scripts`, create a new script, rename it `Launcher`, edit it, and replace its contents with the following code:

```
using UnityEngine;
using UnityEngine.SceneManagement;
```

Creating a Physics Simulation Based on a Pen and Paper Sketch

```
#if PLATFORM_ANDROID
using UnityEngine.Android;
#endif


namespace com.nummist.rollingball {

    public class Launcher : MonoBehaviour {

        void Start() {

#if PLATFORM_ANDROID
            if (!Permission.HasUserAuthorizedPermission(
                Permission.Camera))
            {
                // Ask the user's permission for camera access.
                Permission.RequestUserPermission(Permission.Camera);
            }
#endif

            SceneManager.LoadScene("Rollingball");
        }
    }
}
```

Upon `Start`, this script checks whether the user has already granted permission to access the camera. If not, the script requests permission by showing a standard Android permission request dialog. The `Start` method finishes by loading the `Rollingball` scene that we created previously.

Save the script and drag it from the **Project** pane to the `Launcher` object in the **Hierarchy**. Click on the `Launcher` object and confirm that its **Inspector** looks like the following:

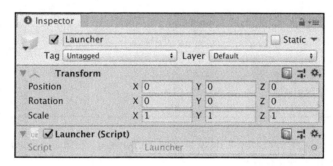

Our launcher scene is complete. All that remains is to configure, build, and test our project.

Tidying up and testing

Let's return to the **Build Settings** window (**File | Build Settings...**). We no longer want the OpenCV for Unity demos in our build. Remove them by either unchecking them or selecting and deleting them (*Delete* on Windows or *Cmd + Del* on Mac). Then, add the `Launcher` and `Rollingball` scenes by dragging them from the **Project** pane into the **Scenes In Build** list. When you are finished, the **Build Settings** window should look like the following screenshot:

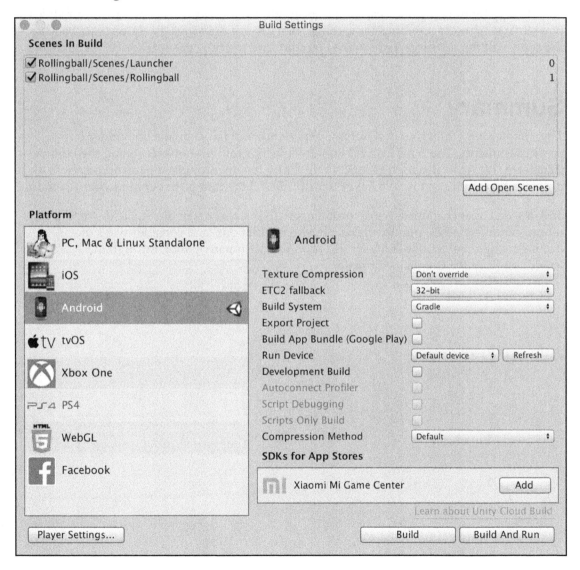

Click on the **Build and Run** button, overwrite any previous builds, and let the good times roll!

 If you are building for iOS, remember to follow the additional instructions in OpenCVForUnity/ReadMe.pdf. Particularly, ensure that the project's **Camera Usage Description** is set to a helpful descriptive string, for example Rollingball uses the camera to detect circles and lines (obviously!) and that the **Target minimum iOS Version** is set to 8.0.

Test the app by drawing and scanning dots and lines of various sizes, with various styles of pen strokes. Also, try scanning some things that are not drawings. Feel free to go back to the code, edit the detectors' parameters, rebuild, and see how the sensitivity has changed.

Summary

This chapter has really rounded out our experience and has drawn a line under our accomplishments. You have learned how to detect primitive shapes by using the Hough transform. We have also used OpenCV and Unity together to turn a pen and paper drawing into a physics toy. We have even surpassed the things that Q can make a pen do!

Still, a secret agent cannot solve all problems with ink and paper alone. Next, we will take off our reading glasses, put down our physics simulations, and consider ways of deconstructing real motion in the world around us. Prepare to look through the kaleidoscope of the frequency domain!

Section 3: The Big Reveal

Visualize things that are normally invisible. Simulate a different timescale or a different spectrum of vision. Integrate with a wider range of cameras and imaging pipelines.

The following chapters will be covered in this section:

- `Chapter 7`, *Seeing a Heartbeat with a Motion-Amplifying Camera*
- `Chapter 8`, *Stopping Time and Seeing like a Bee*

7
Seeing a Heartbeat with a Motion-Amplifying Camera

"Remove everything that has no relevance to the story. If you say in the first chapter that there is a rifle hanging on the wall, in the second or third chapter it absolutely must go off. If it's not going to be fired, it shouldn't be hanging there."
— *Anton Chekhov*

"King Julian: I don't know why the sacrifice didn't work. The science seemed so solid."
— *Madagascar: Escape 2 Africa (2008)*

Despite their strange design and mysterious engineering, Q's gadgets always prove useful and reliable. Bond has such faith in the technology that he never even asks how to charge the batteries.

One of the more inventive ideas in the Bond franchise is that even a lightly equipped spy should be able to see and photograph concealed objects, anyplace, anytime. Let's consider a timeline of a few relevant gadgets in the movies, as follows:

- **1967 (*You Only Live Twice*)**: An X-ray desk scans guests for hidden firearms.
- **1979 (*Moonraker*)**: A cigarette case contains an X-ray imaging system that is used to reveal the tumblers of a safe's combination lock.
- **1989 (*License to Kill*)**: A Polaroid camera takes X-ray photos. Oddly enough, its flash is a visible, red laser.
- **1995 (*GoldenEye*)**: A tea tray contains an X-ray scanner that can photograph documents beneath the tray.
- **1999 (*The World is Not Enough*)**: Bond wears a stylish pair of blue-lensed glasses that can see through one layer of clothing to reveal concealed weapons. According to the *James Bond Encyclopedia* (2007), which is an official guide to the movies, the glasses display infrared video after applying special processing to them. Despite using infrared, they are commonly called **X-ray specs**, a misnomer.

These gadgets deal with unseen wavelengths of light (or radiation) and are broadly comparable to real-world devices such as airport security scanners and night-vision goggles. However, it remains difficult to explain how Bond's equipment is so compact and how it takes such clear pictures under diverse lighting conditions and through diverse materials. Moreover, if Bond's devices are active scanners (meaning they emit X-ray radiation or infrared light), they will be clearly visible to other spies using similar hardware.

To take another approach, what if we avoid unseen wavelengths of light but instead focus on unseen frequencies of motion? Many things move in a pattern that is too fast or too slow for us to easily notice. Suppose a man is standing in one place. If he shifts one leg more than the other, perhaps he is concealing a heavy object, such as a gun, on the side that he shifts more. Equally, we might also fail to notice deviations from a pattern; suppose the same man has been looking straight ahead but suddenly, when he believes no one is looking, his eyes dart to one side. Is he watching someone?

We can make motions of a certain frequency more visible by repeating them, like a delayed afterimage or a ghost, with each repetition appearing fainter (or less opaque) than the last. The effect is analogous to an echo or a ripple and is achieved using an algorithm called **Eulerian video magnification**.

By applying this technique, we will build a desktop app that allows us to simultaneously see the present and selected slices of the past. The idea of experiencing multiple images simultaneously is, to me, quite natural because, for the first 26 years of my life, I had **strabismus**—commonly called a **lazy eye**—which caused double vision. A surgeon corrected my eyesight and gave me depth perception but in memory of strabismus, I would like to name this application `Lazy Eyes`.

Let's take a closer look, or two or more closer looks, at the fast-paced, moving world that we share with other secret agents.

The following topics will be covered in this chapter:

- Understanding what Eulerian video magnification can do
- Extracting repeating signals from video using the fast Fourier transform
- Compositing two images using image pyramids
- Implementing the Lazy Eyes app
- Configuring and testing the app for various motions

Technical requirements

This chapter's project has the following software dependencies:

- **A Python environment with the following modules**: OpenCV, NumPy, SciPy, PyFFTW, wxPython

Where not otherwise noted, setup instructions are covered in `Chapter 1`, *Preparing for the Mission*. Setup instructions for PyFFTW are covered in the current chapter, in the section *Choosing and setting up an FFT library*. Always refer to the setup instructions for any version requirements. Basic instructions for running Python code are covered in `Appendix C`, *Running with Snakes (or, First Steps with Python)*.

The complete project for this chapter can be found in this book's GitHub repository, `https://github.com/PacktPublishing/OpenCV-4-for-Secret-Agents-Second-Edition`, in the `Chapter007` folder.

Planning the Lazy Eyes app

Of all our apps, `Lazy Eyes` has the simplest user interface. It just shows a live video feed with a special effect that highlights motion. The parameters of the effect are quite complex and, moreover, modifying them at runtime would have a big effect on performance. Thus, we do not provide a user interface to reconfigure the effect, but we do provide many parameters in code to allow a programmer to create many variants of the effect and the app. Below the video panel, the app displays the current frame rate, measured in **frames per second** (**FPS**). The following screenshot illustrates one configuration of the app. This screenshot shows me eating cake. Because my hands and face are moving, we see an effect that looks like light and dark waves rippling near moving edges (the effect is more graceful in a live video than in a screenshot):

For more screenshots and an in-depth discussion of the parameters, see the *Configuring and testing the app for various motions* section later in this chapter.

Regardless of how it is configured, the app loops through the following actions:

1. Capture an image.
2. Copy and downsample the image while applying a blur filter and, optionally, an edge-finding filter. We will downsample using so-called **image pyramids**, which will be discussed in the *Compositing two images using image pyramids* section later in this chapter. The purpose of downsampling is to achieve a higher frame rate by reducing the amount of image data that's used in subsequent operations. The purpose of applying a blur filter and, optionally, an edge-finding filter is to create halos that are useful in amplifying motion.
3. Store the downsampled copy in a history of frames, with a timestamp. The history has a fixed capacity. Once it is full, the oldest frame is overwritten to make room for the new one.
4. If the history is not yet full, continue to the next iteration of the loop.
5. Calculate and display the average frame rate based on the timestamps of the frames in the history.
6. Decompose the history into a list of frequencies describing fluctuations (motion) at each pixel. The decomposition function is called a **fast Fourier transform** (**FFT**). We will discuss it in the*Extracting repeating signals from video using the fast Fourier transform* section later in this chapter.
7. Set all frequencies to zero except a chosen range of interest. In other words, filter out the data on motions that are faster or slower than certain thresholds.
8. Recompose the filtered frequencies into a series of images that are motion maps. Areas that are still (with respect to our chosen range of frequencies) become dark, and areas that are moving remain bright. The `recomposition` function is called an **inverse fast Fourier transform** (**IFFT**), which we will discuss later.
9. Upsample the latest motion map (again, using image pyramids), intensify it, and overlay it additively atop the original camera image.
10. Show the resulting composite image.

That's it—a simple plan that requires rather nuanced implementation and configuration. So, with that in mind, let's prepare ourselves by doing a little background research first.

Understanding what Eulerian video magnification can do

Eulerian video magnification is inspired by a model in fluid mechanics called **Eulerian specification of the flow field**. Let's consider a moving, fluid body, such as a river. The Eulerian specification describes the river's velocity at a given position and time. The velocity would be fast in the mountains in springtime and slow at the river's mouth in winter. The velocity would also be slower at a silt-saturated point at the river's bottom, compared to a point where the river's surface hits a rock and sprays. An alternative to the Eulerian specification is the **Lagrangian specification**, which describes the position of a given particle at a given time. For example, a given bit of silt might make its way down from the mountains to the river's mouth over a period of many years and then spend eons drifting around a tidal basin.

For a more formal description of the Eulerian specification, the Lagrangian specification, and their relationship, refer to the following Wikipedia article at `http://en.wikipedia.org/wiki/Lagrangian_and_Eulerian_specification_of_the_flow_field`.

The Lagrangian specification is analogous to many computer vision tasks in which we model the motion of a particular object or feature over time. However, the Eulerian specification is analogous to our current task, in which we model any motion occurring in a particular position and a particular window of time. Having modeled a motion from an Eulerian perspective, we can visually exaggerate the motion by overlaying the model's results for a blend of positions and times.

Let's set a baseline for our expectations of Eulerian video magnification by studying other people's projects, which include the following:

- Michael Rubenstein's webpage at MIT (`http://people.csail.mit.edu/mrub/vidmag/`): Gives an abstract of his team's pioneering work on Eulerian video magnification, along with demo videos.
- Bryce Drennan's eulerian-magnification library (`https://github.com/brycedrennan/eulerian-magnification`): Implements the algorithm using NumPy, SciPy, and OpenCV. This implementation is good inspiration for us, but is designed for processing prerecorded videos and is not sufficiently optimized for real-time input.

Now, let's move on and understand the functions that are the building blocks of these projects and ours.

Extracting repeating signals from video using the fast Fourier transform

An audio signal is typically visualized as a bar chart or wave. The bar or wave is high when the sound is loud and low when it is soft. We recognize that a repetitive sound, such as a metronome's beat, makes repetitive peaks and valleys in the visualization. When audio has multiple channels (such as a stereo or surround-sound recording), each channel can be considered a separate signal and can be visualized as a separate bar chart or wave.

Similarly, in a video, every channel of every pixel can be considered a separate signal, rising and falling (becoming brighter and dimmer) over time. Imagine that we use a stationary camera to capture a video of a metronome. In this case, certain pixel values will rise and fall at a regular interval as they capture the passage of the metronome's needle. If the camera has an attached microphone, its signal values will rise and fall at the same interval. Based on either the audio or the video, we can then measure the metronome's frequency—its **beats per minute (bpm)** or its beats per second (Hertz or Hz). Conversely, if we change the metronome's bpm setting, the effect on both the audio and the video will be predictable. From this thought experiment, we can learn that a signal—be it audio, video, or any other kind—can be expressed as a function of time and, *equivalently*, a function of frequency.

Consider the following pair of graphs. They express the same signal, first as a function of time and then as a function of frequency. Within the time domain, we see one wide peak and valley (in other words, a tapering effect) spanning many narrow peaks and valleys. Within the frequency domain, we can see a low-frequency peak and a high-frequency peak, as shown in the following diagram:

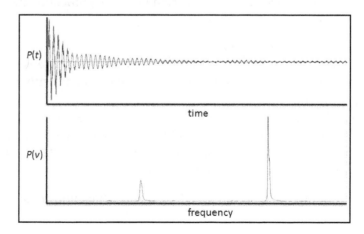

The transformation from the time domain to the frequency domain is called the **Fourier transform** (FT). Conversely, the transformation from the frequency domain to the time domain is called the **inverse Fourier transform**. Within the digital world, signals are discrete, not continuous, so we use the terms **discrete Fourier transform** (DFT) and **inverse discrete Fourier transform** (IDFT). There is a variety of efficient algorithms for computing the DFT or IDFT, and such an algorithm might be described as a FFT or IFFT.

For algorithmic descriptions, refer to the following Wikipedia article at http://en.wikipedia.org/wiki/Fast_Fourier_transform.

The result of the FT (including its discrete variants) is a function that maps a frequency to an amplitude and phase. The **amplitude** represents the magnitude of the frequency's contribution to the signal. The **phase** represents a temporal shift; it determines whether the frequency's contribution starts on a high or a low. Typically, the amplitude and phase are encoded in a complex number, `a+bi`, where `amplitude=sqrt(a^2+b^2)` and `phase=atan2(a, b)`.

For an explanation of complex numbers, see the following Wikipedia article: http://en.wikipedia.org/wiki/Complex_number.

The FFT and IFFT are fundamental to a field of computer science called **digital signal processing**. Many signal processing applications, including `Lazy Eyes`, involve taking the signal's FFT, modifying or removing certain frequencies in the FFT result, and then reconstructing the filtered signal in the time domain using the IFFT. For example, this approach allows us to amplify certain frequencies while leaving others unchanged.

Now, where do we find this functionality?

Choosing and setting up an FFT library

Several Python libraries provide FFT and IFFT implementations that can process NumPy arrays (and thus OpenCV images). The five major contenders are as follows:

- *NumPy*, which provides FFT and IFFT implementations in a module called `numpy.fft` (http://docs.scipy.org/doc/numpy/reference/routines.fft.html). The module also offers other signal processing functions for working with the output of the FFT.

- *SciPy*, which provides FFT and IFFT implementations in a module called `scipy.fftpack` (http://docs.scipy.org/doc/scipy/reference/fftpack.html). This SciPy module is closely based on the `numpy.fft` module, but adds some optional arguments and dynamic optimizations based on the input format. The SciPy module also adds more signal processing functions for working with the output of the FFT.
- *OpenCV* itself has implementations of FFT (`cv2.dft`) and IFT (`cv2.idft`). The following official tutorial provides examples and a comparison to NumPy's FFT implementation: https://docs.opencv.org/master/d8/d01/tutorial_discrete_fourier_transform.html. Note that OpenCV's FFT and IFT interfaces are not directly interoperable with the `numpy.fft` and `scipy.fftpack` modules, which offer a broader range of signal processing functionality. (They format the data very differently.)
- *PyFFTW* (https://hgomersall.github.io/pyFFTW/), which is a Python wrapper around a C library called the **Fastest Fourier Transform in the West (FFTW)** (http://www.fftw.org/). FFTW provides multiple implementations of FFT and IFFT. At runtime, it dynamically selects implementations that are well-optimized for given input formats, output formats, and system capabilities. Optionally, it takes advantage of multithreading (and its threads may run on multiple CPU cores, as the implementation releases Python's **Global Interpreter Lock (GIL)**). PyFFTW provides optional interfaces matching NumPy's and SciPy's FFT and IFFT functions. These interfaces have a low overhead cost (thanks to good caching options that are provided by PyFFTW) and they help to ensure that PyFFTW is interoperable with a broad range of signal processing functionality, as implemented in `numpy.fft` and `scipy.fftpack`.
- *Reinka* (http://reikna.publicfields.net/en/latest/), which is a Python library for GPU-accelerated computations, uses either PyCUDA (http://mathema.tician.de/software/pycuda/) or PyOpenCL (http://mathema.tician.de/software/pyopencl/) as a backend. Reinka provides FFT and IFFT implementations in a module called `reikna.fft`. Reinka internally uses PyCUDA or PyOpenCL arrays (not NumPy arrays) and provides interfaces for conversion from NumPy arrays to these GPU arrays and back. The converted NumPy output is compatible with other signal processing functionality, as implemented in `numpy.fft` and `scipy.fftpack`. However, this compatibility comes at a high overhead cost due to the need to lock, read, and convert the contents of GPU memory.

NumPy, SciPy, OpenCV, and PyFFTW are open source libraries under the BSD license. Reinka is an open-source library under the MIT license.

I recommend PyFFTW because of its optimizations and its interoperability (at a low overhead cost), and all the other functionality that interests us in NumPy, SciPy, and OpenCV. For a tour of PyFFTW's features, including its NumPy- and SciPy-compatible interfaces, see the official tutorial at https://hgomersall.github.io/pyFFTW/sphinx/tutorial.html.

Depending on our platform, we can set up PyFFTW in one of the following ways:

- On Mac, the third-party MacPorts package manager offers PyFFTW packages for some versions of Python, currently including Python 3.6 but not Python 3.7. To install PyFFTW with MacPorts, open a Terminal and run something like the following command (but substitute your Python version if it differs from py36):

    ```
    $ sudo port install py36-pyfftw
    ```

- Alternatively, on any system, use Python's package manager, pip, to install PyFFTW. Open a command prompt and run something like the following command (depending on your system, you might need to replace pip with pip3 in order to install PyFFTW for Python 3):

    ```
    $ pip install --user pyFFTW
    ```

Some versions of pip's pyFFTW package have installation bugs that affect some systems. If pip fails to install the pyFFTW package, try again, but manually specify version 10.4 of the package by running the following command:

```
$ pip install --user pyFFTW==0.10.4
```

Note that some old versions of the library are called PyFFTW3. We do not want PyFFTW3. On Ubuntu 18.04 and its derivatives, the python-fftw package in the system's standard apt repository is an old PyFFTW3 version.

We have our FFT and IFFT needs covered by the Fastest Fourier Transform in the West (and if we were cowboys instead of secret agents, we could say, *Cover me!*). For additional signal processing functionality, we will use SciPy, which can be set up in the way we described in Chapter 1, *Preparing for the Mission*, in the *Setting up a development machine* section.

Signal processing is not the only new material that we must learn about for Lazy Eyes, so let's look at other functionality that is provided by OpenCV.

Compositing two images using image pyramids

Running an FFT on a full-resolution video feed would be slow. The resulting frequencies may also reflect localized phenomena at each captured pixel, so that the motion map (the result of filtering the frequencies and then applying the IFFT) might appear noisy and overly sharp. To address these problems, we need a cheap, blurry downsampling technique. However, we also want the option to enhance edges, which are important to our perception of motion.

Our need for a blurry downsampling technique is fulfilled by a **Gaussian image pyramid**. A **Gaussian filter** blurs an image by making each output pixel a weighted average of multiple input pixels in the neighborhood. An image pyramid is a series in which each image is a fraction of the width and height of the previous image. Often, the fraction is one half. The halving of image dimensions is achieved by *decimation*, meaning that every other pixel is simply omitted. A Gaussian image pyramid is constructed by applying a Gaussian filter before each decimation operation.

Our need to enhance edges in downsampled images is fulfilled by a **Laplacian image pyramid**, which is constructed in the following manner. Suppose we have already constructed a Gaussian image pyramid. We take the image at level `i+1` in the Gaussian pyramid, upsample it by duplicating pixels, and apply a Gaussian filter to it again. We then subtract the result from the image at level `i` in the Gaussian pyramid to produce the corresponding image at level `i` of the Laplacian pyramid. Thus, the Laplacian image is the difference between a blurry, downsampled image and an even blurrier image that was downsampled, downsampled again, and upsampled.

You might wonder how such an algorithm is a form of edge-finding. Consider that edges are areas of local contrast, while non-edges are areas of local uniformity. If we blur a uniform area, it is still uniform—there is zero difference. If we blur a contrasting area, however, it becomes more uniform—there is a non-zero difference. Thus, the difference can be used to find edges.

 The Gaussian and Laplacian image pyramids are described in detail in the following journal article: E. H. Adelson, C. H. Anderson, J. R. Bergen, P. J. Burt, and J. M. Ogden. "Pyramid methods in image processing". RCA Engineer, Vol. 29, No. 6, November/Dececember 1984. It can be downloaded from `http://persci.mit.edu/pub_pdfs/RCA84.pdf`.

Besides using image pyramids to downsample the FFT's input, we can also use them to upsample the most recent frame of the IFFT's output. This upsampling step is necessary for creating an overlay that matches the size of the original camera image so that we can composite the two. Like in the construction of the Laplacian pyramid, upsampling consists of duplicating pixels and applying a Gaussian filter.

OpenCV implements the relevant downsizing and upsizing functions as `cv2.pyrDown` and `cv2.pyrUp`. These functions are useful in compositing two images in general (whether or not signal processing is involved), because they allows us to soften differences while preserving edges. The OpenCV documentation includes a good tutorial on this topic at https://docs.opencv.org/master/dc/dff/tutorial_py_pyramids.html.

Now that we are armed with the necessary knowledge, it's time to implement `Lazy Eyes`!

Implementing the Lazy Eyes app

Let's create a new folder for Lazy Eyes and, in this folder, create copies of or links to the `ResizeUtils.py` and `WxUtils.py` files from any of our previous Python projects, such as *The Living Headlights* from Chapter 5, *Equipping Your Car with a Rearview Camera and Hazard Detection*. Alongside the copies or links, let's create a new file, `LazyEyes.py`. Edit it and enter the following `import` statements:

```
import collections
import threading
import timeit

import numpy
import cv2
import wx

import pyfftw.interfaces.cache
from pyfftw.interfaces.scipy_fftpack import fft
from pyfftw.interfaces.scipy_fftpack import ifft
from scipy.fftpack import fftfreq

import ResizeUtils
import WxUtils
```

Besides the modules that we have used in the previous projects, we are now using the standard library's `collections` module for efficient collections, as well as the `timeit` module for precise timing. For the first time, we are also using the signal processing functionality from PyFFTW and SciPy.

Like our other Python applications, `Lazy Eyes` is implemented as a class that extends `wx.Frame`. The following code block contains the declarations of the class and its initializer:

```
class LazyEyes(wx.Frame):

    def __init__(self, maxHistoryLength=360,
                 minHz=5.0/6.0, maxHz=1.0,
                 amplification=32.0, numPyramidLevels=2,
                 useLaplacianPyramid=True,
                 useGrayOverlay=True,
                 numFFTThreads=4, numIFFTThreads=4,
                 cameraDeviceID=0, imageSize=(640, 480),
                 title='Lazy Eyes'):
```

The initializer's arguments affect the app's frame rate and the manner in which motion is amplified. These effects are discussed in detail in the section *Configuring and testing the app for various motions* later in this chapter. The following is just a brief description of the arguments:

- `maxHistoryLength` is the number of frames (including the current frame and preceding frames) that are analyzed for motion.
- `minHz` and `maxHz`, respectively, define the slowest and fastest motions that are amplified.
- `amplification` is the scale of the visual effect. A higher value means motion is highlighted more brightly.
- `numPyramidLevels` is the number of pyramid levels by which frames are downsampled before signal processing is done. Each level corresponds to downsampling by a factor of 2. Our implementation assumes `numPyramidLevels>0`.
- If `useLaplacianPyramid` is `True`, frames are downsampled using a Laplacian pyramid before signal processing is done. The implication is that only edge motion is highlighted. Alternatively, if `useLaplacianPyramid` is `False`, a Gaussian pyramid is used, and motion in all areas is highlighted.
- If `useGrayOverlay` is `True`, frames are converted to grayscale before signal processing is done. The implication is that motion is only highlighted in areas of grayscale contrast. Alternatively, if `useGrayOverlay` is `False`, motion is highlighted in areas that have contrast in any color channel.
- `numFFTThreads` and `numIFFTThreads`, are the numbers of threads that are used in FFT and IFFT computations, respectively.
- `cameraDeviceID` and `imageSize` are our usual capture parameters.

The initializer's implementation begins in the same way as our other Python apps. It sets flags to indicate that the app is running and should be mirrored by default. It creates the capture object and configures its resolution to match the requested width and height, if possible. Failing that, the device's fallback capture resolution is used. The initializer also declares variables to store images, and creates a lock to manage thread-safe access to the images. The relevant code is as follows:

```
self.mirrored = True

self._running = True

self._capture = cv2.VideoCapture(cameraDeviceID)
size = ResizeUtils.cvResizeCapture(
        self._capture, imageSize)
w, h = size

self._image = None

self._imageFrontBuffer = None
self._imageFrontBufferLock = threading.Lock()
```

Next, we need to determine the shape of the history of frames. We already know that it has at least three dimensions—a number of frames, and a width and height for each frame. The width and height are downsampled from the capture width and height based on the number of pyramid levels. If we are concerned with color motion, and not just grayscale motion, the history also has a fourth dimension that consists of three color channels. The following code calculates the history's shape:

```
self._useGrayOverlay = useGrayOverlay
if useGrayOverlay:
    historyShape = (maxHistoryLength,
                    h >> numPyramidLevels,
                    w >> numPyramidLevels)
else:
    historyShape = (maxHistoryLength,
                    h >> numPyramidLevels,
                    w >> numPyramidLevels, 3)
```

Note the use of >>, the right bitshift operator, in the preceding code; it's used to divide the dimensions by a power of two. The power is equal to the number of pyramid levels.

We now need to store the specified maximum history length. For the frames in the history, we will create a NumPy array of the shape we just determined. For timestamps of the frames, we will create a **double-ended queue (deque)**, a type of collection that allows us to cheaply add or remove elements from either end, as shown in the following code:

```
self._maxHistoryLength = maxHistoryLength
self._history = numpy.empty(historyShape,
                            numpy.float32)
self._historyTimestamps = collections.deque()
```

We will store the remaining arguments because we will need to pass them to the pyramid functions and signal processing functions for each frame later, as follows:

```
self._numPyramidLevels = numPyramidLevels
self._useLaplacianPyramid = useLaplacianPyramid

self._minHz = minHz
self._maxHz = maxHz
self._amplification = amplification

self._numFFTThreads = numFFTThreads
self._numIFFTThreads = numIFFTThreads
```

To ensure meaningful error messages and early termination in the case of invalid arguments, we could add code such as the following for each argument:

```
assert numPyramidLevels > 0, \
    'numPyramidLevels must be positive.'
```

For brevity, such assertions are omitted from our code samples.

We now need to call the following two functions to tell PyFFTW to cache its data structures (notably, its NumPy arrays) for a period of at least 1.0 seconds from their last use. (The default is 0.1 seconds.) Caching is a critical optimization for the PyFFTW interfaces that we are using, so we will choose a period that is more than long enough to keep the cache alive from frame to frame, as follows:

```
pyfftw.interfaces.cache.enable()
pyfftw.interfaces.cache.set_keepalive_time(1.0)
```

[268]

As shown in the following code, the initializer's implementation ends with code to set up a window, event bindings, a video panel, a layout, and a background thread, which are all familiar tasks from our previous Python projects:

```python
style = wx.CLOSE_BOX | wx.MINIMIZE_BOX | \
        wx.CAPTION | wx.SYSTEM_MENU | \
        wx.CLIP_CHILDREN
wx.Frame.__init__(self, None, title=title,
                  style=style, size=size)

self.Bind(wx.EVT_CLOSE, self._onCloseWindow)

quitCommandID = wx.NewId()
self.Bind(wx.EVT_MENU, self._onQuitCommand,
          id=quitCommandID)
acceleratorTable = wx.AcceleratorTable([
    (wx.ACCEL_NORMAL, wx.WXK_ESCAPE,
     quitCommandID)
])
self.SetAcceleratorTable(acceleratorTable)

self._videoPanel = wx.Panel(self, size=size)
self._videoPanel.Bind(
        wx.EVT_ERASE_BACKGROUND,
        self._onVideoPanelEraseBackground)
self._videoPanel.Bind(
        wx.EVT_PAINT, self._onVideoPanelPaint)

self._videoBitmap = None

self._fpsStaticText = wx.StaticText(self)

border = 12

controlsSizer = wx.BoxSizer(wx.HORIZONTAL)
controlsSizer.Add(self._fpsStaticText, 0,
                  wx.ALIGN_CENTER_VERTICAL)

rootSizer = wx.BoxSizer(wx.VERTICAL)
rootSizer.Add(self._videoPanel)
rootSizer.Add(controlsSizer, 0,
              wx.EXPAND | wx.ALL, border)
self.SetSizerAndFit(rootSizer)

self._captureThread = threading.Thread(
        target=self._runCaptureLoop)
self._captureThread.start()
```

We must now modify our usual `_onCloseWindow` callback to disable PyFFTW's cache. Disabling the cache ensures that resources are freed and that PyFFTW's threads terminate normally. The callback's implementation is shown in the following code:

```
def _onCloseWindow(self, event):
    self._running = False
    self._captureThread.join()
    pyfftw.interfaces.cache.disable()
    self.Destroy()
```

The escape key is bound to our usual `_onQuitCommand` callback, which just closes the app, as follows:

```
def _onQuitCommand(self, event):
    self.Close()
```

The video panel's erase and paint events are bound to our usual callbacks, `_onVideoPanelEraseBackground` and `_onVideoPanelPaint`, as shown in the following code:

```
def _onVideoPanelEraseBackground(self, event):
    pass

def _onVideoPanelPaint(self, event):
    self._imageFrontBufferLock.acquire()

    if self._imageFrontBuffer is None:
        self._imageFrontBufferLock.release()
        return

    # Convert the image to bitmap format.
    self._videoBitmap = \
        WxUtils.wxBitmapFromCvImage(self._imageFrontBuffer)

    self._imageFrontBufferLock.release()

    # Show the bitmap.
    dc = wx.BufferedPaintDC(self._videoPanel)
    dc.DrawBitmap(self._videoBitmap, 0, 0)
```

The loop running on our background thread is similar to the one used in other Python apps. For each frame, it calls a helper function, `_applyEulerianVideoMagnification`. The loop's implementation is as follows:

```
def _runCaptureLoop(self):

    while self._running:
```

```
                success, self._image = self._capture.read(
                        self._image)
                if self._image is not None:
                    self._applyEulerianVideoMagnification()
                    if (self.mirrored):
                        self._image[:] = numpy.fliplr(self._image)

                    # Perform a thread-safe swap of the front and
                    # back image buffers.
                    self._imageFrontBufferLock.acquire()
                    self._imageFrontBuffer, self._image = \
                            self._image, self._imageFrontBuffer
                    self._imageFrontBufferLock.release()

                    # Send a refresh event to the video panel so
                    # that it will draw the image from the front
                    # buffer.
                    self._videoPanel.Refresh()
```

The `_applyEulerianVideoMagnification` helper function is quite long, so we will consider its implementation in several chunks. First, we need to create a timestamp for the frame and copy the frame to a format that is more suitable for processing. Specifically, we will use a floating point with either one gray channel or three color channels, depending on the configuration, as shown in the following code:

```
        def _applyEulerianVideoMagnification(self):

            timestamp = timeit.default_timer()

            if self._useGrayOverlay:
                smallImage = cv2.cvtColor(
                        self._image, cv2.COLOR_BGR2GRAY).astype(
                                numpy.float32)
            else:
                smallImage = self._image.astype(numpy.float32)
```

Using this copy, we will calculate the appropriate level in the Gaussian or Laplacian pyramid, as follows:

```
            # Downsample the image using a pyramid technique.
            i = 0
            while i < self._numPyramidLevels:
                smallImage = cv2.pyrDown(smallImage)
                i += 1
            if self._useLaplacianPyramid:
                smallImage[:] -= \
                        cv2.pyrUp(cv2.pyrDown(smallImage))
```

For the purposes of the history and signal processing functions, we will refer to this pyramid level as *the image* or *the frame*.

Next, we need to check the number of history frames that have been filled so far. If the history has more than one unfilled frame (meaning the history still won't be full after adding the frame), we will append and timestamp the new image, before returning it early, so that no signal processing is done until a later frame. This can be seen in the following code:

```
historyLength = len(self._historyTimestamps)

if historyLength < self._maxHistoryLength - 1:

    # Append the new image and timestamp to the
    # history.
    self._history[historyLength] = smallImage
    self._historyTimestamps.append(timestamp)

    # The history is still not full, so wait.
    return
```

If the history is just one frame short of being full (meaning the history will be full after adding this frame), we will append the new image and timestamp, as follows:

```
if historyLength == self._maxHistoryLength - 1:
    # Append the new image and timestamp to the
    # history.
    self._history[historyLength] = smallImage
    self._historyTimestamps.append(timestamp)
```

If the history is already full, we will drop the oldest image and timestamp and append the new image and timestamp, as follows:

```
else:
    # Drop the oldest image and timestamp from the
    # history and append the new ones.
    self._history[:-1] = self._history[1:]
    self._historyTimestamps.popleft()
    self._history[-1] = smallImage
    self._historyTimestamps.append(timestamp)

# The history is full, so process it.
```

The history of image data is a NumPy array and, as such, we are using the terms *append* and *drop* loosely. NumPy arrays are immutable, meaning that they cannot grow or shrink. Moreover, we are not recreating this array because it is large, and reallocating each frame would be expensive. Instead, we are just overwriting data within the array by moving old data leftward and copying new data in.

Based on the timestamps, we will calculate the average time per frame in the history, and we will display the frame rate, as seen in the following code:

```
# Find the average length of time per frame.
startTime = self._historyTimestamps[0]
endTime = self._historyTimestamps[-1]
timeElapsed = endTime - startTime
timePerFrame = \
        timeElapsed / self._maxHistoryLength
fps = 1.0 / timePerFrame
wx.CallAfter(self._fpsStaticText.SetLabel,
             'FPS: %.1f' % fps)
```

We will then proceed with a combination of signal processing functions, collectively called a **temporal bandpass filter**. This filter blocks (zeros out) some frequencies and allows others to pass and remain unchanged. Our first step in implementing this filter is to run the `pyfftw.interfaces.scipy_fftpack.fft` function using the history and number of threads as arguments. Also, with the `axis=0` argument, we will specify that the history's first axis is the time axis, as follows:

```
# Apply the temporal bandpass filter.
fftResult = fft(self._history, axis=0,
                threads=self._numFFTThreads)
```

We will pass the FFT result and the time per frame to the `scipy.fftpack.fftfreq` function. This function will then return an array of midpoint frequencies (in Hz, in our case) corresponding to the indices in the FFT result. (This array answers the question, *Which frequency is the midpoint of the bin of frequencies represented by index i in the FFT?*) We will find the indices whose midpoint frequencies lie closest to our initializer's `minHz` and `maxHz` parameters (a minimum of absolute value difference). Then, we will modify the FFT result by setting the data to zero in all ranges that do not represent frequencies of interest, as follows:

```
frequencies = fftfreq(
        self._maxHistoryLength, d=timePerFrame)
lowBound = (numpy.abs(
        frequencies - self._minHz)).argmin()
```

```
highBound = (numpy.abs(
        frequencies - self._maxHz)).argmin()
fftResult[:lowBound] = 0j
fftResult[highBound:-highBound] = 0j
fftResult[-lowBound:] = 0j
```

> The FFT result is symmetrical—`fftResult[i]` and `fftResult[-i-1]` pertain to the same bin of frequencies. Thus, we modify the FFT result symmetrically.

> Remember, the Fourier transform maps a frequency to a complex number that encodes an amplitude and phase. Thus, while the indices of the FFT result correspond to frequencies, the values contained at those indices are complex numbers. Zero as a complex number is written in Python as `0+0j` or `0j`.

Having filtered out the frequencies that do not interest us, we will now finish applying the temporal bandpass filter by passing the data to the `pyfftw.interfaces.scipy_fftpack.ifft` function, as follows:

```
ifftResult = ifft(fftResult, axis=0,
                  threads=self._numIFFTThreads)
```

From the IFFT result, we will take the most recent frame. It should somewhat resemble the current camera frame, but should be black in areas that do not exhibit recent motion that matches our parameters. We will multiply this filtered frame so that the non-black areas become bright. Then, we will upsample it (using a pyramid technique) and add the result to the current camera frame so that areas of motion are lit up. The relevant code, which concludes the `_applyEulerianVideoMagnification` method, is as follows:

```
# Amplify the result and overlay it on the
# original image.
overlay = numpy.real(ifftResult[-1]) * \
            self._amplification
i = 0
while i < self._numPyramidLevels:
    overlay = cv2.pyrUp(overlay)
    i += 1
if self._useGrayOverlay:
    overlay = cv2.cvtColor(overlay,
                           cv2.COLOR_GRAY2BGR)
cv2.add(self._image, overlay, self._image,
        dtype=cv2.CV_8U)
```

This concludes the implementation of the `LazyEyes` class. Our module's `main` function just instantiates and runs the app, as seen in the following code:

```
def main():
    app = wx.App()
    lazyEyes = LazyEyes()
    lazyEyes.Show()
    app.MainLoop()

if __name__ == '__main__':
    main()
```

That's all! Now, it's time to run the app and stay still while it builds up its history of frames. Until the history is full, the video feed will not show any special effects. At the history's default length of 360 frames, it fills in about 50 seconds on a machine. Once it is full, you should start to see ripples moving through the video feed in areas of recent motion—or perhaps even everywhere if the camera moves or the lighting or exposure changes. The ripples should then gradually settle and disappear in areas of the scene that become still, with new ripples appearing in new areas of motion. Feel free to experiment on your own. Now, let's discuss a few recipes for configuring and testing the parameters of the `LazyEyes` class.

Configuring and testing the app for various motions

Currently, our `main` function initializes the `LazyEyes` object with the default parameters. If we were to fill in the same parameter values explicitly, we would have the following statement:

```
lazyEyes = LazyEyes(maxHistoryLength=360,
                    minHz=5.0/6.0, maxHz=1.0,
                    amplification=32.0,
                    numPyramidLevels=2,
                    useLaplacianPyramid=True,
                    useGrayOverlay=True,
                    numFFTThreads=4,
                    numIFFTThreads=4,
                    imageSize=(640, 480))
```

This recipe calls for a capture resolution of *640 x 480* and a signal processing resolution of *160 x 120* (as we are downsampling by 2 pyramid levels, or a factor of 4). We are amplifying the motion only at frequencies of 0.833 Hz to 1.0 Hz, only at edges (as we are using the Laplacian pyramid), only in grayscale, and only over a history of 360 frames (about 20 to 40 seconds, depending on the frame rate). Motion is exaggerated by a factor of 32. These settings are suitable for many subtle upper-body movements such as a person's head swaying side to side, shoulders heaving with breathing, nostrils flaring, eyebrows rising and falling, and eye scanning to and fro. For performance, FFT and IFFT are each using 4 threads.

How the app looks when it runs with its default parameters is shown in the following screenshot. Moments before taking the screenshot, I smiled before returning to my normal expression. Note that my eyebrows and mustache are visible in multiple positions, including their current low positions and their previous high positions. For the sake of capturing the motion amplification effect in a still image, this gesture is quite exaggerated. However, in a moving video, we can see the amplification of more subtle movements, too:

The following screenshot illustrates an example where my eyebrows appear taller after being raised and then lowered:

The parameters interact with each other in complex ways. Consider the following relationships:

- Frame rate is greatly affected by the size of the input data for the FFT and IFFT functions. The size of the input data is determined by maxHistoryLength (a shorter length provides less input and thus a faster frame rate), numPyramidLevels (more levels implies less input), useGrayOverlay (True implies less input), and imageSize (a smaller size is less input).
- Frame rate is also greatly affected by the level of multithreading of the FFT and IFFT functions, as determined by numFFTThreads and numIFFTThreads (a greater number of threads is faster up to some point).

- Frame rate is slightly affected by `useLaplacianPyramid` (`False` implies a faster frame rate), as the Laplacian algorithm requires extra steps beyond the Gaussian.
- Frame rate determines the amount of time that `maxHistoryLength` represents.
- Frame rate and `maxHistoryLength` determine how many repetitions of motion (if any) can be captured in the `minHz` to `maxHz` range. The number of captured repetitions, together with `amplification`, determines how greatly a motion or a deviation from the motion will be amplified.
- The inclusion or exclusion of noise is affected by `minHz` and `maxHz` (depending on which frequencies of noise are characteristic of the camera), `numPyramidLevels` (more levels implies a less noisy image), `useLaplacianPyramid` (`True` is less noisy), `useGrayOverlay` (`True` is less noisy), and `imageSize` (a smaller size implies a less noisy image).
- The inclusion or exclusion of motion is affected by `numPyramidLevels` (fewer means the amplification is more inclusive of small motions), `useLaplacianPyramid` (`False` is more inclusive of motion in non-edge areas), `useGrayOverlay` (`False` is more inclusive of motion in areas of color contrast), `minHz` (a lower value is more inclusive of slow motion), `maxHz` (a higher value is more inclusive of fast motion), and `imageSize` (a bigger size is more inclusive of small motions).
- Subjectively, the visual effect is always more impressive when the frame rate is high, noise is excluded, and small motions are included. Again subjectively, other conditions for including or excluding motion (edge versus non-edge, grayscale contrast versus color contrast, or fast versus slow) are application-dependent.

Now, let's try our hand at reconfiguring `Lazy Eyes`, starting with the `numFFTThreads` and `numIFFTThreads` parameters. We want to determine the numbers of threads that maximize Lazy Eyes' frame rate on a given machine. The more CPU cores there are, the more threads one can gainfully use. However, experimentation is the best guide for picking a number.

Run `LazyEyes.py`. Once the history fills up, the history's average FPS will be displayed in the lower left corner of the window. Wait until this average FPS value stabilizes. It might take a minute for the average to adjust to the effect of the FFT and IFFT functions. Take note of the FPS value, close the app, adjust the thread count parameters, and test again. Repeat these steps until you feel that you have enough data to pick a good number of threads to use on the relevant hardware.

By activating additional CPU cores, multithreading can cause your system's temperature to rise. As you experiment, monitor your machine's temperature, fans, and CPU usage statistics. If you become concerned, reduce the number of FFT and IFFT threads. Having a sub-optimal frame rate is better than overheating your machine.

Now, experiment with other parameters to see how they affect FPS; the `numPyramidLevels`, `useGrayOverlay`, and `imageSize` parameters should all have a considerable effect. At a threshold of approximately 12 FPS, a series of frames starts to look like continuous motion instead of *a slide show*. The higher the frame rate, the smoother the motion will appear. Traditionally, hand-drawn animated movies run at 12 drawings per second for most scenes, and 24 drawings per second for fast action.

Besides the software parameters, external factors can also greatly affect the frame rate. Examples include the camera parameters, the lens parameters, and the scene's brightness.

Let's try another recipe. Whereas our default recipe accentuates motion at edges that have high grayscale contrast, this next recipe accentuates motion in all areas (edge or non-edge) that have either high color or grayscale contrast. By considering three color channels instead of one grayscale channel, we are tripling the amount of data that is processed by the FFT and IFFT. To offset this change, we need to cut each dimension of the capture resolution to half of its default value, thus reducing the amount of data to 1/2 * 1/2 = 1/4 times the default amount. As a net change, the FFT and IFFT process 3 * 1/4 = 3/4 times the default amount of data, a small decrease. The following initialization statement shows our new recipe's parameters:

```
lazyEyes = LazyEyes(useLaplacianPyramid=False,
                    useGrayOverlay=False,
                    imageSize=(320, 240))
```

Note that we are still using the default values for most parameters. If you found non-default values that work well for `numFFTThreads` and `numIFFTThreads` on your machine, enter them as well.

The following screenshots show the effects of our new recipe. Let's look at a non-extreme example first. I was typing on my laptop when this was taken. Note the halos around my arms, which move a lot when I type, and a slight distortion and discoloration of my left cheek (your left in this mirrored image). My left cheek twitches a little when I think. Apparently, it is a tic already known to my friends and family, but rediscovered by me with the help of computer vision:

If you are viewing the color version of this image in the e-book, you should see that the halos around my arms take a green hue from the shirt and a red hue from the sofa. Similarly, the halos on my cheek take a magenta hue from my skin and a brown hue from my hair.

Now, let's consider a more fanciful example. If we were Jedi instead of secret agents, we might wave a steel ruler in the air and pretend it was a lightsaber. While testing the theory that Lazy Eyes could make the ruler *look like a real lightsaber*, I took the following screenshot. This screenshot shows two pairs of light and dark lines in two places where I was waving the lightsaber ruler. One of the pairs of lines passes through each of my shoulders. The Light Side (the light line) and the Dark Side (the dark line) show opposite ends of the ruler's path as it moved. The lines are especially clear in the color version in the e-book:

Finally, the moment for which we have all been waiting—a recipe for amplifying a heartbeat! If you have a heart rate monitor, start by measuring your heart rate. Mine is approximately 87 **beats per minute** (**bpm**) as I type these words and listen to inspiring ballads by Canadian folk singer Stan Rogers. To convert bpm to Hz, divide the bpm value by 60 (the number of seconds per minute), which gives (87 / 60) Hz = 1.45 Hz in my case. The most visible effect of a heartbeat is that a person's skin changes color, becoming more red or purple when blood is pumped through an area. Thus, let's modify our second recipe, which is able to amplify color motions in non-edge areas. Choosing a frequency range centered on 1.45 Hz, we have the following initializer:

```
lazyEyes = LazyEyes(minHz=1.4, maxHz=1.5,
                    useLaplacianPyramid=False,
                    useGrayOverlay=False,
                    imageSize=(320, 240))
```

Customize `minHz` and `maxHz` based on your own heart rate. Remember to also specify `numFFTThreads` and `numIFFTThreads` if non-default values work best for you on your machine.

Seeing a Heartbeat with a Motion-Amplifying Camera

Even when amplified, a heartbeat is difficult to show in still images; it is much clearer in the live video when running the app. However, take a look at the following pair of screenshots. My skin in the left-hand screenshot is more yellow (and lighter), whereas in the right-hand screenshot it is more purple (and darker). For comparison, note that there is no change in the cream-colored curtains in the background:

Three recipes are a good start, and they're certainly enough to fill a cooking TV show. So, why not go and observe some other motions in your environment, try to estimate their frequencies, and then configure Lazy Eyes to amplify them. How do they look with grayscale amplification versus color amplification? Edge (Laplacian) versus area (Gaussian)? What about when different history lengths, pyramid levels, and amplification multipliers are used?

 Check this book's GitHub repository, https://github.com/PacktPublishing/OpenCV-4-for-Secret-Agents-Second-Edition, for additional recipes, and feel free to share your own by mailing me at josephhowse@nummist.com.

Summary

This chapter has introduced the relationship between computer vision and digital signal processing. We have considered a video feed as a collection of many signals—one for each channel value of each pixel—and we have learned that repetitive motions create wave patterns in some of these signals. We have used the fast Fourier transform and its inverse to create an alternative video stream that only sees certain frequencies of motion. Finally, we have superimposed this filtered video atop the original to amplify the selected frequencies of motion. There, we summarized Eulerian video magnification in 100 words!

Our implementation adapts Eulerian video magnification to real-time by running the FFT repeatedly on a sliding window of recently captured frames, rather than running it once on an entire prerecorded video. We have considered optimizations such as limiting our signal processing to grayscale, recycling large data structures rather than recreating them, and using several threads.

Seeing things in different light

Although we began this chapter by presenting Eulerian video magnification as a useful technique for visible light, it is also applicable to other kinds of light or radiation. For example, a person's blood beneath the skin (in veins and bruises) is more visible when imaged in **ultraviolet** (**UV**) or in **near infrared** (**NIR**) than in visible light. This is because blood is darker in UV light than in visible light, and skin is more transparent in NIR light than in visible light. Thus, a UV or NIR video might be an even better input when trying to magnify a person's pulse.

We will experiment with invisible light in the next chapter, `Chapter 8`, *Stopping Time and Seeing like a Bee*. Q's gadgets will inspire us once again!

8
Stopping Time and Seeing like a Bee

"You never can tell with bees."
  – A. A. Milne, Winnie-the-Pooh (1926)

The silent threat of radiation is everywhere in James Bond's world. Of course, stolen nuclear warheads are one cause for concern, but the excessively sunny weather is almost as bad, exposing the hero and his lovely traveling companions to an overdose of UV rays. Then, in *Moonraker* (1979), there is a high-budget mission to outer space, where the radiation hazards include cosmic rays, solar flares, and the turquoise lasers that everyone is shooting.

James Bond is not afraid of all this radiation. Perhaps he is able to take a cool, rational view of it by reminding himself that *electromagnetic radiation* can refer to various kinds of waves that move at the speed of light, including the rainbow-colored range of *visible light* we all see and love, but also including radio waves, microwaves, thermal infrared emissions, near-infrared light, ultraviolet light, X-rays, and gamma rays.

With specialized cameras, it is possible to capture images of other kinds of radiation besides visible light. Moreover, it is possible to capture videos at high frame rates, revealing patterns of motion or of pulsing light that are too fast for human vision to perceive. These capabilities would nicely complement the `Lazy Eyes` application that we developed in Chapter 7, *Seeing a Heartbeat with a Motion-Amplifying Camera*. Recall that `Lazy Eyes` implements the Eulerian video magnification algorithm, which amplifies a specified range of frequencies of motion. If we can increase the frame rate, we can improve the precision of this range of frequencies; thus, we can isolate high frequencies (fast motion) more effectively. This could also be described as an improvement in **selectivity**.

From a programming perspective, our goal in this chapter is simply to develop a variant of `Lazy Eyes` with support for more types of cameras. We will name this variant `Sunbaker`. We will make `Sunbaker` compatible with the Point Grey brand of industrial cameras from FLIR Systems. These cameras can be controlled using a C++ library called **Spinnaker SDK**, which has a Python wrapper called `PySpin`. We will learn how to integrate PySpin (and, in principle, any Python module for camera control) seamlessly with OpenCV.

PySpin (with a capital *P* and capital *S*) should not be confused with pyspin (all lowercase letters). The latter is a different Python library that can display spinning icons in a Terminal.

More broadly, our objective is to learn about some of the specialized cameras available on the market today, work with images from them, and understand how these kinds of imaging relate to the natural world. Did you know that a honey bee flies at an average speed of 24 kilometers (15 miles) per hour, and that it can see ultraviolet patterns on flowers? A different camera can give us an appreciation of how this creature might perceive the passing of light and time.

Technical requirements

This chapter's project has the following software dependencies:

- **A Python environment with the following modules**: OpenCV, NumPy, SciPy, PyFFTW, and wxPython.
- **Optional**: Spinnaker SDK and PySpin. These are available for Windows and Linux, but not Mac.

Where not otherwise noted, setup instructions are covered in `Chapter 1`, *Preparing for the Mission*. Setup instructions for PyFFTW are covered in `Chapter 7`, *Seeing a Heartbeat with a Motion-Amplifying Camera*, in the *Choosing and setting up an FFT library* section. Setup instructions for Spinnaker SDK and PySpin are covered in the current chapter, in the *Installing Spinnaker SDK and PySpin* section. Always refer to the setup instructions for any version requirements. Basic instructions for running Python code are covered in `Appendix C`, *Running with Snakes (or First Steps with Python)*.

The completed project for this chapter can be found in the book's GitHub repository, `https://github.com/PacktPublishing/OpenCV-4-for-Secret-Agents-Second-Edition`, in the `Chapter008` folder.

Planning the Sunbaker app

Compared to `Lazy Eyes`, `Sunbaker` has the same GUI and, substantially, the same implementation of Eulerian video magnification. However, `Sunbaker` can capture input from a Point Grey industrial camera if one is connected. The following screenshot shows `Sunbaker` running with a high-speed monochrome camera called the **Point Grey Grasshopper 3 GS3-U3-23S6M-C**:

The preceding screenshot shows my monochromatic friend, Eiffel Einstein Rocket. The effect of the Eulerian video magnification is visible as a halo along the edge of his back, which is moving as he breathes. The frame rate (98.7 **frames per second** (**FPS**) as shown in the screenshot) happens to be limited by the processing of the images; on a faster system, the camera could potentially capture up to 163 FPS.

Stopping Time and Seeing like a Bee

As a fallback, if PySpin is unavailable or no PySpin-compatible camera is connected, Sunbaker can also capture input from any OpenCV-compatible camera. The following screenshot shows Sunbaker running with an OpenCV-compatible ultraviolet webcam called the **XNiteUSB2S-MUV**:

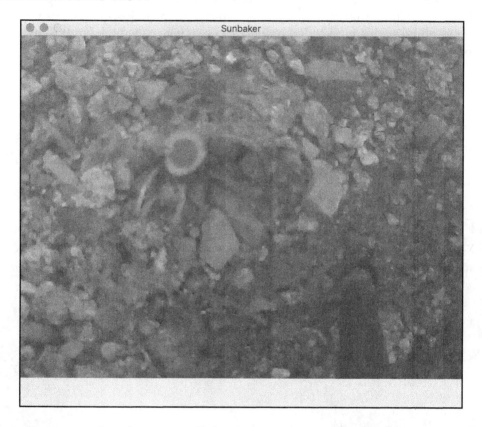

The preceding screenshot shows a small dandelion. Of course, in visible light, a dandelion's petals are entirely yellow. However, to the ultraviolet camera, the dandelion petals look like a dark circle inside a bright circle. This bull's-eye pattern is what a bee would see. Note that, in this screenshot, Sunbaker is still building up its history of frames, so it does not yet show a frame rate yet or an Eulerian video magnification effect. Potentially, Eulerian video magnification could amplify the pattern of the petals' motion in the wind.

Next, let's take a moment to put the capabilities of an *ultraviolet webcam* in context by looking at the electromagnetic spectrum.

Understanding the spectrum

The universe is flooded with light, or electromagnetic radiation, and astronomers can use all wavelengths to capture images of distant objects. However, the Earth's atmosphere partly or wholly reflects some wavelengths of light or radiation back into outer space, so typically we deal with more limited ranges of wavelengths in imaging on Earth. NASA provides the following illustration, showing various wavelengths of electromagnetic radiation, their day-to-day importance to human beings, and their ability (or inability) to penetrate the Earth's atmosphere:

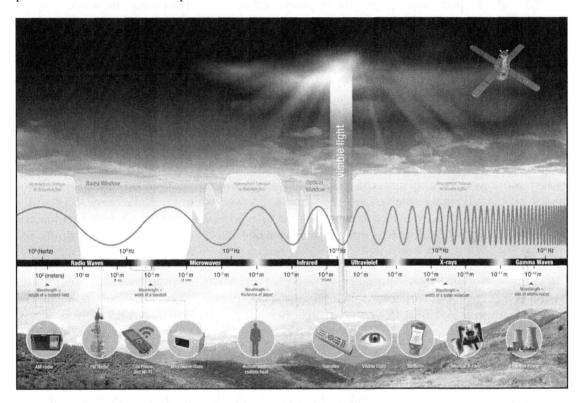

Note that the axis in the preceding diagram runs from longer wavelengths on the left to shorter wavelengths on the right. The Earth's atmosphere is relatively opaque in the range from the longest radio wavelengths down to the short end of the shortwave band (10 m). This **opacity** or **reflectivity** is an important principle in worldwide radio broadcasting, as it enables certain radio wavelengths to propagate around the Earth by bouncing back and forth between the surface and the upper atmosphere.

Next in the spectrum, the atmosphere is relatively transparent in the so-called **radio window**, including very high frequency or FM radio (which does not propagate beyond the horizon), cellular and Wi-Fi ranges, and the longer part of the microwave range. Then, the atmosphere is relatively opaque to the shorter part of the microwave range and the longer part of the **infrared** (**IR**) range (which starts around 1 mm).

Longwave infrared is also called **thermal infrared** or **far infrared** (**FIR**), and shortwave infrared is also called **near infrared** (**NIR**). Here, the terms *far* and *near* mean *farther from visible light* and *nearer to visible light*, respectively. So, past the opposite end of the visible range, longwave ultraviolet is also called **near ultraviolet** (**NUV**), and shortwave ultraviolet is also called **far ultraviolet** (**FUV**).

The radio and microwave ranges have relatively poor potential for terrestrial (earthbound) imaging. Only low-resolution imaging would be possible in these ranges because wavelength is a limiting factor of resolution. On the other hand, starting in the IR range, it becomes feasible to capture recognizable images of human-sized or smaller objects. Fortunately, there are good sources of natural illumination in the IR and visible ranges. Warm-blooded animals and other warm objects emit FIR radiation, which makes them visible to thermal cameras (even at night and even behind cold obstacles such as trees or walls). Moreover, the atmosphere is relatively transparent in the so-called **optical window**, including the NIR range, the visible range, and to a lesser extent the NUV range. NIR and NUV cameras produce images that look fairly similar to visible-light images, but with some differences in objects' coloration, opacity, and sharpness.

Throughout most of the UV range, as well as the X-ray and gamma ranges, the Earth's atmosphere is relatively opaque again. This is also fortunate—perhaps not from a computer vision perspective, but certainly from a biological perspective. Shortwave radiation can penetrate unprotected skin, flesh, and even bone, quickly causing burns and more slowly causing cancer. However, in short, controlled exposures from an artificial source, **ultraviolet** (**UV**) and X-ray imaging can be very useful in medicine. For example, UV imaging can record invisible bruises that are deep beneath the surface of the skin, and this kind of image is often used as forensic evidence in domestic abuse cases. X-ray imaging, of course, can go even deeper to reveal the bones or the inside of the lungs. Shortwave or *hard* X-rays, as well as gamma rays, are widely used to scan the inside of containers and vehicles, for example at security checkpoints.

For many decades, X-ray images have been commonplace in much of the world. During the 1950s and 1960s in the Soviet Union, discarded X-ray slides were sufficiently plentiful that music bootleggers used them as a cheap substitute for vinyl records. People listened to *jazz on bones* or *rock on bones* because this banned, foreign music was unobtainable in any other form. However, in contrast to a world where an X-ray scan might be less troublesome than a jazz record, the world in 1895-1896 was astonished by the first X-ray images. *I have seen my death,* said Anna Bertha Ludwig, the wife of the pioneering X-ray scientist Wilhelm Röntgen, when she first saw a skeletal scan of her hand. She, and other viewers at the time, had never imagined that a photograph could uncover the skeleton of a living person.

Today, specialized imaging technology is continuing to become more pervasive, and it will continue to change the way people see themselves and the world. For example, IR and UV cameras are now widely used for surveillance and detection in police work, many members of the public are aware of this due to police dramas on television, and we might begin to question our old assumptions about what can and cannot be seen. Forget about secret agents and even police detectives for a moment; we might even see a thermal camera on a **do-it-yourself** (**DIY**) show, since FIR imaging can be used to locate a cold draft around a window or a hot water pipe inside a wall. IR and UV cameras are becoming more affordable even for home use, and we will consider some examples of these and other specialized cameras in the next section.

Finding specialized cameras

The following table provides a few examples of cameras that can capture video at high frame rates, in IR, or in UV:

Name	Price	Purpose	Modes	Optics	Compatibility
XNiteUSB2S-MUV	$135	Monochrome imaging in near ultraviolet	Monochrome *1920 x 1080* @ 30 FPS Monochrome *1280 x 720* @ 60 FPS Monochrome *640 x 480* @ 120 FPS (and other modes)	Diagonal field of view—86 degrees 3.6 mm lens on 1/2.7" sensor	OpenCV on Windows, Mac, Linux

Camera	Price	Purpose	Modes	Optics	Software
XNiteUSB2S-IR715	$135	Monochrome imaging in NIR	Monochrome 1920 x 1080 @ 30 FPS Monochrome 1280 x 720 @ 60 FPS Monochrome 640 x 480 @ 120 FPS (and other modes)	Diagonal field of view—86 degrees 3.6 mm lens on 1/2.7" sensor	OpenCV on Windows, Mac, Linux
Sony PlayStation Eye	$10	High-speed color imaging in visible light	Color 640 x 480 @ 60 FPS Color 320 x 240 @ 187 FPS	Diagonal field of view—75 degrees or 56 degrees (two zoom settings)	OpenCV on Linux only (V4L backend)
Point Grey Grasshopper 3 GS3-U3-23S6C-C	$1045	High-speed color imaging in visible light	Color 1920 x 1200 @ 162 FPS (and other modes)	C-mount lens (not included) on 1/1.2" sensor	Spinnaker SDK and PySpin on Windows, Linux
Point Grey Grasshopper 3 GS3-U3-23S6M-C	$1045	High-speed monochrome imaging in visible light	Monochrome 1920 x 1200 @ 162 FPS (and other modes)	C-mount lens (not included) on 1/1.2" sensor	Spinnaker SDK and PySpin on Windows, Linux
Point Grey Grasshopper 3 GS3-U3-41C6NIR-C	$1359	Monochrome imaging in NIR	Monochrome 2048 x 2048 @ 90 FPS (and other modes)	C-mount lens (not included) on 1" sensor	Spinnaker SDK and PySpin on Windows, Linux

Of course, there are many other specialized cameras on the market besides these few examples. Many industrial cameras, including the Point Grey cameras previously listed, conform to an industry standard called **GenICam**, which, in principle, makes them compatible with third-party software libraries that are based on this standard. Harvesters (https://github.com/genicam/harvesters) is an example of an open source Python library that can control GenICam-compliant cameras. You may want to look into Harvesters if you are interested in support for additional brands of industrial cameras and additional platforms (Mac as well as Windows and Linux). For now, though, let's discuss some of the cameras in the preceding table in more detail.

XNiteUSB2S-MUV

The XNiteUSB2S-MUV, available from MaxMax.com (https://maxmax.com/), is a true UV camera in the sense that it blocks out visible and infrared light in order to capture ultraviolet light alone. This is accomplished by means of a permanently attached lens filter that is opaque to visible light but relatively transparent to part of the NUV range. The lens's glass itself also filters out some ultraviolet light, and the result is that the camera captures the range from 360 nm to 380 nm. The following photograph of the camera and a black-eyed Susan (a North American flower with yellow petals and black stamens) shows an opaque reflection of the flower in the lens filter:

Stopping Time and Seeing like a Bee

The following photo, captured by the UV camera, shows the same flower with petals that are dark at the base and bright at the tip, forming a typical ultraviolet bull's-eye pattern:

To a bee, this big splash of two contrasting colors would stand out like a fast-food logo. Pollen is here!

 The XNiteUSB2S-MUV can capture images outdoors in sunlight, but if you want to use it indoors, you will need a UV light source that covers the camera's range of sensitivity, 360 nm to 380 nm. MaxMax.com can provide sales advice on UV light sources, and on options to customize the XNiteUSB2S-MUV with a quartz lens that extends the range of sensitivity down to approximately 300 nm (at a significantly higher cost). See the camera's product page at `https://maxmax.com/maincamerapage/uvcameras/usb2-small` and MaxMax.com's contact page at `https://maxmax.com/contact-us`.

MaxMax.com also offers a series of infrared cameras that have the same electronics and lens as the XNiteUSB2S-MUV, only they use a different filter in order to block out visible and ultraviolet light while capturing part of the NIR range. The XNiteUSB2S-IR715 captures the broadest part of the NIR range, down to a wavelength of approximately 715 nm (for comparison, visible red starts at 700 nm). The product lineup includes several similarly named alternatives for other wavelength cutoffs.

Sony PlayStation Eye

The PlayStation Eye holds a unique position as a low-cost camera with a high maximum frame rate (albeit at a low resolution). Sony released the Eye in 2007 as an accessory for the PlayStation 3 game console, and game developers used the camera to support motion tracking, face tracking, or simply video chat. Later, the Eye's driver was reverse-engineered for other platforms, and the device gained popularity among computer vision experimenters. The Linux kernel (specifically, the Video4Linux or V4L module) officially supports the Eye. So, on Linux (and only on Linux), OpenCV can use the Eye just like an ordinary webcam.

PS3EYE Driver (https://github.com/inspirit/PS3EYEDriver) is an open-source C++ library that can control the PlayStation Eye on Windows or Mac. Potentially, you could write your own wrapper around PS3EYEDriver to provide an OpenCV-friendly interface. PS3EYEDriver reuses a lot of code from the Eye's Linux driver, which is GPL-licensed, so be careful about the licensing implications of using PS3EYE Driver; it might not be right for you unless your project is also GPL-licensed.

Here is a screenshot of Sunbaker running at a high frame rate with a PlayStation Eye camera on Linux:

The preceding photo shows my monochromatic friend, Eiffel Einstein Rocket, at rest. As he breathes, the effect of the Eulerian video magnification is visible as a halo along the edge of his back. Note that the frame rate (60.7 FPS, as displayed) is actually limited by the processing of the images; we could approach or even reach the camera's maximum rate of 187 FPS on a faster system.

Point Grey Grasshopper 3 GS3-U3-23S6M-C

The Point Grey Grasshopper 3 GS3-U3-23S6M-C is a highly configurable, monochrome camera with interchangeable lenses and a high-speed USB 3 interface. Depending on the configuration and the attached lens, it can capture detailed images of a wide variety of subjects, under a wide variety of conditions, at a high frame rate. Consider the following set of images. We see a headshot of the author, a close-up shot of veins in the author's eye, and a long-distance shot of the moon, all captured with the GS3-U3-23S6M-C camera and various low-cost lenses (each $50 or less):

The camera uses a type of lens mount called a **C-mount**, and its sensor size is the so-called **1/1.2" format**. This is the same lens mount and nearly the same sensor size as two formats called **16 mm** and Super 16, which have been popular in amateur movie cameras ever since 1923. So, the camera is compatible with a wide range of inexpensive, old *cine* (cinematography) lenses, as well as newer and more expensive machine vision lenses.

Before even sending the frames through USB, the camera itself can efficiently perform some image processing operations, such as cropping the image and binning (summing) neighboring pixels to increase brightness and reduce noise. We will see how to control these features later in this chapter, in the *Capturing images from industrial cameras using PySpin* section.

The Point Grey Grasshopper 3 GS3-U3-23S6C-C is the same as the camera described previously, except it captures visible light in color instead of in monochrome. The Point Grey Grasshopper 3 GS3-U3-41C6NIR-C also belongs to the same family of cameras, but it is a monochrome NIR camera with a larger sensor (1" format), higher resolution, and lower frame rate. There are many other interesting Point Grey cameras, and you can search through a list of the available models and features at `https://www.flir.com/browse/camera-cores--components/machine-vision-cameras`.

Next, let's look at how we can set up software libraries to control Point Grey cameras.

Installing Spinnaker SDK and PySpin

To obtain drivers and libraries that will enable us to interface with Point Grey cameras, let's take the following steps:

1. Go to the Spinnaker SDK section of the FLIR website at `https://www.flir.com/products/spinnaker-sdk/`. Click the **DOWNLOAD NOW** button. You will be prompted to go to a different download site. Click the **DOWNLOAD FROM BOX** button.
2. You will see a page that allows you to navigate a file structure to find the available downloads. Select the folder that matches your operating system, such as Windows or Linux/Ubuntu18.04.
3. Within the selected folder or its subfolders, find and download a version of Spinnaker SDK that matches your operating system and architecture. (For Windows, you may choose either the Web installer or the Full SDK.) Also, find and download a version of PySpin (the Python Spinnaker bindings) that matches your Python version, operating system, and architecture, such as `spinnaker_python-1.20.0.15-cp36-cp36m-win_amd64.zip` for 64-bit Python 3.6 on Windows.

4. Close the web browser.
5. The instructions for installation for the various systems are as follows:

    - For Windows, the Spinnaker SDK installer is an `.exe` installer. Run it and follow the installer's prompts. If you are prompted to select an **Installation Profile**, choose **Application Development**. If you are prompted to select **Installation Components**, choose **Documentation, Drivers**, and any other components you want.
    - For Linux, the Spinnaker SDK download is a `TAR.GZ` archive. Unzip it to any destination, which we will refer to as `<spinnaker_sdk_unzip_destination>`. Open a Terminal, run `$ cd <spinnaker_sdk_unzip_destination> && ./install_spinnaker.sh`, and answer all the installer's prompts by entering `Yes`.

6. The Python Spinnaker download is a ZIP archive (for Windows) or a TAR archive (for Linux). Unzip it to any destination. We will refer to its unzip destination as `<PySpin_whl_unzip_destination>` because it contains a WHL file, such as `spinnaker_python-1.20.0.15-cp36-cp36m-win_amd64.whl`. We will refer to the `WHL` file as `<PySpin_whl_file>`. The WHL file is a package that can be installed using Python's package manager, `pip`. Open a Terminal and run the following commands (but substitute the actual folder name and filename):

```
$ cd <PySpin_whl_unzip_destination>
$ pip install --user <PySpin_whl_file>
```

For some Python 3 environments, you may need to run `pip3` instead of `pip` in the preceding command.

At this point, we have all the software we need in order to control Point Grey cameras from Python scripts. Let's proceed to write a Python class that supports interoperability between PySpin and OpenCV.

Capturing images from industrial cameras using PySpin

Let's create a file called `PySpinCapture.py`. Not surprisingly, we will begin its implementation with the following `import` statements:

```
import PySpin
import cv2
```

As a practical introduction to `PySpin`, let's add the following function, which returns the number of PySpin-compatible cameras currently connected to the system:

```
def getNumCameras():
    system = PySpin.System.GetInstance()
    numCameras = len(system.GetCameras())
    system.ReleaseInstance()
    return numCameras
```

Here, we see that our standalone `getNumCameras` function (like any self-contained module of code that uses `PySpin`) is responsible for acquiring and releasing a reference to the `PySpin` system. We also see that the `PySpin` system is a gateway, providing access to any connected PySpin-compatible cameras.

Our primary goal in this file is to implement a class, `PySpinCapture`, which will provide some of the same public methods as the `cv2.VideoCapture` class in OpenCV's Python bindings. An instance of `PySpinCapture` will provide access to a single PySpin-compatible camera in a self-contained way. However, the class can be instantiated multiple times for simultaneous access to different cameras through different instances. `PySpinCapture` will implement the following methods to partly mimic the behavior of `cv2.VideoCapture`:

- `get(propId)`: This method returns the value of the camera property identified by the `propId` argument. We will support two of OpenCV's `propId` constants, namely `cv2.CAP_PROP_FRAME_WIDTH` and `cv2.CAP_PROP_FRAME_HEIGHT`.
- `read(image=None)`: This method reads a camera frame and returns a tuple, `(retval, image_out)`, where `retval` is a Boolean indicating success (`True`) or failure (`False`), and `image_out` is the captured frame (or `None` if the capture failed). If the `image` argument is not `None` and the capture succeeds, then `image_out` is the same object as `image`, but it contains new data.

- `release()`: This method releases the camera's resources. `cv2.VideoCapture` is implemented such that the destructor calls `release`, and `PySpinCapture` will be implemented this way too.

Other Python scripts will be able to call these methods on an object without needing to know whether the object is an instance of `cv2.VideoCapture`, `PySpinCapture`, or some other class that has the same methods. This is the case even though these classes have no relationship in terms of object-oriented inheritance. This feature of Python is called **duck typing**. *If it looks like a duck, swims like a duck, and quacks like a duck, then it probably is a duck,* or so the saying goes. If it provides a `read` method that returns a frame, then it probably *is* a frame-capture object. Later in this chapter, in the *Adapting the Lazy Eyes app to make Sunbaker* section, we will instantiate `PySpinCapture` if `PySpin` is available, and `cv2.VideoCapture` otherwise; then, we will use the instantiated object without further concern about its type.

Point Grey cameras are more configurable than most cameras supported by `cv2.VideoCapture`. Our `__init__` method for `PySpinCapture` will accept the following arguments:

- `index`: This is the camera's device index.
- `roi`: This is a region of interest in the (`x`, `y`, `w`, `h`) format, relative to the camera's native image dimensions. Data outside the region of interest will not be captured. For example, if the native image dimensions are *800 x 600* pixels, and the `roi` is (`0, 300, 800, 300`), the captured image will cover only the bottom half of the image sensor.
- `binningRadius`: This is `1` if an unfiltered image should be captured, and `2` or more if neighboring pixels in the specified radius should be summed to produce a smaller, brighter, less noisy image.
- `isMonochrome`: This is `True` if the captured image should be grayscale, and `False` if it should be BGR.

The following code shows how we declare the `PySpinCapture` class and its `__init__` method:

```
class PySpinCapture:


    def __init__(self, index, roi, binningRadius=1,
            isMonochrome=False):
```

PySpin and the underlying Spinnaker SDK are organized around a hierarchical model of a system, the cameras in the system, and the respective configurations of the cameras. Each camera's configuration is organized into a so-called **node map**, which defines properties, their supported values, and their current current values. To begin the implementation of our __init__ method, we get an instance of the system, a list of cameras, and a specific camera by index. We initialize this camera and get its node map. All of this is seen in the following code:

```
self._system = PySpin.System.GetInstance()

self._cameraList = self._system.GetCameras()

self._camera = self._cameraList.GetByIndex(index)
self._camera.Init()

self._nodemap = self._camera.GetNodeMap()
```

We are interested in capturing a continuous series of video frames, rather than isolated still images. To support video capture, `PySpin` allows us to set a camera's `'AcquisitionMode'` property to a value for a `'Continuous'` capture:

```
# Enable continuous acquisition mode.
nodeAcquisitionMode = PySpin.CEnumerationPtr(
        self._nodemap.GetNode('AcquisitionMode'))
nodeAcquisitionModeContinuous = \
        nodeAcquisitionMode.GetEntryByName(
                'Continuous')
acquisitionModeContinuous = \
        nodeAcquisitionModeContinuous.GetValue()
nodeAcquisitionMode.SetIntValue(
        acquisitionModeContinuous)
```

For more information about nodes, their names, and relevant documentation, see the technical note *Spinnaker Nodes* on the FLIR website at https://www.flir.com/support-center/iis/machine-vision/application-note/spinnaker-nodes/.

Next, we set a property called `'PixelFormat'` to either a value called `'Mono8'` or a value called `'BGR8'`, depending on whether our __init__ method's `isMonochrome` argument is `True`. Here is the relevant code:

```
# Set the pixel format.
nodePixelFormat = PySpin.CEnumerationPtr(
    self._nodemap.GetNode('PixelFormat'))
if isMonochrome:
    # Enable Mono8 mode.
```

```
            nodePixelFormatMono8 = PySpin.CEnumEntryPtr(
                    nodePixelFormat.GetEntryByName('Mono8'))
            pixelFormatMono8 = \
                    nodePixelFormatMono8.GetValue()
            nodePixelFormat.SetIntValue(pixelFormatMono8)
        else:
            # Enable BGR8 mode.
            nodePixelFormatBGR8 = PySpin.CEnumEntryPtr(
                    nodePixelFormat.GetEntryByName('BGR8'))
            pixelFormatBGR8 = nodePixelFormatBGR8.GetValue()
            nodePixelFormat.SetIntValue(pixelFormatBGR8)
```

Similarly, we set a `'BinningVertical'` property based on our `binningRadius` argument (the horizontal binning radius is automatically set to the same value as the vertical binning radius). Here is the relevant code:

```
        # Set the vertical binning radius.
        # The horizontal binning radius is automatically set
        # to the same value.
        nodeBinningVertical = PySpin.CIntegerPtr(
                self._nodemap.GetNode('BinningVertical'))
        nodeBinningVertical.SetValue(binningRadius)
```

Likewise, based on the `roi` argument, we set the values of properties named `'OffsetX'`, `'OffsetY'`, `'Width'`, and `'Height'`, as seen in the following code:

```
        # Set the ROI.
        x, y, w, h = roi
        nodeOffsetX = PySpin.CIntegerPtr(
                self._nodemap.GetNode('OffsetX'))
        nodeOffsetX.SetValue(x)
        nodeOffsetY = PySpin.CIntegerPtr(
                self._nodemap.GetNode('OffsetY'))
        nodeOffsetY.SetValue(y)
        nodeWidth = PySpin.CIntegerPtr(
                self._nodemap.GetNode('Width'))
        nodeWidth.SetValue(w)
        nodeHeight = PySpin.CIntegerPtr(
                self._nodemap.GetNode('Height'))
        nodeHeight.SetValue(h)
```

cv2.VideoCapture starts a capture session as soon as it is constructed, so we want to do the same thing in PySpinCapture. So, we finish the __init__ method's implementation with the following line of code, which tells the camera to start acquiring frames:

```
self._camera.BeginAcquisition()
```

We use the node map again in the implementation of the get method. If cv2.CAP_PROP_FRAME_WIDTH is requested, we return the value of the 'Width' property. If, instead, cv2.CAP_PROP_FRAME_HEIGHT is requested, we return the value of the 'Height' property. For any other request, we return 0.0. Here is the method's implementation:

```
def get(self, propId):
    if propId == cv2.CAP_PROP_FRAME_WIDTH:
        nodeWidth = PySpin.CIntegerPtr(
            self._nodemap.GetNode('Width'))
        return float(nodeWidth.GetValue())
    if propId == cv2.CAP_PROP_FRAME_HEIGHT:
        nodeHeight = PySpin.CIntegerPtr(
            self._nodemap.GetNode('Height'))
        return float(nodeHeight.GetValue())
    return 0.0
```

We begin the implementation of the read method by telling the camera to capture a frame. If this fails, we return False and None (no image). Otherwise, we get the frame's dimensions and number of channels, get its data as a NumPy array, and reshape this array to match the format that OpenCV expects. We copy the data, release the original frame, and then return True and the copied image. Here is the method's implementation:

```
def read(self, image=None):

    cameraImage = self._camera.GetNextImage()
    if cameraImage.IsIncomplete():
        return False, None

    h = cameraImage.GetHeight()
    w = cameraImage.GetWidth()
    numChannels = cameraImage.GetNumChannels()
    if numChannels > 1:
        cameraImageData = cameraImage.GetData().reshape(
            h, w, numChannels)
    else:
        cameraImageData = cameraImage.GetData().reshape(
            h, w)

    if image is None:
```

```
            image = cameraImageData.copy()
        else:
            image[:] = cameraImageData

        cameraImage.Release()

        return True, image
```

We implement the `release` method by telling the camera to stop acquiring frames, de-initializing and deleting the camera, clearing the list of cameras, and releasing the `PySpin` system. Here is the relevant code:

```
    def release(self):

        self._camera.EndAcquisition()
        self._camera.DeInit()
        del self._camera

        self._cameraList.Clear()

        self._system.ReleaseInstance()
```

To complete the implementation of the `PySpinCapture` class, we provide the following destructor or `__del__` method, which simply calls the `release` method that we implemented previously:

```
    def __del__(self):
        self.release()
```

Next, let's look at how to use `PySpinCapture` or `cv2.VideoCapture` interchangeably in our application.

Adapting the Lazy Eyes app to make Sunbaker

As we discussed at the start of this chapter, `Sunbaker` is a variant of `Lazy Eyes` with support for more cameras. As a starting point, make a copy of the completed `LazyEyes.py` script from Chapter 7, *Seeing a Heartbeat with a Motion-Amplifying Camera*, and rename it `Sunbaker.py`. The supported cameras in `Sunbaker` will vary depending on the modules that are available at runtime.

Add the following `try`/`except` block after the other `import` statements in `Sunbaker.py`:

```
try:
    import PySpinCapture
except ImportError:
    PySpinCapture = None
```

The preceding block of code tries to import our `PySpinCapture` module, which contains our `getNumCameras` function and our `PySpinCapture` class. The `PySpinCapture` module, in turn, imports the `PySpin` module, as we saw earlier in this chapter in the *Capturing images from industrial cameras using PySpin* section. If the `PySpin` module is not found, `ImportError` is thrown. The preceding block of code catches this error and it defines `PySpinCapture = None` as a way to note that we failed to import an optional dependency, namely the `PySpinCapture` module. Later in `Sunbaker.py`, we will use the `PySpinCapture` module only when `PySpinCapture` is not `None`.

We must modify the `__init__` method of the `Sunbaker` class to remove the `cameraDeviceID` and `imageSize` arguments, and instead add a `capture` argument and an `isCaptureMonochrome` argument. The `capture` argument can be either a `cv2.VideoCapture` object or a `PySpinCapture` object. We assume that `capture` argument's width, height, and other properties are already fully configured before `capture` is passed to `__init__`. So, we have no need to call `ResizeUtils.cvResizeCapture` in `__init__` (and we can remove `ResizeUtils` from the list of imports). We attempt to get the image dimensions and format (grayscale or not) from an actual frame. If this fails, we will instead rely on getting the dimensions from the `capture` argument's properties and the format from the `isCaptureMonochrome` argument. The modifications to `__init__` are marked in bold in the following code:

```
class Sunbaker(wx.Frame):

    def __init__(self, capture, isCaptureMonochrome=False,
            maxHistoryLength=360,
            minHz=5.0/6.0, maxHz=1.0,
            amplification=32.0, numPyramidLevels=2,
            useLaplacianPyramid=True,
            useGrayOverlay=True,
            numFFTThreads=4, numIFFTThreads=4,
            title='Sunbaker'):

        self.mirrored = True

        self._running = True

        self._capture = capture
```

```
        # Sometimes the dimensions fluctuate at the start of
        # capture.
        # Discard two frames to allow for this.
        capture.read()
        capture.read()

        success, image = capture.read()
        if success:
            # Use the actual image dimensions.
            h, w = image.shape[:2]
            isCaptureMonochrome = (len(image.shape) == 2)
        else:
            # Use the nominal image dimensions.
            w = int(capture.get(cv2.CAP_PROP_FRAME_WIDTH))
            h = int(capture.get(cv2.CAP_PROP_FRAME_HEIGHT))
        size = (w, h)
        if isCaptureMonochrome:
            useGrayOverlay = True
        self._isCaptureMonochrome = isCaptureMonochrome

        # ... The rest of the method is unchanged ...
```

The `_applyEulerianVideoMagnification` method needs minor modifications to support the possibility that the input is not a BGR image, but rather a grayscale image from a monochrome camera. Again, the modifications are marked in bold in the following code:

```
    def _applyEulerianVideoMagnification(self):

        timestamp = timeit.default_timer()

        if self._useGrayOverlay and \
                not self._isCaptureMonochrome:
            smallImage = cv2.cvtColor(
                    self._image, cv2.COLOR_BGR2GRAY).astype(
                            numpy.float32)
        else:
            smallImage = self._image.astype(numpy.float32)

        # ... The middle part of the method is unchanged ...

        # Amplify the result and overlay it on the
        # original image.
        overlay = numpy.real(ifftResult[-1]) * \
                        self._amplification
        i = 0
        while i < self._numPyramidLevels:
            overlay = cv2.pyrUp(overlay)
            i += 1
```

```
        if self._useGrayOverlay and \
                not self._isCaptureMonochrome:
            overlay = cv2.cvtColor(overlay,
                                   cv2.COLOR_GRAY2BGR)
        cv2.add(self._image, overlay, self._image,
                dtype=cv2.CV_8U)
```

Finally, the `main` function needs modifications to provide appropriate `capture` and `isCaptureMonochrome` arguments to `Sunbaker` application's `__init__` method. As an example, let's suppose that if `PySpin` is available, we want to use a monochrome camera with a binning radius of 2 and a capture resolution of *960 x 600*. (The GS3-U3-23S6M-C camera supports this configuration.) Alternatively, if `PySpin` is unavailable or if no PySpin-compatible camera is connected, let's use an OpenCV-compatible camera with a capture resolution of *640 x 480* at 60 FPS. The relevant modifications are marked in bold in the following code:

```
def main():

    app = wx.App()

    if PySpinCapture is not None and \
            PySpinCapture.getNumCameras() > 0:
        isCaptureMonochrome = True
        capture = PySpinCapture.PySpinCapture(
                0, roi=(0, 0, 960, 600), binningRadius=2,
                isMonochrome=isCaptureMonochrome)
    else:
        # 320x240 @ 187 FPS
        #capture.set(cv2.CAP_PROP_FRAME_WIDTH, 320)
        #capture.set(cv2.CAP_PROP_FRAME_HEIGHT, 240)
        #capture.set(cv2.CAP_PROP_FPS, 187)

        # 640x480 @ 60 FPS
        capture.set(cv2.CAP_PROP_FRAME_WIDTH, 640)
        capture.set(cv2.CAP_PROP_FRAME_HEIGHT, 480)
        capture.set(cv2.CAP_PROP_FPS, 60)

    # Show motion at edges with grayscale contrast.
    sunbaker = Sunbaker(capture, isCaptureMonochrome)

    sunbaker.Show()
    app.MainLoop()
```

You might need to modify the preceding code based on the capture modes that are supported by your cameras. If you are interested in using the PlayStation Eye camera at its maximum frame rate, you should comment out the lines of code that pertain to *640 x 480* resolution at 60 FPS, and uncomment the lines of code that pertain to *320 x 240* resolution at 187 FPS.

This brings us to the end of the code revisions. Now, you can test `Sunbaker` with either a Point Grey camera or an OpenCV-compatible camera such as a USB webcam. Take some time to adjust the camera parameters, as well as the parameters of the Eulerian video magnification algorithm (the latter are described in detail in `Chapter 7`, *Seeing a Heartbeat with a Motion-Amplifying Camera*, in the *Configuring and testing the app for various motions* section). Experiment with a variety of subjects and lighting conditions, including outdoor sunlight. If you are using a UV camera, remember to look at the flowers!

Summary

This chapter has broadened our view of the things cameras can see. We have considered video capture at high frame rates and at wavelengths of light that are invisible to the human eye. As programmers, we have learned to wrap a third-party camera API in a way that allows us to use industrial cameras and OpenCV-compatible webcams interchangeably, thanks to Python's duck typing. As experimenters, we have extended our study of Eulerian video magnification into higher frequencies of motion, as well as more surprising patterns of pulsing light beyond the visible spectrum.

Let's reflect on all our progress. From finding the head of SPECTRE to exploring the electromagnetic spectrum, our journey as secret agents has taken us far. At this proud moment, however, our adventure must reach its conclusion. We will meet again. Look out for future books, webcasts, and presentations, to be announced on my website at `http://nummist.com/opencv`. Also, email me at `josephhowse@nummist.com` to report issues, ask questions, and tell me how you are using OpenCV.

The book is ending now and I am waiting to find out whether I disappear into the sunset with a femme fatale or whether I have a melancholy debriefing with M.

Making WxUtils.py Compatible with Raspberry Pi

In Chapter 2, *Searching for Luxury Accommodations Worldwide*, we wrote a file, WxUtils.py, that contains a utility function, wxBitmapFromCvImage, to convert OpenCV images to wxPython bitmaps. We used this utility function in our Python projects throughout this book.

Our implementation of wxBitmapFromCvImage relied in part on wxPython's wx.BitmapFromBuffer function. On some versions of Raspberry Pi and Raspbian, wx.BitmapFromBuffer suffers from a platform-specific bug that causes it to fail. As a workaround, we can do a less efficient, two-step conversion using the wx.ImageFromBuffer and wx.BitmapFromImage functions. Here is some code to check whether we are running on an early model of Raspbperry Pi (based on the CPU model) and to implement our wxBitmapFromCVImage function appropriately:

```
import numpy # Hint to PyInstaller
import cv2
import wx


WX_MAJOR_VERSION = int(wx.__version__.split('.')[0])

# Try to determine whether we are on Raspberry Pi.
IS_RASPBERRY_PI = False
try:
    with open('/proc/cpuinfo') as f:
        for line in f:
            line = line.strip()
            if line.startswith('Hardware') and \
                    line.endswith('BCM2708'):
                IS_RASPBERRY_PI = True
                break
except:
    pass

if IS_RASPBERRY_PI:
    def wxBitmapFromCvImage(image):
        image = cv2.cvtColor(image, cv2.COLOR_BGR2RGB)
        h, w = image.shape[:2]
```

Making WxUtils.py Compatible with Raspberry Pi

```
            wxImage = wx.ImageFromBuffer(w, h, image)
            if WX_MAJOR_VERSION < 4:
                bitmap = wx.BitmapFromImage(wxImage)
            else:
                bitmap = wx.Bitmap(wxImage)
            return bitmap
    else:
        def wxBitmapFromCvImage(image):
            image = cv2.cvtColor(image, cv2.COLOR_BGR2RGB)
            h, w = image.shape[:2]
            # The following conversion fails on Raspberry Pi.
            if WX_MAJOR_VERSION < 4:
                bitmap = wx.BitmapFromBuffer(w, h, image)
            else:
                bitmap = wx.Bitmap.FromBuffer(w, h, image)
            return bitmap
```

If you replace the contents of WxUtils.py with the code shown previously, our wxBitmapFromCvImage utility function will work on Raspberry Pi, as well as other systems.

Learning More about Feature Detection in OpenCV

In Chapter 4, *Controlling a Phone App with Your Suave Gestures*, we used the Good Features to Track algorithm to detect trackable features in images. OpenCV offers implementations of several more feature-detection algorithms. Two of the other algorithms, called minimum eigenvalue corners and Harris Corners, are precursors to Good Features to Track, which improves upon them. An official tutorial illustrates the use of eigenvalue corners and Harris Corners in a code sample at https://docs.opencv.org/master/d9/dbc/tutorial_generic_corner_detector.html.

Some of the other, more-advanced feature-detection algorithms in OpenCV are named FAST, ORB, SIFT, SURF, and FREAK. Compared to Good Features to Track, these more-advanced alternatives evaluate a much larger set of potential features, at a much greater computational cost. They are overkill for a basic optical flow task such as ours. Once we have detected a face, we do not need many features in this region in order to distinguish between vertical motions (nodding) and horizontal motions (shaking). For our gesture-recognition task, running at a fast frame rate is far more important than running with a large number of features. On the other hand, some computer vision tasks require a large number of features. Image recognition is a good example. If we put red lipstick on a poster of the *Mona Lisa*, the resulting image is not the Mona Lisa (or at least not Leonardo's version of her). An image's details may be considered fundamental to its identity. However, a change in lighting or perspective does not change an image's identity, so the feature-detection and matching system still needs to be robust with respect to some changes.

For a project that covers image recognition and tracking, refer to *Chapters 4*, *Chapter 5*, and *Chapter 6* of *Android Application Programming with OpenCV 3*, by Packt Publishing.

Learning More about Feature Detection in OpenCV

For benchmarks of several feature detectors and matchers in OpenCV, refer to the series of articles on Ievgen Khvedchenia's blog, including `http://computer-vision-talks.com/2011-07-13-comparison-of-the-opencv-feature-detection-algorithms/`. Also, you can find more up-to-date benchmarks in the *Example comparative performance tests of algorithms* section in *Chapter 9, Finding the Best OpenCV Algorithm for the Job* in *Mastering OpenCV 4*, by Roy Shilkrot and David Millán Escrivá (Packt Publishing, 2018).

For tutorials on several algorithms and their OpenCV implementations, see the *Feature Detection and Description* section of the official OpenCV-Python Tutorials at `http://docs.opencv.org/master/db/d27/tutorial_py_table_of_contents_feature2d.html`.

Running with Snakes (or, First Steps with Python)

This appendix assumes that you have already set up a Python environment and OpenCV's Python bindings, as instructed in Chapter 1, *Preparing for the Mission*. Now, if you are new to Python, you are probably wondering how to test this environment and run Python code.

Python offers an interactive interpreter, so you can test code without even having to save your source code to a file. Open the operating system's Terminal or Command Prompt, and enter the following command:

```
$ python
```

Python will print its version information and then show a prompt, >>>, for its interactive interpreter. You can enter code at this prompt and Python will print the code's return value, if any. For example, if we enter 1+1, we should see the following text:

```
>>> 1+1
2
```

Now, let's try to import the OpenCV Python module, which is called cv2:

```
>>> import cv2
```

If your OpenCV installation is in good shape, this line of code should run silently. On the other hand, if you see an error, you should go back and review the setup steps. If the error says, ImportError: No module named 'cv2', this suggests that Python did not find the cv2.pyd file (the OpenCV Python module) in Python's site-packages folder. On Windows, if the error says, ImportError: DLL load failed. This suggests that Python succeeded in finding the cv2.pyd file, but failed to find one of the module's DLL dependencies, such as one of the OpenCV DLLs or (in a custom build using TBB) the TBB DLL; perhaps the folder containing the DLL is missing from the system's Path.

Assuming that we succeeded in importing `cv2`, now we can get its version number, as seen in the following snippet:

```
>>> cv2.__version__
'4.0.1'
```

Make sure the output matches the OpenCV version you believed you had installed. If not, go back and review the setup steps.

When you are ready to exit the Python interactive interpreter, enter the following command:

```
>>> quit()
```

Throughout this book's projects, when you encounter a Python script (a `.py` file) with a `__main__` section in the code, Python can execute this script if you pass it as an argument to the Python interpreter. For example, let's suppose that we want to run the `Luxocator.py` script from Chapter 2, *Searching for Luxury Accommodations Worldwide*. At the operating system's Terminal or Command Prompt, we would run the following command:

```
$ python Luxocator.py
```

Then, Python would execute the `__main__` section of `Luxocator.py`. This section of the script would, in turn, invoke other sections.

You do not need any special tools to create and edit `.py` files. A text editor will suffice, and minimalists may prefer it. Alternatively, a variety of dedicated Python editors and IDEs offer features such as autocompletion. I sometimes use a text editor and other times an IDE called **PyCharm** (https://www.jetbrains.com/pycharm/), which has a free community edition.

Here, we have covered just the bare minimum to enable you to run and edit Python code. This book does not include a guide to the Python language per se, although, certainly, the book's projects can help you learn Python (and other languages) by example. If you want to supplement your reading of this book with a more language-focused resource, you can find many options in the official *Python For Beginners* guide at https://www.python.org/about/gettingstarted/, and on Packt Publishing's Python tech page at https://www.packtpub.com/tech/Python.

Other Books You May Enjoy

If you enjoyed this book, you may be interested in these other books by Packt:

Mastering OpenCV 4 - Third Edition
Roy Shilkrot, David Millán Escrivá

ISBN: 9781789533576

- Build real-world computer vision problems with working OpenCV code samples
- Uncover best practices in engineering and maintaining OpenCV projects
- Explore algorithmic design approaches for complex computer vision tasks
- Work with OpenCV's most updated API (v4.0.0) through projects
- Understand 3D scene reconstruction and Structure from Motion (SfM)
- Study camera calibration and overlay AR using the ArUco Module

Learn OpenCV 4 By Building Projects - Second Edition
David Millán Escrivá, Vinícius G. Mendonça, Prateek Joshi

ISBN: 9781789341225

- Install OpenCV 4 on your operating system
- Create CMake scripts to compile your C++ application
- Understand basic image matrix formats and filters
- Explore segmentation and feature extraction techniques
- Remove backgrounds from static scenes to identify moving objects for surveillance
- Employ various techniques to track objects in a live video
- Work with new OpenCV functions for text detection and recognition with Tesseract
- Get acquainted with important deep learning tools for image classification

Leave a review - let other readers know what you think

Please share your thoughts on this book with others by leaving a review on the site that you bought it from. If you purchased the book from Amazon, please leave us an honest review on this book's Amazon page. This is vital so that other potential readers can see and use your unbiased opinion to make purchasing decisions, we can understand what our customers think about our products, and our authors can see your feedback on the title that they have worked with Packt to create. It will only take a few minutes of your time, but is valuable to other potential customers, our authors, and Packt. Thank you!

Index

A

activity 149
algorithmic descriptions
  reference link 261
amplitude 261
Android Studio
  project, setting up 132, 134, 137
  setting up 28
  URL, for installing 28
Angora Blue app
  building, for distribution 125
  implementing 118, 120, 122, 123, 124
  planning 117
app
  building 251, 252
  configuring, for motions 275, 276, 277, 280, 281, 282
  requisites, specifying 139
  testing 251, 252
  testing, for motions 275, 276, 277, 280, 281, 282
aspect fill 59
audio clips
  playing, as question-and-answer sequence 144, 148
audio file 138

B

back buffer 91
back-and-forth gestures
  tracking 141
Banana Pi M3
  reference link 37
beats per minute (bpm) 260, 281
binarization 171
blob 206

blob detection 171
blue, green, and red (BGR) 90, 156

C

C-mount 296
California Institute of Technology (Caltech) 102
camera preview
  laying out, as main view 140
Camera Serial Interface (CSI) 34
Canny algorithm 207
cascade 83
cascade file 138
cat-detection model
  planning 101, 102, 103
  training script, implementing 103, 105, 108, 110, 111, 112, 115, 117
cells 207
CentOS
  OpenCV, setting up 27
  Python, setting up 27
chroma 173, 179
circles
  detecting 206, 207, 208, 209
classifier
  training, with reference images 48, 49
CMake
  about 14, 23
  URL, for downloading 14
color histogram analysis 39, 42
components 217
coroutine 236

D

Debian Jessie
  OpenCV, setting up 22
  Python, setting up 22
derivative 207

development machine
  OpenCV, setting up on CentOS 26
  OpenCV, setting up on Debian Jessie 22
  OpenCV, setting up on Fedora 26
  OpenCV, setting up on Linux Mint 23
  OpenCV, setting up on Mac 17
  OpenCV, setting up on openSUSE 27
  OpenCV, setting up on Raspbian 23
  OpenCV, setting up on RHEL 26
  OpenCV, setting up on Ubuntu 23
  Python, setting up on CentOS 26
  Python, setting up on Debian Jessie 22
  Python, setting up on Fedora 26
  Python, setting up on Linux Mint 22
  Python, setting up on Mac 17
  Python, setting up on openSUSE 27
  Python, setting up on Raspbian 22
  Python, setting up on RHEL 26
  Python, setting up on Ubuntu 22
  Python, setting up on Windows 13
  setting up 11
digital signal processing 261
discrete Fourier transform (DFT) 261
distance estimation techniques
  3D feature tracking 177
  stereo camera 176
  Structure from Motion (SfM) 176
  time-of-flight (ToF) 176
distances
  estimating 174, 175, 176
do-it-yourself (DIY) 291
double buffering 91

E

edginess 207
Enox Software
  URL 29
equalized 97
Etcher
  about 30
  URL, for downloading 30
Eulerian video magnification 256, 259
eulerian-magnification library
  reference link 259

F

faces
  tracking, in activity 149, 152, 155, 159, 162, 165
false alarm rate 112
false positive rate 112
far infrared (FIR) 290
far ultraviolet (FUV) 290
fast Fourier transform (FFT)
  about 258
  selecting 261, 262, 263
  setting up 261, 262, 263
  used, for extracting signals from video 260
Fastest Fourier Transform in the West (FFTW)
  about 262
  URL 262
feature 82
Fedora
  OpenCV, setting up 27
  Python, setting up 27
Fourier transform (FT) 261
frames per second (FPS) 257, 287
front buffer 91

G

game objects 217
Gaussian filter 264
Gaussian image pyramid 264
GenICam 293
Global Interpreter Lock (GIL) 262
Global Positioning System (GPS) 223
Goldgesture app
  planning 128
Good Features to Track (GFTT) 131
grid 207
GUI
  integrating 61, 62, 63, 65, 67, 70

H

Haar cascade 82, 83, 85
Haar cascade, in OpenCV
  reference link 83
Harvesters
  reference link 293

histograms
  comparing 42, 43, 46, 48
  creating 42, 43, 46, 48
  storing 42, 43, 46, 48
hit rate 112
Hough circle detection 207
Hough line detection 207
Hough transform 207
Hue 173

I

IEEE Conference on Open Systems (ICOS) 175
image pyramids
  about 258
  used, for compositing images 264, 265
images
  acquiring, from Bing Image Search 52, 54, 56, 58
  acquiring, from web 50, 51
  capturing, from industrial cameras using PySpin 299
  capturing, in activity 149, 152, 155, 159, 162, 165
  compositing, image pyramids used 264, 265
  preparing, for app 59, 61
indoor 43
infrared radiation (IR) 34
Integrated Development Environment (IDE) 28
Interactive Recognizer app
  implementing 86, 88, 90, 91, 94, 96, 97, 98, 99
  planning 80, 82
intersection 42
inverse discrete Fourier transform (IDFT) 261
inverse fast Fourier transform (IFFT) 258
inverse Fourier transform 261

J

Java API documentation
  reference link 36

L

Lagrangian specification 259
Laplacian image pyramid 264
launcher scene
  creating, in Unity 248, 250

lazy eye 256
Lazy Eyes app
  adapting, to Sunbaker 304
  implementing 265, 266, 267, 268, 272, 273, 275
  planning 257, 258
lights
  detecting, as blobs 171, 173, 174
lines
  detecting 206, 207, 208, 209
Living Headlights app
  implementing 177, 178, 179, 180, 181, 182, 186, 188, 191
  planning 169, 170, 171
  testing, at home 192, 193, 194, 195
  testing, in car 195, 196, 198, 199, 200
Local Binary Pattern Histograms (LBPH) 82, 83, 85
Local Binary Patterns (LBP) 82
Luxocator app
  building, for distribution 71, 74
  executing 70, 71
  planning 40, 41
Luxury 43

M

Mac
  OpenCV, setting up 17
  Python, setting up 17
  with Homebrew 20
  with MacPorts 18
machine learning 79
MacPorts
  URL, for installing 19
materials
  creating 219, 220, 221
MaxMax
  URL 293
miss rate 112
mutex 91
mutual exclusion lock 91

N

near infrared (NIR) 34
near ultraviolet (NUV) 290

negative training set 83

O

Odroid XU4
  reference link 37
opacity 290
Open Source Software (OSS) 18
OpenCV Android pack
  URL, for downloading 28
OpenCV documentation
  finding 36
  reference link 36
OpenCV for Unity 29, 203
OpenCV help
  finding 36
OpenCV sources
  URI, for downloading 25
OpenCV updates
  finding 36
OpenCV Win pack
  URL, for downloading 15
OpenCV, source code archive
  reference link 18
OpenCV-Python
  reference link 80
OpenCV
  building, on Debain Jessie 23
  building, on Windows with CMake 14
  building, on Windows with Visual Studio 14
  building, with CMake 23
  building, with GCC 23
  setting up 28, 29
  setting up, for Unity 209, 211
  setting up, on CentOS 27
  setting up, on Fedora 27
  setting up, on Linux Mint 22
  setting up, on Mac 17
  setting up, on openSUSE 27
  setting up, on Raspbian 22
  setting up, on RHEL 27
  setting up, on Ubuntu 22
  setting up, on Windows 13
opencv_contrib
  URL, for downloading 15
openSUSE

OpenCV, setting up 28
  Python, setting up 28
optical flow 130
optical window 290
Orange Pi 3
  reference link 37
overfit 112

P

phase 261
physics materials, properties
  Bounce Combine 222
  Bounciness 222
  Dynamic Friction 222
  Friction Combine 222
  Static Friction 222
physics materials
  creating 222
PlayStation Eye 295
Point Grey Grasshopper 3 GS3-U3-23S6M-C 287
Portfile 18
positive training set 83
prefab
  creating 224, 226
PyImageSearch
  reference link 36
PySpin
  installing 297
  used, for capturing images from industrial
    cameras 299
Python
  setting up, on CentOS 26
  setting up, on Fedora 26
  setting up, on Linux Mint 22
  setting up, on Mac 17
  setting up, on openSUSE 27
  setting up, on Raspbian 22
  setting up, on RHEL 26
  setting up, on Ubuntu 22
  setting up, on Windows 13
  URL 13

R

radio window 289
Raspberry Pi

alternatives 37
camera module, setting up 34, 36
reference link 32
setting up 30, 33
Raspbian disk image
　URL, for downloading 30
recall rate 112
Red Hat Enterprise Linux (RHEL)
　about 10
　OpenCV, setting up 27
　Python, setting up 27
red, green, blue, and alpha (RGBA) 157
reference images
　used, for training classifier 48, 49
reflectivity 289
reinforcement learning 80
Remote Desktop Viewer 34
resources
　preparing, for app 59, 61
RGB (red, green, and blue) 156
Rollingball app
　planning 203, 204, 205
Rollingball scene
　creating, in Unity 216, 217, 218
Rollingball script
　writing 230, 231, 234, 239, 244, 248

S

Saturation 173
selectivity 285
sensitivity rate 112
shader
　about 219
　writing 219, 220, 221
Shi-Tomasi algorithm 131
signals
　extracting, from video using fast Fourier
　　transform 260, 261
single-board computer (SBC) 30
sparse 45
Special Executive for Counterintelligence,
　Terrorism, Revenge, and Extortion (SPECTRE)
　77
specialized cameras
　finding 291

PlayStation Eye 295
Point Grey Grasshopper 3 GS3-U3-23S6M-C
　296
XNiteUSB2S-MUV 293
spectrum 289
Sphere 224
Spinnaker SDK
　about 286
　installing 297
SSL problem
　troubleshooting 70, 71
strabismus 256
Sunbaker app
　planning 287

T

TBB
　URL, for downloading 15
Tegra Android Development Pack (TADP) 21
temporal bandpass filter 273
thermal infrared 290
Thread Building Blocks (TBB) 14
true positive rate 112

U

Unity Asset Store
　reference link 29
Unity assets
　adding, to scene 219
　creating, to scene 219
　materials, creating 219, 220, 221
　physics materials, creating 222
　prefab, creating 224, 226
　Rollingball script, writing 230, 231, 234, 239,
　　244, 248
　shaders, writing 219, 220, 221
　Unity script, writing 228, 229, 230
Unity Hub
　URL, for downloading 29
Unity project
　building 212, 216
　configuring 212, 216
Unity
　about 12
　launcher scene, creating 248, 250

setting up 29
URL 29
used, for setting up OpenCV 209, 211
unsupervised learning 79
Urtho 102
USB Video Class (UVC) 11

V

Video for Linux 2 (V4L2) 36
Video4Linux (V4L) 25
Virtual Network Computing (VNC) 32
Visual Object Classes Challenge 2007 (VOC2007) 101
Visual Studio

URL, for downloading 14
VNC Viewer
  URL, for downloading 33
vote 207

W

window 82
Windows
  OpenCV, setting up 13
  Python, setting up 13

X

X-ray specs 255
XNiteUSB2S-MUV 288, 293

Printed by BoD"in Norderstedt, Germany